SCHOLASTIC BOOK OF
OUTSTANDING
AMERICANS

★ ★ ★

SHEILA KEENAN

For Kevin, *carpe diem*

Special thanks to Mary Varilla Jones, an outstanding editor,
and Nancy Sabato, a great art director.
Thanks also to Elysa Jacobs for her good suggestions.
Special thanks also go to Manuela Soares, Dwayne Howard, and
Heidi Robinson, who all helped make this book a reality.

The author acknowledges use of her book
Scholastic Encyclopedia of Women in the United States

★   ★   ★

Library of Congress Cataloging-in-Publication Data
Keenan, Sheila. ★ Scholastic book of outstanding Americans / Sheila Keenan. ★ p. cm. Summary: Brief biographies of nearly 500 men and women who shaped United States history including, for each, a photograph or picture, birth and death dates, and a brief essay describing why that person is notable. ★ Includes bibliographical references and index. ★ 1. United States—Biography—Juvenile literature. [1. United States—Biography.] I. Title.

CT217 .K44 2003
920.073—dc21   2002073341

0-439-28358-2

10 9 8 7 6 5 4 3 2 1   03 04 05 06 07

Printed in the U.S.A.
First printing, July 2003

Book design by Nancy Sabato ★ Composition by Kay Petronio and Nancy Sabato
Cover design by Red Herring Design

Front cover photos: Clockwise from top left: (Albert Einstein) Bettmann/CORBIS; (Jacqueline Kennedy Onassis) John F. Kennedy Library, Boston, MA; (Tiger Woods) Reuters NewMedia/CORBIS; (George Washington) New Bedford Public Library/Superstock; (Madonna) AP/Wide World Photos; (Cesar Chavez) AP/Wide World Photos; (Sojourner Truth) The Granger Collection; (Sacajawea) North Wind Picture Archives, Alfred, ME

Back cover photos: Clockwise from top left: (Maya Lin) AP/Wide World Photos; (Bill Gates) AFP/CORBIS; (Mia Hamm) Getty Images; (Bill Cosby) Lynn Goldsmith/CORBIS; (Wilma Mankiller) AP/Wide World Photos; (Celia Cruz) AP/Wide World Photos

Title page photos: From left (Cesar Chavez) AP/Wide World Photos; (Sojourner Truth) The Granger Collection; (George Washington) New Bedford Public Library/Superstock

Henry Aaron
baseball player ★ 1934—

On April 8, 1974, 53,775 baseball fans filled the Atlanta Braves' stadium. Thirty-five million more people tuned in by television or radio. In the fourth inning, Hammerin' Hank stepped up to the plate and smashed a fastball over the fence—and right through **Babe Ruth's** home-run record.

Playing for the Braves' minor league club in 1953, Henry (Hank) Aaron was one of five players to integrate the all-white South Atlantic League. On the field, he was voted Most Valuable Player; on the road, he couldn't eat or sleep in the same places as his white teammates.

Aaron made it to the major league in 1954. He played shortshop, second base, third base, and right field. By 1973, Aaron had slugged 713 home runs. He was closing in on Ruth's record of 714—but not everyone was happy about a black man setting a new home-run record. Racists taunted and threatened Aaron. Hammerin' Hank kept his eye on the ball and triumphed in the end. His career stats included 755 home runs, 2,297 runs batted in, 6,856 bases. His batting averages topped .300 fourteen times, his career average was .305.

Hank Aaron retired from baseball in 1975 and is now an executive with the Atlanta Braves and Turner Broadcasting.

Bud Abbott and Lou Costello
comedians ★ 1896—1974 (Abbott);
1908—1959 (Costello)

Bud Abbott was the tall, thin, straight man. Lou Costello was the short, chubby clown. Together, they were one of the funniest comedy acts of the 1940s and 1950s.

Abbott and Costello teamed up in 1936. They were a hit in the vaudeville shows. Two years later, they became household names. The comedians did their now classic "Who's on First?" routine on a radio program. The hilarious baseball skit became Abbott and Costello's trademark.

Abbott and Costello made 36 movie comedies together, including box-office hits like *Buck Privates* (1941), *The Naughty Nineties* (1945), and *The Time of Their Lives* (1946). From 1952 to 1954, they kept television audiences laughing with *The Abbott and Costello Show*. They created funny TV routines around everything from bingo games to barber shops.

Abbott and Costello inspired many contemporary comedians. Their movies are still shown on television—and still make millions laugh.

Bud Abbott (l.) and Lou Costello (r.) in Pardon My Sarong *(1942).*

★ ★ ★ ★ ★ ★ ★ ★ Introduction ★ ★ ★ ★ ★ ★ ★ ★

What's it like to write a book like the *Scholastic Book of Outstanding Americans?*

Sometimes you cry. I did when I listened to a recording of Dr. Martin Luther King, Jr.'s "I Have a Dream" speech.

Sometimes you cheer. I did when I read about Michael Jordan and "The Shot."

Sometimes you're outraged. I was when I learned what happened to Chief Joseph and the Nez Percé.

Sometimes you're proud. I was when I read about Susan B. Anthony refusing to pay a $100 fine for trying to vote.

And sometimes you laugh. (Nothing beats watching the Marx Brothers in *Monkey Business* to get that perfect quote!)

This book is about more than 450 people who shaped, shook up, challenged, or changed American culture. Every one of them is an outstanding American. (That means they "stood out." Outstanding doesn't always mean upright: Check out Calamity Jane or Joseph McCarthy.) There are thousands of people who could have been included here. The people in this book were chosen to reflect the diversity of the American experience over the last five centuries. You'll find Native American figures; patriots of the American Revolution; abolitionists and suffragists; Civil War and world war heroes; presidents, first ladies, and politicians; labor, civil rights, and equal rights leaders; record-breaking athletes; visionary artists; incredible entertainers; groundbreaking scientists; and go-getter entrepreneurs.

Naturally, you can't compress a person's whole life into 200 words or less. So these biographical profiles are not strict chronological stories. Rather, each alphabetical entry focuses on what a person did that's so important, what influenced them, and how they influenced us. The people profiled here took part in major events, movements, and discoveries. It would be impossible to fully describe these events and movements within a given entry, so there is a glossary at the back of the book to help you with dates and definitions of key words and phrases.

What's it like to read a book like the *Scholastic Book of Outstanding Americans?* Turn the page and find out!

— *Sheila Keenan*

★ ★

April 5, 1984. Kareem Abdul-Jabbar (l.) soars. The famous Skyhook . . . yes!

Kareem Abdul-Jabbar
basketball player ★ 1947—

When Lew Alcindor was 14, he stood 6 feet 8 inches tall. He could *touch* a basketball rim.

Ferdinand Lewis Alcindor, Jr., played for the University of California at Los Angeles (UCLA) Bruins and was the country's number one college basketball player. He also became deeply involved in studying Islam. In 1968, Alcindor converted and took a Muslim name, Kareem Abdul-Jabbar.

After college, Abdul-Jabbar signed with the Milwaukee Bucks. He played center with grace, speed, and agility, a whole new style for the position. In 1971, the Bucks' 7-foot 2-inch center was named the National Basketball Association's Most Valuable Player. It was the first of his record-breaking six NBA MVP awards.

Four years later, Abdul-Jabbar was bounding out of a new locker room, that of the Los Angeles Lakers. He had perfected his famous "Skyhook" shot, which would help bring the Lakers six NBA championships.

Kareem Abdul-Jabbar retired in 1989, but nothing could retire his legend. He had scored 38,387 points and blocked 3,189 shots—both records—and he had played more game minutes than any other NBA player.

Abigail Adams
first lady ★ 1744–1818

Abigail Adams wrote vivid reports of her life in hundreds of letters to family, friends, and her beloved husband, **John Adams**. Her letters chronicle everything from the birth of her children to the birth of our nation.

Adams was smart, curious, and completely self-taught. She married John Adams, a young lawyer, in 1764. John's appointment to the Continental Congress in Philadelphia meant Abigail was on her own with their children in Braintree, Massachusetts. Throughout their 54-year marriage, the Adamses were often separated for months, even years, and sometimes by whole continents.

*Many political leaders, including her husband and her son, **John Quincy Adams**, were influenced by Abigail Adams's ideas.*

Abigail Adams ran the farm, dealt with finances, and educated the children. Meanwhile, the American Revolution raged right outside her door. Adams's detailed letters were an important source of information to Congress. After the war, Adams stood by her husband as he held a series of important political positions at home and abroad. Throughout her life, she argued for education for women.

Ansel Adams

photographer ★ 1902–1984

This photo of Ansel Adams was taken in 1980.

Ansel Adams traveled to the Yosemite Valley in 1916 with his new Brownie Box camera. He was headed on a trip that would last a lifetime.

Adams became America's most celebrated nature photographer. His haunting black-and-white photographs of the West and Southwest capture the awesome beauty of the world. They are also proof of Adams's artistic understanding of light and shadow, shapes, perspective, and patterns.

His first portfolio of prints was published in 1927. At that time, photographers were still fighting to be fully recognized by art museums. Ansel Adams and other influential photographers formed Group f/64. Their mission was to promote photography as a unique art form. In 1937, Adams had six photographs in the first photography exhibit ever held at New York City's prestigious Museum of Modern Art (MOMA).

In a career that spanned nearly 70 years, Adams never stopped shooting photos. He was awarded the Presidential Medal of Freedom by President **Jimmy Carter** in 1980.

John Adams

second president ★ 1735–1826

The U.S. was a new nation when John Adams became president in 1797. But Adams was an old hand at politics. He had served in the Continental Congress from 1774 to 1777 and helped draft the Declaration of Independence. For ten years (1778–1788), he had been an American diplomat in Europe. He helped negotiate the 1783 Treaty of Paris, which ended the American Revolution.

John and **Abigail Adams** and their children were the first presidential family to live in the White House. They moved there in 1800.

John Adams, a native of Massachussetts, played key roles during the American Revolution and was **George Washington**'s vice president. In 1796, he successfully ran for president in what was the nation's first real campaign.

Like other Federalists, Adams believed in a strong central government. While president, he created the first U.S. Naval Department and kept the country out of a costly war with France. He also signed the controversial Alien and Sedition Acts of 1798. This was supposed to protect America by controlling immigration. The acts limited criticism of the government, too, all of which also protected Adams's political party. Adams lost his bid for a second term to **Thomas Jefferson**.

"Witness the magic

John Quincy Adams
sixth president ★ 1767–1848

The son of **Abigail Adams** and former president **John Adams**, John Quincy Adams's political career began when he was only 14. He was the secretary to the American minister to Russia. He later represented President **George Washington** in several European capitals and was President **James Monroe**'s secretary of state.

Adams ran for president in 1824. None of the four candidates won the electoral majority. So the House of Representatives had to decide the election. They chose Adams.

President Adams had big plans for the country. He wanted roads, canals, a naval academy, and a national university built. But this sharp-tongued, unpopular president wasn't able to get all of his plans through Congress. Adams did sign the 1828 "Tariff of Abominations," though. The tariff, or tax, protected American manufactured goods, but it also raised prices. Adams wasn't reelected.

John Quincy Adams was the first president to be photographed.

Massachusetts elected the former president to the House of Representatives. Adams served for 17 years. He fought, and after eight years, in 1844, overturned the House "gag rule," which banned debate on antislavery petitions. Adams was a public servant to the end. In 1848, he had a stroke on the House floor and could be moved only as far as the Speaker's Room. Two days later, he died in that Congressional chamber.

Samuel Adams
American Revolution leader ★ 1722–1803

Sam Adams understood what it took to fan the flames of the American Revolution: agitation and communication. He was a master at both.

Adams led Massachusetts patriots in the fight against the Stamp Act. His fiery—though inaccurate—account of the Boston Massacre (1770) set even more colonists against the British.

In 1772, Adams set up the Committee of Correspondence. This network of letter-writers helped keep leaders throughout the colonies aware of what the British were doing. An organizer of the patriotic Sons of Liberty, Adams, along with **John Hancock**, masterminded the Boston Tea Party (1773).

In 1776, Adams was among the signers of the Declaration of Independence. He later became governor of Massachusetts.

*Samuel Adams, who was **John Adams's** cousin.*

that is our world." —ANSEL ADAMS

"I believe in the goodness

Jane Addams was very
active in the international
peace movement.

Jane Addams
social reformer ★ 1860–1935

In 1889, Jane Addams bought Hull House, an old mansion in a run-down
neighborhood in Chicago. She transformed it into a settlement house
offering education, work training, child care, and arts programs for poor
people and immigrants.

Though Addams was a college-educated member of Illinois's wealthy
class, she moved into Hull House herself. She was not above delivering
a baby or even getting a job as a garbage inspector to improve services in
the neighborhood. Addams's commitment to social reform broadened. She
campaigned for workers' rights and for the rights of children. She helped
establish the country's first juvenile court in 1899. Jane Addams realized that
two things would help move social reform forward: voting and organizing.
She served as vice president of the National American Women's Suffrage
Association (1911–1914), which lobbied for women's right to vote. She joined
W. E. B. Du Bois and other prominent leaders in organizing the National Association for the
Advancement of Colored People in 1909. In 1920, she helped found the American Civil Liberties
Union. A devoted pacifist, Addams was awarded the Nobel Peace Prize in 1931.

Alvin Ailey
choreographer, dancer ★ 1931–1989

Alvin Ailey moved to New York from Los
Angeles in 1954. He studied with influential
dance teachers like Katherine Dunham and
Martha Graham. He appeared in several
plays and dance pieces. His performances
were well received. Then, in 1958, Ailey
choreographed and performed in *Blues Suite*,
a piece celebrating black culture. The dance
world took notice of this powerful new talent.

The following year, he established the
Alvin Ailey American Dance Theater with
eight African-American dancers. In 1960, he

Members of the Alvin Ailey American Dance Theater in a 1993 rehearsal
of Revelations.

choreographed his most famous piece, *Revelations*. Still performed, Ailey's masterpiece was
inspired by gospel music. It is at once deeply spiritual, poignantly humorous, and with its jazzy
dance movements, energetic.

During his career, Ailey choreographed more than 75 pieces for his company. He collaborated
with **Duke Ellington** on *The River* (1970). He celebrated the music of **Charlie Parker** in *For
Bird—With Love* (1984). He created innovative dance set to folk, jazz, blues, and classical pieces.
Ailey received numerous prizes, including the 1988 Kennedy Center Honor.

Secretary of State Madeleine Albright greets soldiers serving in Kosovo in 1999.

Madeleine Albright
secretary of state ★ 1937—

Madeleine Albright's first experiences of international politics were personal: She was a refugee. Born in Prague, Czechoslovakia, she fled the Nazi invasion as a child, then the Communist takeover, then moved with her family to the United States.

President **Jimmy Carter** made Albright congressional liaison to the National Security Council in 1976. But it was when President **Bill Clinton** appointed her U.S. representative to the United Nations (UN) in 1992 that Albright really came into her own. Representative Albright was feisty and forthright. She strongly championed sending a UN peacekeeping force into war-ravaged Bosnia and Kosovo. She lobbied hard to extend NATO (North Atlantic Treaty Organization) membership to emerging democracies in Eastern Europe. When Clinton later nominated her for secretary of state, she was unanimously approved by the Senate, 99–0. On January 23, 1997, Madeleine Albright was sworn in. She became the highest-ranking woman ever in U.S. government.

Secretary of State Albright's agenda included Middle East peace talks, visiting North Korea to discuss missile controls, and dealing with sensitive relations with China. She lobbied for the 1999 NATO bombing of Yugoslavia and military intervention in Bosnia and Kosovo.

Louisa May Alcott
author ★ 1832—1888

As a child, Louisa May Alcott spent hours filling her "imagination book" with wild stories of adventure and exotic places far from her native Massachusetts. But her real fame would come from writing novels about what she knew best: domestic life.

She moved to Boston, Massachusetts, and in the 1850s made a living teaching, and writing thrillers, sensational stories, romances, and poems. Women's writing was not taken seriously at the time, so Louisa used male-sounding pen names like "A. M. Barnard" to help sell her work.

In 1862, Louisa put aside her writing and went to Washington, D.C., to nurse wounded Civil War soldiers. A keen observer, she turned her experiences into what became her first successful book, *Hospital Sketches* (1863). A few years later, she wrote a novel for young women using her own family life for inspiration. *Little Women* (1868–1869) sold more than 38,000 copies in its first year. Alcott received $12,000, more money than any other American writer of the time had earned.

"...I don't have to be what you want me

Muhammad Ali
boxer ∗ 1942—

Muhammad Ali made things simple for boxing fans: "I am the greatest," he boasted. Then he stepped into the ring and proved it.

Cassius Marcellus Clay was born in Louisville, Kentucky. He took his Muslim name, Muhammad Ali, when he joined the Nation of Islam, a black Muslim religious movement, in 1964.

Ali started boxing when he was 12. Six years later, he won the 1960 Olympic gold medal for light heavyweight boxing and then turned pro. He brought a whole new wit and style to boxing.

"Float like a butterfly, sting like a bee" was Ali's motto. His quick, dancing footwork and powerful left jab helped him win all of his first 20 pro bouts. In 1964, Ali stepped into the ring with rough, tough Sonny Liston. The odds were seven to one against him. Ali surprised everyone but himself. He beat Liston to become heavyweight champion of the world.

Muhammad Ali's reputation was built on his fists and his lips. He was brash, outspoken, and funny, an athlete with attitude. He recited poems about his opponents and bragged that "They all must fall/in the round I call." One opponent didn't fall though—the U.S. government.

In 1967, Ali was drafted by the army for the controversial war in Vietnam. He refused to go because "I ain't got no quarrel with them Vietcong" and because his faith prohibited him from bearing arms. Ali was fined and sentenced to jail. He was stripped of his title and barred from boxing. Ali was out of the ring for three and a half years before the U.S. Supreme Court reversed his conviction in 1971. During that time, he became a popular speaker on college campuses and at Muslim meetings.

Ali had to fight his way back to his title. In "The Fight of the Century" (1971), he was outslugged by the reigning champ, Joe Frazier. But at the 1974 "Rumble in the Jungle" in Zaire, Ali used his famous "rope-a-dope" feint to tire George Foreman before knocking him out to win the heavyweight championship. In 1975, Frazier fell before Ali in "The Thrilla in Manila" bout in the Philippines.

Ali defended his title until 1978, when he lost it to newcomer Leon Spinks. Spinks, 12 years younger than Ali, couldn't hold on to the title, though. Ali won the rematch seven months later. Once again, he reigned as heavyweight champ.

Muhammad Ali retired from boxing in 1980. He now suffers from Parkinson's syndrome. But to many of the three billion people who watched Ali light the 1996 Olympic torch in Atlanta, he's still a champ.

Muhammad Ali won the world heavyweight boxing title three times.

The cannons Ethan Allen captured at Ticonderoga were used by General **George Washington** to drive the British out of Boston. This drawing of the attack is actually from the 19th century.

Ethan Allen
American Revolution leader ★ 1738—1789

Ethan Allen caught the British with their pants down.

The American Revolution commander led his rough-and-tumble Green Mountain Boys on a secret, nighttime assault on Fort Ticonderoga, New York, on May 10, 1775. The fort's British commander was so surprised that he didn't have time to pull on his trousers. Surrender quickly followed. Shortly after, Allen and his men had captured 60 pieces of much-needed artillery from British troops in nearby Crown Point.

Allen was a big, burly, tough-talking native of Connecticut who could back up his mouth with muscle. He moved to the area between New Hampshire and New York (now Vermont). In the 1770s, he formed the Green Mountain Boys to defend this area from being absorbed by either colony.

During the American Revolution, Allen and the Green Mountain Boys became part of the Continental army. Allen later helped establish Vermont as a republic.

Richard Allen
religious leader ★ 1760—1831

In 1816, Richard Allen became the founder and bishop of the African Methodist Episcopal (AME) church. It was the first independent African-American church in the country.

Born into slavery in Philadelphia, Pennsylvania, Allen and his family were sold to a Delaware farmer. When he was 17, he had a religious awakening after listening to Methodist preachers. Allen joined that church. By the time he was 20, he had purchased his freedom and embarked on a life of faith.

Allen's spirited preaching drew in audiences of all colors. He was appointed assistant minister in a racially diverse church in Philadelphia. But he couldn't ignore the prejudices that African Americans faced, even from their fellow Methodists, many of whom opposed slavery. The Bethel African Methodist Episcopal church was his answer.

Richard Allen helped found the Free African Society in Philadelphia in 1787. This benevolent group offered comfort and aid to free African Americans.

The tiny congregation first met in a blacksmith shop. By 1794, Bethel had a church. By 1813, it had 1,200 members. In 1799, Richard Allen had been ordained as the first African-American Methodist minister. The AME church has grown into a powerful religious and social institution in many African-American communities, north and south.

Marian Anderson

opera singer ★ 1902–1993

Marian Anderson's vocal range was so great that she could sing all four of the major voice parts: bass, alto, tenor, and soprano. In the 1920s and 1930s she toured Europe, where she was hailed as one of the great voices of the century. But when she wanted to sing at Constitution Hall in Washington, D.C., in 1939, the Daughters of the American Revolution, who owned the hall, said no. People were outraged that one of America's greatest opera singers was not allowed to sing because of her skin color. **Eleanor Roosevelt** arranged for Anderson to sing at the Lincoln Memorial instead. More than 75,000 people showed up to hear her.

After the 1939 concert, Anderson continued to perform and to win awards. In 1955, she became the first African American to sing with the famous Metropolitan Opera in New York. Anderson's legendary performances earned her the Presidential Medal of Freedom in 1963 and a Grammy for Lifetime Achievement in 1991.

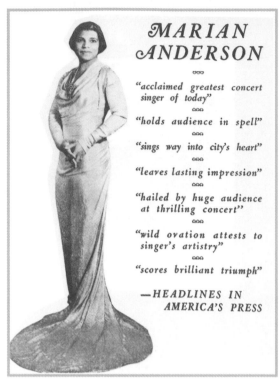

A concert advertisement from the 1930s praises Marian Anderson's incredible voice.

Maya Angelou

author ★ 1928–

In *I Know Why the Caged Bird Sings*, Maya Angelou describes her childhood in St. Louis, Missouri, during the Great Depression. The book deals with the hardships and racism she faced. When she was only seven years old, Angelou was raped. The assault shocked her into not speaking for five years. When she later found her voice as a writer, she liberated herself and her audience.

Angelou has worked onstage, in film, and in television. *I Know Why the Caged Bird Sings* (1970) was nominated for the National Book Award. Her collection of poems, *Just Give Me a Cool Drink of Water 'fore I Diiie* (1971) was nominated for a Pulitzer prize. Angelou received an Emmy Award nomination for her acting in the TV miniseries *Roots* (1977), and a Tony Award nomination in 1978 for her role in the Broadway play *Look Away*. By 1993, her list of published work included several more collections of poetry and autobiographies, and the best-selling essay collections, *Wouldn't Take Nothing for my Journey Now* (1993) and *Even the Stars Look Lonesome* (1997). Angelou has been the Reynolds Professor of American Studies at Wake Forest University in North Carolina since 1981 and has received more than 50 honorary academic degrees.

*Maya Angelou reads her poem "On the Pulse of Morning" at President **Bill Clinton**'s 1993 inauguration.*

"Failure is impossible."

Susan B. Anthony and Elizabeth Cady Stanton

suffragists ★ 1820—1906 (Anthony); 1815—1902 (Stanton)

Elizabeth Cady Stanton(l.) and Susan B. Anthony (r.)

Susan B. Anthony was active in the education, temperance, and abolition movements of the 1840s. She was annoyed that women were given limited roles in each. Elizabeth Cady Stanton had helped plan the First Women's Rights Convention in 1848. She shocked attendees with her bold Declaration of Sentiments, which began, "We hold these truths to be self-evident, that all men *and women* are created equal."

In 1851, **Amelia Bloomer** introduced the two women to each other. Susan B. Anthony and Elizabeth Cady Stanton formed an historic personal and political friendship that lasted more than 50 years.

In 1852, Stanton and Anthony founded the Woman's State Temperance Society in New York. They actively campaigned for temperance laws (bans on alcohol), for married women's rights, and for more liberal divorce laws.

In 1863, during the Civil War, Anthony and Stanton formed an abolitionist, or antislavery, group, the Women's Loyal National League. The league collected more than 300,000 signatures supporting the 13th Amendment, which would end slavery. After the war, Anthony and Stanton had great hopes that both African Americans and women would get the vote. They were quickly disappointed. The proposed 15th Amendment gave only black men the right to vote. The suffrage movement split in 1869 and two groups emerged. **Lucy Stone**'s conservative American Woman's Suffrage Association (AWSA) backed the African-American male suffrage movement and women's suffrage at state levels. Stanton, Anthony, and **Lucretia Mott**'s more liberal National Woman Suffrage Association (NWSA) lobbied for a constitutional amendment giving women the vote. In 1872, Susan B. Anthony even tried to vote in the presidential elections herself. She was arrested, jailed, and fined $100. Anthony refused to pay.

Stanton and Anthony began publishing a weekly women's newspaper, *The Revolution,* in 1868. The two women traveled around the country, lecturing on women's suffrage. Their trips were long and difficult. Suffragists didn't always get a warm reception—sometimes they got rotten eggs and flying vegetables. Still, Stanton convinced a California senator to introduce a women's suffrage amendment to Congress in 1878.

In 1890, AWSA and NWSA finally merged and became the National American Woman Suffrage Association (NAWSA). Elizabeth Cady Stanton was elected the new organization's first president. The call for women's rights got louder. The women's suffrage amendment was brought before Congress every year . . . for 42 years! Finally, in 1920, the 19th Amendment passed, giving women the right to vote. Susan B. Anthony and Elizabeth Cady Stanton did not live long enough to cast their ballots, but thanks to them, millions of American women now can.

Lance Armstrong
Olympian ★ 1971—

Texan Lance Armstrong was among the world's top cyclists in 1996. He competed in the 1992 Olympics before turning pro. The following year he won 10 titles, including 1993 World Champion and the Thrift Drug Triple Crown. In 1995, Armstrong finished first at the Tour Du Pont and the Classico San Sebastian. Now he faced his toughest challenge: cancer.

Armstrong was diagnosed with testicular cancer in 1996. He had a 50–50 chance of surviving the disease and its aggressive treatment. Armstrong did everything he could to beat those odds. Not only that, he planned a cycling comeback.

On July 25, 1999, Armstrong proved what a champion he truly is. He won the 2,286-mile Tour de France, the toughest bike race in world. In 2002, he became the first American to win the Tour de France four times in a row.

July 25, 1999. Paris goes wild as cancer survivor Lance Armstrong wins the Tour de France with a 7-minute, 37-second lead.

Louis Armstrong
musician ★ c.1901—1971

Louis Armstrong had several nicknames, including "Pop" and "Satchel Mouth" (because of his big mouth), which became "Satchmo."

When Louis Armstrong wailed on his trumpet, he could hit 50 high-C notes *in a row*! When he started humming and singing the new form of wordless "scat" music, he turned his own voice into a musical instrument.

Armstrong grew up in poverty in New Orleans, Louisiana. He learned to play the cornet horn in a reform school band. Between 1918 and 1924 he played with famous big bands in New York and Chicago. He switched to the trumpet soon after.

Armstrong created a whole new jazz sound by adding a modern swing tempo and emphasizing solos. In 1925, he formed his own band, the Hot Spot Five. They recorded hits like "Heebie Jeebies," where Armstrong also sang scat in his signature gravelly voice. The Hot Spot Five's recordings (1925–1928) are among the most important works in jazz history. One of those recordings, Armstrong's song "West End Blues," is one of the most famous jazz songs of all time.

During the 1930s and 1940s, Armstrong was "America's Ambassador of Jazz," touring the United States and Europe. In the 1950s and 1960s, swing music became less popular, but Armstrong held steady with hits like "Mack the Knife" and "Hello, Dolly!"

"**I would rather do without**

Neil Armstrong
astronaut ★ 1930—

"That's one small step for a man, one giant leap for mankind."
Millions of people around the world had just watched Neil
Armstrong take that step . . . out onto the moon!

Armstrong, a former test-plane pilot, joined NASA's
astronaut training program in 1962. NASA launched *Apollo 11*
on July 16, 1969. Armstrong, Michael Collins, and Edwin
"Buzz" Aldrin were headed for the moon. Collins would keep
the command module orbiting. Armstrong and Aldrin would
shoot off in the lunar module (code-named *The Eagle*) and land
on the moon—300 miles away.

On July 20, 1969, Armstrong relayed the unbelievable news:
"*The Eagle* has landed." The lunar module was on the moon's Sea
of Tranquility. At 10:56 P.M. (EST), Armstrong's historic step was
televised. Aldrin joined him. The astronauts spent 2 hours 48
minutes on the moon. They shot photos and collected lunar rocks
and soil. They planted an American flag, and Armstrong read from a plaque to be left on the moon:
"We came in peace for all mankind."

*Some scientists worried astronauts would sink when
they stepped onto the moon. Neil Armstrong's
footprint proved the moon was solid.*

The words Benedict Arnold *are now used to
mean a traitor or a betrayal. But in this
painting (c.1776), an anonymous artist
imagines how he looked as a hero.*

Benedict Arnold
American Revolution leader ★ 1741—1801

Benedict Arnold was a great American Revolution hero—and
traitor.

Arnold was a brilliant but difficult commander. He fought
bravely on the field but also picked fights with his fellow officers.

Arnold took part in the stunning victory at Fort Ticonderoga,
New York, in 1775. That same year, he was one of the commanders
on a doomed invasion of Canada. The American forces were defeated
by smallpox, snowstorms, starvation, and, finally, by the British.

In 1877, Arnold led a surprise charge against British general
John Burgoyne near Saratoga, New York. The redcoats were forced
to retreat. Arnold was then given command of Philadelphia,
Pennsylvania.

Still, Benedict Arnold felt underappreciated by the Continental
Congress. He thought Congress had not promoted him properly.
Arnold contacted the British. He agreed to sell them information
that would help them capture key Continental forces at West Point,
New York. Luckily, the plot was uncovered.

Arnold switched uniforms and fought two battles *against* the patriots. He was never captured,
and in 1791 moved to England, where he died 10 years later.

food than music." —LOUIS ARMSTRONG

"From what we get, we can

Arthur Ashe
tennis player ★ 1943–1993

Arthur Ashe was a champ on the tennis court and a winner at promoting equality and justice.

Ashe broke barriers in the 1960s, when he became the first African-American man to win national standing as a tennis player (1961), the first to be a U.S. Men's Hardcourt champ (1963), and the first named to the U.S. Davis Cup team (1963).

In 1968, Ashe's grace and power on court earned him both the U.S. Amateur and the U.S. Open Championships. He also helped the U.S. team take home the Davis Cup. He was considered the number one tennis player in the country. The next year Ashe turned pro. In 1975, he defeated Jimmy Connors and became the first African-American man to win the prestigious Wimbledon singles.

In 11 years of pro tennis, Ashe racked up an impressive score: 33 singles titles. After several heart attacks he retired in 1980. Ashe then cofounded Artists and Athletes Against Apartheid, which fought against South Africa's policy of racial discrimination, and chaired many charitable committees.

In 1988, Ashe was diagnosed with AIDS, caused by an infected blood transfusion. He faced it with the same courage he showed on court. Before he died in 1992, he founded the Arthur Ashe Foundation for the Defeat of AIDS.

Fred Astaire and Ginger Rogers
dancers, film stars ★ 1899–1987 (Astaire); 1911–1995 (Rogers)

Fred and Ginger. They were Hollywood's most famous couple in the 1930s . . . on-screen.

Fred Astaire was dapper and elegant. Ginger Rogers was sexy, athletic, and all-American. In 1933, the two were paired in the movie *Flying Down to Rio*. They were airborne!

Astaire and Rogers made nine glorious films between 1933 and 1939. No other dancers have ever achieved the on-screen magic Fred and Ginger sparked in movies like *Top Hat* (1935) and *Shall We Dance* (1937). Astaire also brought exciting new ideas about choreography, filming, editing, and music to their movies.

Astaire and Rogers pursued individual careers from the 1940s on. Rogers won an Academy Award for Best Actress for *Kitty Foyle* (1940). Astaire made 38 films and was given a special Academy Award in 1949 for his contribution to movies.

Fred Astaire and Ginger Rogers in Swing Time *(1936).*

make a living. What we give, however, makes a life." — ARTHUR ASHE

John Jacob Astor
fur trade entrepreneur ★ 1763–1848

John Jacob Astor was America's first millionaire. When he died, the *New York Herald* called him a "self-inventing money-making machine."

Astor emigrated to New York from Germany in 1783. He learned the fur trade and within three years set up his own business. Astor traveled through northern New York and Canada to get the otter, fox, mink, and especially beaver furs that were so popular in Europe. He bartered with trappers and Native Americans, exchanging guns, metal goods, and liquor for animal pelts. Sometimes he paid cash. He also shrewdly invested in New York City real estate.

Astor's business empire spread east. He began a very profitable trade with China in 1800. And it spread west. Astor was inspired by the reports of **Lewis** and **Clark**. In 1808, he founded the American Fur Company to start trading and trapping in the Louisiana Purchase territory. Astor wanted to get rid of competition in the area. His men were not above bribing, beating, or stealing from other fur traders to drive them out of business. Astor himself used his political influence to get favorable trading rights. He monopolized the fur trade by the 1820s.

John Jacob Astor owned much of midtown Manhattan, including Times Square, which he paid $25,000 for in 1803.

Crispus Attucks
American Revolution hero ★ c.1723–1770

He got his name in the *Boston Gazette* twice: once in an advertisement to recapture him as a runaway slave and the other when he became the first American to die in the fight for independence.

In 1750, Crispus Attucks, a tall man of African and Native American descent, fled slavery in Framingham, Massachusetts. He may have worked as a sailor, which could explain why he ended up in the port of Boston. British soldiers had also sailed into Boston, and the city's inhabitants were not happy with having to feed, house, and put up with harassment from the "Red Coats."

On March 5, 1770, a British soldier beat a barber's apprentice. Angry Bostonians gathered. Attucks strode to the head of the crowd and urged them to storm the guards at the Boston Customs House. The British main guard rallied. Accounts vary on what happened next, but the outcome was fatal: the soldiers fired. Attucks was felled by two musket balls. Four other men were killed, too. The *Boston Gazette* covered the funeral of Attucks and the other heroes of the "Boston Massacre." The city's bells all tolled in their honor.

The Crispus Attucks memorial on the Boston Common in Massachusetts is the first American monument to honor an African American.

John James Audubon
naturalist painter ★ 1785—1851

John James Audubon was a keen observer of nature, especially birds. (He was the first to put small bands around birds' legs to track their movements.)

But in 1819, Audubon was bankrupt. He'd failed at several businesses in Kentucky and Missouri. One reason was the amount of time he spent out in the wilderness, drawing and note-taking. Now, all he had was his sketches. So in 1820, Audubon decided to produce a multivolume book of paintings of all the birds in North America.

Audubon left his family in New Orleans, Louisiana, and traveled widely, seeking subjects for his paintings. In 1826, he went to Europe to exhibit his work and find sponsors for his book. People loved Audubon's vivid paintings. His birds were life-size and realistically posed in detailed, elaborate backgrounds.

Audobon's masterpiece, *The Birds of America,* was published between 1827 and 1838. Audubon also published *The Viviparous Quadrupeds of North America* (1845–1854). The National Audubon Society, a wildlife protection group founded in 1886, was named in honor of this naturalist.

Osprey, c.1829. Audubon often shot birds and used wire to position them as models for his paintings.

Joan Baez
musician ★ 1941—

In July 1959, a young singer talked her way onto the stage of the Newport Folk Festival. She sang two spirituals and the crowd went wild. Joan Baez had just become the new queen of folk music.

After her stunning success, Baez signed a record contract. Her first solo album, *Joan Baez,* got rave reviews when it was released in 1960. Her live performances on the folk music circuit were packed. People loved hearing her strong, beautiful soprano bring new power to traditional folk songs. Baez's music also included her own work, which reflected her liberal politics. During the 1960s and 1970s, her stirring protest songs inspired civil rights marchers and anti–Vietnam War demonstrators. Her live performances of songs like "Joe Hill" and "We Shall Overcome" are legendary.

Baez has released 47 albums to date. Her album, *Diamonds and Rust* (1975) went gold. Throughout her career, Joan Baez has often used her name and her voice to support activist causes.

*Joan Baez introduced **Bob Dylan** to her audiences. In the early 1960s, the two reigned as king and queen of the folk-singing world.*

"You don't get to choose how you're going to die. Or when. You can decide how you're going to live now." —JOAN BAEZ

18

George Balanchine (l.) studied ballet and music theory. This gave him an extraordinary feel for the relationship between movement and music.

George Balanchine
choreographer ★ 1904–1983

Russian-born George Balanchine transformed American ballet. Balanchine defected from a 1924 tour with the Soviet State Dancers. He joined Sergei Diaghilev's famous Ballets Russes in Paris in 1924. Nine years later, he arrived in the United States with American dance patron Lincoln Kirstein, Balanchine founded the School of American Ballet in 1934 and the American Ballet Company the following year. Their goal was to develop an American dance troupe that rivaled those in Europe. Ballets like *Serenade* (1934) established Balanchine as a bold new choreographer, one who could infuse classical ballet with contemporary dance movement and style.

In 1946, Balanchine and Kirstein founded the Ballet Society, which became the New York City Ballet in 1948. Balanchine served as the company's artistic director for 35 years.

During his long career, Balanchine choreographed 425 dances. He created some of ballet's most important works, such as *Apollo* (1928), *The Four Temperaments* (1946), *Firebird* (1949), and *Agon* (1957). He was awarded the Presidential Medal of Freedom in 1983.

Lucille Ball
actress ★ 1911–1989

A classic Lucille Ball moment.

Huge, long-lashed eyes. Wide, lipsticked mouth. A face that stretched and twisted like rubber. The great comic actress Lucille Ball used them all as props.

In the 1930s and 1940s, Ball appeared in 43 movies. Most of them weren't memorable. She moved on to a new medium, television.

The *I Love Lucy* show ran from 1951 to 1957. Ball played a ditzy housewife always dreaming up ways to break into showbiz or make money. Most of her schemes backfired . . . hilariously! Ball was a slapstick queen, a master of comic timing and gestures. *I Love Lucy* became America's number one TV show for most of its run.

Ball and her husband, Cuban bandleader Desi Arnaz (costar of *I Love Lucy*), insisted on innovative formats for their show. Their ideas changed the whole TV industry. *I Love Lucy* ushered in the half-hour sitcom. It was shot on high-quality film in a studio in front of a live audience. Desilu became one of the world's largest television producers. After their 1960 divorce, Ball took over Desilu, becoming the first woman to head a major studio.

Benjamin Banneker

astronomer, inventor ★ 1731–1806

Benjamin Banneker, a free descendent of slaves, grew up on the family farm in Maryland and went to a Quaker school. In his spare time he made up complicated math puzzles.

When he was 20, Banneker took apart a neighbor's watch, sketched each component, and memorized its position. Then he started carving. Two years later, he had built an accurate wooden clock that chimed on the hour for 50 years.

Though he continued farming, Banneker borrowed a telescope from his neighbor and took up astronomy at age 58. A friend then persuaded President **George Washington** to appoint Banneker to the surveying committee planning the nation's new capital. His calculations told the building crew where to chop down trees to create Washington, D.C.'s wide avenues.

Once home, Banneker went back to work, calculating the times of sunrise, sunset, eclipses, and other astronomical events. From 1792 to 1797, he published his findings as *Benjamin Banneker's Almanac*. Banneker sent a copy of his first almanac to **Thomas Jefferson**. He wanted to show by example of his own work that African Americans were not inferior.

In 1980, the U.S. Post Office issued this stamp commemorating Benjamin Banneker's achievements.

P. T. Barnum

showman ★ 1810–1891

P. T. Barnum knew people loved the kinds of shows he produced—and that they would pay for the entertainment.

For 25¢ you could enter Phineas Taylor Barnum's American Museum in New York City and see trained dogs and trained fleas, mimes and marionettes, and the not-so-real Feejee Mermaid (actually, a shriveled monkey skin with fish scales added). Thousands of people eagerly gave up that quarter.

Barnum was America's biggest and brashest showman in the 19th century. He got his start by touring Joice Heth, a black woman who claimed to be 160 years old *and* to have been George Washington's nurse. In 1842, Barnum introduced one of his biggest stars, a midget nicknamed General Tom Thumb.

When he was 60, Barnum, along with partners, helped create one of America's earliest mass entertainments: the circus. The "Barnum & Bailey Greatest Show on Earth, The World's Largest, Grandest, Best Amusement Institution" opened in Brooklyn, New York, in 1871.

"There's a sucker born

Clara Barton

nurse ★ 1821–1912

Mathew Brady photographed Clara Barton in Washington, D.C., in the 1860s.

Born in Oxford, Massachusetts, Clara Barton went to work in the U.S. Patent Office in Washington, D.C. She was the first woman hired for a government job.

Barton was in the capital when the Civil War broke out. She recruited women to help gather and prepare supplies for the front lines. She bypassed government and military authorities. Barton worked in some of the Civil War's worst battles. The "Angel of the Battlefield" comforted, nursed, and cooked for thousands of wounded soldiers she called "my boys."

In 1868, Clara Barton traveled to Switzerland for a rest. There, she heard about the International Committee of the Red Cross, a neutral agency that brought medical aid to all sides during wartime. Barton returned home and spent five years drumming up government and public support for a similar group. The American National Red Cross was formed in 1881. Clara Barton served as its president until she retired in 1904.

Alexander Graham Bell

inventor ★ 1847–1922

Alexander Graham Bell was looking for a way to improve the telegraph—instead, he invented the telephone.

Bell was a professor of vocal physiology at Boston University. He was fascinated by how the vocal chords worked and wondered if those sounds could be transmitted through wires. In the 1870s, Bell and his assistant, Thomas Watson, a mechanical whiz, were working on ways to send multiple telegrams over one telegraph line. Watson was in one room. He tuned a thin metal strip. In another room nearby, Bell heard plucking on a wire. It was the sounds of Watson's tuning, which had transmitted along the wire. Bell realized what the possibilities were and went to work. On March 7, 1876, Bell received a patent for his new machine. Three days later, he uttered into it historic words: "Mr. Watson. Come here, I want to see you." It was the first telephone call.

Within 40 years of its invention, nearly the whole country was wired for telephones, and 1.5 million phones were in use. Bell became quite wealthy. Still, he spent hours working on his new inventions, like the "vacuum jacket," an artificial breathing device.

Alexander Graham Bell placing a call from New York to Chicago in 1892, 17 years after he invented his "harmonic telegraph," or telephone.

every minute." — P. T. BARNUM

"God bless America, Land that I love..."

— IRVING BERLIN

Irving Berlin (at the piano) wrote a song while he was in the army in 1918, but it didn't really become a hit for nearly 20 years. The song? "God Bless America," now the "second" national anthem.

Irving Berlin
composer ★ 1888—1989

"There's No Business Like Show Business" was one of Irving Berlin's hit songs. It could also have been his personal theme song.

Berlin, the son of Russian-Jewish immigrants, sang on New York street corners to earn money. Then he started writing music. His piece "Alexander's Ragtime Band" got people across the nation humming and tapping their toes. From then on, through the 1930s, Berlin was the country's top songwriter.

In 1919, Berlin started his own music publishing business and later opened the Music Box Theatre in New York to stage his work. He wrote music for revues, Broadway shows, and Hollywood films. Some of Berlin's classic numbers include "Puttin' on the Ritz" and "Easter Parade." One of the highlights of the box-office hit movie *Holiday Inn* (1942) was when Bing Crosby crooned Berlin's now-famous song "White Christmas." Berlin's long-running musical about **Annie Oakley**, *Annie Get Your Gun* (1946), ran for 1,000 performances, and has been recently revived.

Leonard Bernstein
composer, conductor ★ 1918—1990

To Leonard Bernstein, music was a celebration of life and he wanted to invite everyone to the party.

Schooled at Harvard University and trained at Tanglewood, the summer home of the Boston Symphony, Bernstein became an overnight sensation in 1943. When the conductor fell ill, he stepped in to lead the New York Philharmonic Orchestra. Bernstein's energy and emotion at the podium got rave reviews.

Between 1958 and 1969, Bernstein conducted 939 concerts with the New York Philharmonic Orchestra and was its first American director. He greatly increased the audience for classical music through his popular television broadcasts and educational programs. He traveled around the world, conducting orchestras in Europe and Israel. He made more than 400 records during his career.

Bernstein was an extraordinary composer, too. In 1954, he won an Academy Award for his music for *On the Waterfront*. Three years later, he collaborated on the smash Broadway musical *West Side Story*.

Leonard Bernstein was awarded a Lifetime Achievement Grammy (1985), 11 Emmys, and countless international and academic awards.

Chuck Berry
rock 'n' roll musician ★ 1926—

Chuck Berry. Rock 'n' roll. Many people would say those words are synonyms.

In the early 1950s, Berry played guitar in a trio in clubs around his hometown of St. Louis, Missouri. Legendary bluesman Muddy Waters introduced him to his record producer. Leonard Chess liked the way Berry's two-string guitar licks gave hillbilly music a rocking new rhythm. He signed up the guitarist. "Maybellene" (1955), Berry's first release with Chess Records, was a hit with black and white audiences, especially teenagers. More of his songs made the charts: "Roll over Beethoven" (1956), "Rock and Roll Music" (1957), "Johnny B. Goode" and "Sweet Little Sixteen" (both 1958). Berry's sassy songs about cars, girls, fun, and freedom had an irresistible rock 'n' roll beat. New, young British bands—now the world-famous Beatles and Rolling Stones—picked up this rhythm, recording Berry tunes on their first albums.

After a stint in jail, Chuck Berry came back with hits like "Nadine" and "No Particular Place to Go" in 1964. Most of Chuck Berry's songs are considered rock classics.

The "duckwalk." Chuck Berry says he created his famous move early in his career, to hide the wrinkles in a suit he was wearing.

Mary McLeod Bethune
educator ★ 1875—1955

Mary McLeod Bethune was the daughter of former slaves. Her life's work was to ensure that no African-American child was enslaved by ignorance or poverty.

In 1904, Bethune rented an old cottage in Daytona, Florida. She set up crates for chairs and desks and opened the Daytona Normal and Industrial Institute for Negro Girls in Florida. By 1923, the elementary school had grown into a college. That year, it merged with the Cookman Institute for Men and became Bethune-Cookman College. Bethune served as president for many years and counted **Eleanor Roosevelt** and **Madame C. J. Walker** among her supporters.

Her work was recognized by President **Franklin D. Roosevelt**, who appointed Bethune head of the Office of Minority Affairs of the National Youth Administration in 1936. She was the first African-American woman to hold a government job at this level. Bethune also served as vice president of the National Association for the Advancement of Colored People (NAACP) from 1940 until her death in 1955.

Educator Mary McLeod Bethune founded the National Council of Negro Women in 1935 to fight racism and sexism.

"I am just a guy with a very

Billy the Kid
outlaw ★ c.1859–1881

Billy the Kid shot his first man in a bar fight in Arizona. He was 15.

He was a hired gun in New Mexico's Lincoln County range wars in 1878. There were murder and revenge on all sides of the feuding landowners and cattle grazers. Billy ambushed and killed a sheriff and deputy. In 1879, he worked out a deal with New Mexico's governor to give evidence in return for a pardon. When he was double-crossed, Billy escaped from jail. He continued getting into gunfights and added in a little mail robbery and counterfeiting, too.

Sheriff Pat Garrett of Lincoln County thought he put a stop to all this in 1881, when he captured Billy the Kid. Despite leg and hand irons, Billy shot two deputies. With a bold wave of his hat, he escaped. Garrett was enraged. He tracked Billy the Kid for several months. Finally, in Fort Sumner, Garrett found him in the home of a sweetheart. The sheriff hid in a darkened room, surprised the outlaw, and shot him in the heart. Billy the Kid was dead. He was 21.

Billy the Kid also used the names Kid Antrim and William H. Bonney. This is the only surviving photo of the outlaw.

Game 4 of the 1983–1984 NBA championship. Larry Bird's aggressive playing helped the Celtics come from behind. The Celtics won the title in the seventh game when they beat the Lakers 111–102.

Larry Bird
basketball player ★ 1956—

In his first year, forward Larry Bird helped turn the Boston Celtics around from a basketball team with a 29–53 record to one with 61 wins, 21 losses. He became NBA (National Basketball Association) Rookie of the Year for his efforts.

Bird signed with the Celtics in 1979 for $3.25 million, making him the most highly paid rookie ever in pro basketball. Passing, shooting, rebounding, defense, Bird was an all-around extraordinary forward, especially in clutch plays. In his 13 seasons with the Celtics, Bird led the team to three NBA titles (1981, 1984, 1986). The competition between Bird and Los Angeles Lakers guard **Magic Johnson** was legendary.

Larry Bird was named Most Valuable Player (MVP) three times and MVP of the NBA finals twice. In 1992, Bird joined the Dream Team that scored the Olympic gold medal at Barcelona, Spain. That same year, Bird retired from playing professional basketball. He coached the Indiana Pacers from 1997 to 2000. He was named Coach of the Year (1997–1998).

large bump of curiosity and a gambling instinct."

Clarence Birdseye
inventor ★ 1886—1956

Clarence Birdseye traveled to Labrador, Canada, to seek his fortune in the fur trade. He found it—but in frozen foods.

Birdseye watched Labrador's Native Americans fishing in subzero weather. The fish froze solid the minute they were laid out on the Arctic ice. They were later thawed and eaten, and were still tasty!

Back in New York, Birdseye started experimenting with brine, ice, and an electric fan. He opened his own company, Birdseye Seafood, Inc., and sold chilled fish. By 1925, he had invented a "Quick Freeze Machine." It flash-froze food so fast that large ice crystals couldn't form and ruin the food. Four years later, Birdseye Seafood, Inc., was sold for $22 million to what would become the huge General Foods Corporation. Birdseye became a president within the company.

In 1930, 26 different types of individually packaged frozen fruits, vegetables, meat, and fish were test-marketed in Springfield, Massachusetts. Fourteen years later, people in the rest of the country got their first taste of frozen food. Clarence Birdseye had founded a whole new industry.

Elizabeth Blackwell
doctor ★ 1821—1910

Dr. Elizabeth Blackwell founded the first medical school for women in the United States.

Elizabeth Blackwell applied to 29 different medical schools before Geneva College in New York accepted her in 1847. Even then, she was not taken seriously. The college admitted her as a joke! Blackwell had the last laugh. In 1849, she became the first woman in the U.S. to receive a medical degree.

No American hospital would hire a female doctor, though. Dr. Blackwell, who was born in England, went back to Europe. She worked in a British hospital and studied midwifery in France. In 1851, Dr. Elizabeth Blackwell returned to New York and tried to set up a private practice. No one would rent her office space. Blackwell bought a house and set up her own hospital, the New York Infirmary for Women and Children, in 1857.

During the Civil War, Blackwell and **Dorothea Dix** trained women for the Union army medical corps and helped establish the U.S. Sanitary Commission in 1861. The commission set up and ran war hospitals. In 1868, Blackwell founded the Women's Medical College of the New York Infirmary.

Bonnie Blair
Olympic skater ★ 1964—

Bonnie Blair hit the ice with a tight, low crouch and a long glide. Her strength and style added up to one thing: speed.

Blair first stood up on skates when she was two years old. She was winning races in her hometown of Champaign, Illinois, by the time she was four. As a teenager, she set her sights on the Olympics. After training in Europe, Blair finished eighth in the 500-meter speed-skating sprint at the 1984 Winter Olympics in Sarajevo, Yugoslavia. Then she was off on a record-breaking winning streak. Blair became the first U.S. female athlete to be awarded five Olympic gold medals in her career. She took home the gold for the 500-meter race in 1988, 1992, and 1994. She picked up gold medals for the 1,000-meter race in 1992 and 1994. In 1988, she picked up a bronze medal for this event. These triumphs made her the first speed skater to win the same event in three consecutive Winter Olympics.

Blair still had a personal goal beyond the gold: She wanted to beat the women's world record of 39 seconds for the 500-meter race. She did—*twice*! At the 1994 World Sprint Championship in Calgary, Canada, Blair finished in a close 38.99. The following year, she skated an impressive 38.69. Blair retired in 1995.

Amelia Bloomer
suffragist ★ 1818—1894

Suffragist Amelia Jenks Bloomer founded *The Lily* in 1849. It was the first newspaper journal published, edited, and even typeset by women. Through *The Lily,* Bloom promoted temperance, suffrage, women's rights, health, and dress reform. In the 1860s, a woman might have worn almost 15 pounds of clothing. The uncomfortable dresses, hooped skirts, tight corsets, and petticoats caused physical problems and even accidents. Bloomer wrote about a new style of full-cut pantaloons, or "Turkish trousers," worn under a short skirt. She urged women to adopt this comfortable new fashion and did so herself. People started calling the pants "bloomers." Suffragists like **Elizabeth Cady Stanton**, **Susan B. Anthony**, and **Lucy Stone** wore the outfits publicly. However, people did not take women in pants seriously. Bloomer and the others realized the costume was interfering with their suffrage and reform work. They abandoned bloomers. Amelia did not abandon her activist work, however. She became president of the Iowa Woman Suffrage Society in 1871 and continued to lobby for women's right to vote.

Amelia Bloomer helped start a national craze for "bloomers," like the ones shown here. Some religious leaders branded the outfit "devilish."

laughing off those who would ban them."

Judy Blume is an active leader in the National Coalition Against Censorship. She's seen her own books banned in some schools and libraries because of their topics.

Judy Blume
author ★ 1938—

When she was a child, Judy Blume dreamed of becoming a ballerina or a movie star. Instead, she became a famous author who writes about children's dreams—and fears, and all the other joys and pains of growing up.

Blume was a suburban housewife and mother when she started writing children's books. She struggled through two years of rejections before her first book, *The One in the Middle Is the Green Kangaroo* (1969), was published. Judy got a check for $350. She's now the author of 22 books, which have been translated into more than 20 languages and have sold more than 75 million copies.

Blume opened up a whole new approach to realistic children's fiction. She writes sympathetically and humorously about the things kids worry about, but no one wrote about: first kisses, first bras, menstruation, weight, difficult siblings, divorce, peer pressure. Her best-selling titles include *Are You There God? It's Me, Margaret* (1970); *Tales of a Fourth-grade Nothing* and *Otherwise Known as Sheila the Great* (both 1972); *Blubber* (1974); *Superfudge* (1980); *Here's to You, Rachel Robinson* (1993); and *Double Fudge* (2002).

Nellie Bly
journalist ★ c.1865—1922

Elizabeth Cochrane Seaman took her pen name from a popular song. Under the byline "Nellie Bly" she wrote investigative pieces that got people calling her "the best reporter in America."

In 1887, Nellie took a job with the *New York World* newspaper. She wrote her stories from firsthand experience. One of her early articles exposed conditions in a New York mental institution. Bly faked insanity and got herself committed to the asylum on Blackwell's Island. Her story prompted a grand jury investigation of the institution that resulted in better patient care. Bly also pretended to shoplift, so she would be arrested and could accurately write about life in jail.

Always looking for a challenge, Nellie Bly decided to beat the record of Phileas Fogg, the fictitious hero of Jules Verne's *Around the World in 80 Days*. She sailed from Hoboken, New Jersey, on November 14, 1889, and traveled around the world by boat, train, and even rickshaw. Seventy-two days, 6 hours, and 11 minutes later, on January 25, 1890, Bly arrived in New York City, where she was greeted by fireworks and a parade.

Nellie Bly recorded her experience in Nellie Bly's Book: Around the World in Seventy-two Days (1890).

Humphrey Bogart

actor ★ 1899—1957

Humphrey Bogart was nominated for an Oscar for Casablanca. *He's more famous for on-screen snarls than smiles.*

The brooding loner, the tough guy, the man with a dark past and no hope of a bright future—Humphrey Bogart built a career out of being an antihero.

In the 1930s, Bogart acted in dozens of gangster films. "Bogey" was usually a bad guy. He soon became a *famous* bad guy. He was outstanding as a gritty gangster who still had a soul in *High Sierra* (1941). Bogart followed with another four-star performance as a hard-edged detective in *The Maltese Falcon* (1941).

Casablanca (1943), a tragic love story set in Nazi-occupied Morocco, catapulted Bogart into film history. Bogey smoked and snarled his way through the movie as a jaded nightclub owner who rediscovers love and hope. Bogart himself discovered love with his next leading lady. Bogart and Lauren Bacall burned up the screen in *To Have and Have Not* (1944), *The Big Sleep* (1946), and *Key Largo* (1948). They married in 1945.

Over the next decade, Humphrey Bogart showed his range and depth as an actor. He won an Academy Award for his performance in *The African Queen* (1951).

Daniel Boone

pioneer ★ 1734—1820

This frontiersman never really settled down—but he opened up the way for all the settlers who streamed into Kentucky.

Daniel Boone grew up in Pennsylvania and North Carolina. He married and later moved his family to Virginia. Boone was only a halfhearted farmer. What he really liked was the wilderness. He joined an expedition that explored the swampy interior of Florida and, in 1767, journeyed westward to the Cumberland River area.

In 1775, Boone helped negotiate a deal between the Cherokee and the Transylvania Land Company. The company got 20 million acres of land surrounded by the Ohio, Kentucky, and Cumberland rivers. But settlers had no route into the new holdings. The solution would make Daniel Boone famous.

Following the Cherokees' "Warrior's Path," Boone, and 30 other men bushwhacked, burned, and hacked out the 250-mile-long Wilderness Road over the Blue Ridge Mountains and through the Cumberland Gap, near what is now the borders of Kentucky, Virginia, and Tennessee. The Boones were the first white settlers in what became Kentucky.

"I can't say as ever I was lost, but I was

Margaret Bourke-White
photographer ★ 1906–1971

Margaret Bourke-White turned her lens on the world and made the world take a good look at itself. Her photos document the lives of sharecroppers and mine workers, the horrors of war, and the soaring beauty of skyscrapers.

In 1936, Bourke-White became one of four staff photographers of **Henry Luce**'s new photo magazine, *Life*. She remained with the magazine for 33 years, covering newsworthy events worldwide. One of her early assignments was a study of poverty in the rural South. Bourke-White and her husband, novelist Erskine Caldwell, collected the photos into a powerful book called *You Have Seen Their Faces* (1937).

In 1941, Bourke-White got a major news scoop. She shot photos inside the Soviet Union, which had just been invaded by Germany. Women at that time rarely did war

While covering WWII, Margaret Bourke-White was once aboard a ship that was torpedoed off the coast of North Africa.

reporting, but Bourke-White insisted on covering World War II. She became the U.S. Army's first woman war correspondent in 1942 and traveled with General Patton's army. Her chilling photographs of the Nazi concentration camps shocked the world.

Bradford (standing at right) looks on as Plymouth colonists throw snowballs c. 1621.

William Bradford
Pilgrim leader ★ 1590–1657

He called his new home a "hidious & desolate wilderness, full of wild beasts & willd men." Nonetheless, William Bradford, with his fellow Pilgrims, bravely walked off the *Mayflower* in 1621 onto what would become Plymouth, Massachusetts.

Bradford became the colony's governor in 1622 and served for 30 years. He oversaw the judicial, economic, and legislative decisions that affected the colony. He enforced the Pilgrim's strict religious rules, such as "no gameing or revelling" on Christmas. But Bradford thought it would be wise to have a legal code for the colony, too. He helped draft this in 1636. As governor, he tried to keep religious and civic issues separate. He allowed colonists who did not belong to his church to have the same rights as those who did.

William Bradford kept many records of life in the new colony. His most ambitious work was a two-volume history, *Of Plimouth Plantation, 1620–1647*, which he started in 1630. It is an important account of Pilgrim life and their relations with the Pequot and Wampanoag of the area.

bewildered once for three days."

— DANIEL BOONE

Mathew Brady
photographer ★ 1823–1896

Six hundred thousand people lost their lives in the Civil War. The pain and sorrow of some of those deaths were recorded for all to see by this artist of a new medium: photography.

Samuel Morse introduced Mathew Brady to daguerreotypes, an early type of photograph. Brady quickly became a well-known photographer of the rich and famous.

Mathew Brady (leaning against tree) called the camera the "eye of history." Congress bought his Civil War photo collection in 1875 for $25,000.

When the Civil War broke out, Brady saw the historical and financial possibilities of going to war . . . with a camera. Soldiers on the battlefront and families on the home front wanted to have photos of their faraway loved ones. Brady also organized 300 photographers who lugged heavy camera equipment to battlefields and military camps. Some war photos he shot himself. Most times "photography by Brady" was actually by a Brady employee. But no matter who was behind the lens, the grim, corpse-ridden photos that came out of the camera shocked the nation. Never before had war and death looked so real.

Marlon Brando (r.) as The Godfather.

Marlon Brando
actor ★ 1924—

He seethed with frustration and lust as the brute Stanley Kowalski in *A Streetcar Named Desire* (stage, 1947; film, 1951). He transformed a working-class lug into a gutsy hero in *On the Waterfront* (1954). He swaggered with devil-may-care desperation as a motorcycle tough in *The Wild One* (1954). Marlon Brando brought extraordinary intensity to these roles.

Brando won an Academy Award for *On the Waterfront*, but in the 1960s, his career zigzagged. He was pegged as difficult and unreliable. In 1972, he dominated the screen as Don Corleone in *The Godfather* (1972). Brando won a second Academy Award for his portrayal of the aging Mafia head. His last masterpiece was the acclaimed but controversial *Last Tango in Paris* (1973). Brando was nominated for best supporting actor for *A Dry White Season* (1989). He charmed audiences in the comedy *The Freshman* (1990) and in the quirky *Don Juan de Marco* (1995). In 2001, he starred in *The Score*.

"Country isn't an image, it's a way

CANADA
MOLLY BRANT
KOŃWATSI'TSIAIÉŃNI
POSTAGE POSTES
34

Molly Brant helped run Johnson Hall in Johnstown, New York. Iroquois councils were often held there.

Molly Brant
Mohawk leader ★ 1736—1796

Molly Brant was probably born and raised in the Mohawk Valley, New York. She was the daughter of a Mohawk chief. Her tribal name was Deganwadonti or Kaonwatsi-Tsiaienni. Brant lived with Sir William Johnson, the superintendent of Indian affairs, from around 1759 to his death in 1774. William and Molly had nine children together. She ran Johnson's household and entertained distinguished guests at his New York mansion. Still, in his will, Johnson referred to Brant as his "prudent & Faithfull Housekeeper."

Through Molly's influence, the Iroquois nation sided with the British during the American Revolution. So did her family. Her brother, Joseph Brant, was the war's most famous Native American warrior. Her son, Peter Brant, captured the patriot soldier **Ethan Allen**. Molly herself spied on the patriots for the British, sent ammunition to their troops, and hid their soldiers. After the peace treaties of 1783, she moved on to Kingston, Ontario. Brant received a lifetime annual pension of 100 pounds (£) from the British for her efforts.

Garth Brooks
country-western singer ★ 1962—

Garth Brooks gets his audiences clapping, toe tapping, and line dancing. And this country-western singer is pretty energetic onstage himself!

Brooks plays down-home country music with a little bit of a pop twang. His album *Ropin' the Wind* (1991) was the first ever to debut at number one on the country *and* pop music charts. The Stetson-wearing Oklahoman debuted in Kansas City in 1989. There were only 334 people in the audience. That soon changed. His first album had four songs that hit the charts, including "If Tomorrow Never Comes" and "The Dance." His second album, *No Fences* (1990), sold 700,000 copies. *Double-Live* (1998) sold a record 1.08 million in the first week!

In 2000, Garth Brooks was awarded three American Music Awards: Favorite Country Album, Favorite Male Country Artist, and Artist of the Decade. The release of *Scarecrow* (2001) marked Brooks's 15th album and his first studio album in four years. It shot to number one on the country charts.

Garth Brooks plays the Country Music Awards (2001). His 1997 concert in New York City's Central Park drew nearly one million fans.

# of life put to music."
—GARTH BROOKS

Gwendolyn Brooks
poet ★ 1917—2000

This is the time for Big Poems/roaring up out of the sleaze,/poems from ice, from vomit, and from/tainted blood. Gwendolyn Brooks's poems reflected the hopes, dreams, struggles, frustrations, and pride of her people. Her mastery of words helped make her the first African-American poet to win the Pulitzer prize.

Brooks's first collection of poems, *A Street in Bronzeville* (1945), dealt with questions of race and poverty. It got great reviews and earned Brooks two Guggenheim writing fellowships. Her second book, *Annie Allen*, was a poetic look at inner-city life in Chicago. This time, Brooks got the 1950 Pulitzer.

Brooks's writing during the 1960s was influenced by the Black Power and black arts movements. The movements encouraged the growth of African-American political awareness and cultural pride. Brooks addressed these topics in *In the Mecca*, published in 1968. She was the first African-American woman elected to the National Institute of Arts and Letters (1976) and the first to serve as the Library of Congress's poetry consultant (1985). Brooks wrote more than 20 books and hundreds of poems. She was awarded the National Medal of Arts in 1995.

James Brown
soul singer ★ c.1928—

He spins, slides, falls to his knees. He sweats off seven pounds. He shrieks from his very soul. He's James Brown, "The Hardest Working Man in Show Business."

James Brown exploded onto the music scene in 1955. He was the lead singer for the Famous Flames who had a hit single in "Please, Please, Please." His songwriting took gospel and rhythm and blues and layered them with innovative rhythms and vocals to create a whole new sound. People liked what they heard. Brown's album *Live at the Apollo* (1963) sold a million copies.

Brown was often ahead of his time musically and in touch with the times emotionally. He brought in the funk with albums like "Papa's Got a Brand New Bag," (1965) and classic singles like "I Got You (I Feel Good)" (1966). His anthem song, "Say It Loud—I'm Black and I'm Proud" (1968) captured the pride of the Black Power movement in the 1960s. "Sex Machine" (1970) and "Hot Pants" (1971) provided dance tracks for the party atmosphere of the 1970s.

"God got me in on the ground floor

Jim Brown
football player ★ 1936—

The thing about stopping Cleveland Browns fullback Jim Brown was that first you had to tackle him . . . if you could.

Brown came to pro football with an outstanding college ball reputation. He was All-American in football and helped bring Syracuse University to the 1957 Cotton Bowl.

After graduation, he was drafted by the Cleveland Browns. Brown played with Cleveland from 1957 to 1965 and never missed a game. The formidable fullback developed his own low-to-the-ground running style. With this high-speed glide and his awesome power, Brown built up a great career record: 756 points scored, 12,312 yards rushed, 262 receptions, 126 touchdowns, and 15,459 combined net yards. Brown was the top rusher in eight of the nine seasons he played pro football, averaging 104 yards a game. He was voted the National Football League's Most Valuable Player in 1958 and 1965.

1957 Rookie of the Year Jim Brown went on to play in nine straight Pro Bowls. In 1963, he helped the Browns win the NFL championship.

John Brown
abolitionist ★ 1800—1859

John Brown's last act fired up the antislavery movement.

Brown planned to seize the federal arsenal at Harper's Ferry in what was then Virginia. He was going to give the weapons to slaves. Brown expected them to join him in a violent rebellion against slaveholders.

On October 16, 1859, Brown, 13 other white men, including three of his sons, and five black men quietly captured the arsenal. They didn't hold it long. A howling mob and local militia attacked. Several of Brown's men were killed. A few fled. Others tried to surrender, but were shot instead. Colonel **Robert E. Lee** and the U.S. Marines arrived. They overwhelmed Brown and the four other men still standing. The fiery abolitionist was jailed and charged with murder and treason.

Brown wrote more than 100 letters from his cell. Many of them were published in newspapers. Brown's words rallied Northerners to the antislavery cause, which angered and frightened Southerners. He stood trial lying on a cot because of his severe injuries. The verdict was swift: guilty.

On December 2, 1859, John Brown was hanged. About two years later, the Civil War broke out.

*John Brown confided his plan to other abolitionists like **Frederick Douglass**, **Harriet Tubman**, and **William Lloyd Garrison**.*

# of every kind of music." —JAMES BROWN

"The stakes for America

Blanche K. Bruce
senator ★ 1841—1898

Blanche Kelso Bruce was born a slave and became a senator.

Born in Virginia, Bruce fled to Kansas when the Civil War began in 1861. There he started a school for other escaped slaves. He spent a short time studying at Oberlin College in Ohio, then later moved on and set up Missouri's first state school for African Americans in 1864.

Bruce moved to Mississippi in 1869, after the Civil War. Smart and savvy, he realized there were political opportunities to represent newly freed slaves. He saw there were financial opportunities, too. Bruce purchased an old plantation and soon had a thriving cotton business. Because of his moderate approach, he gained the support of many white officials and was appointed to different jobs in the state's tax, education, levee (flood control), and sheriff's departments.

In 1874, Mississippi's legislature elected Blanche K. Bruce to the U.S. Senate. He served on Congressional committees on education

Blanche K. Bruce was appointed register of the Treasury in 1881. He was the first African American to put his signature on U.S. currency.

and labor. He lobbied for equal rights and more opportunities for African Americans and for fairer treatment for Native Americans and Chinese immigrants.

Aaron Burr
vice president ★ 1756—1836

Thomas Jefferson and Aaron Burr tied for the presidency in 1800. Burr, a senator from New York, expected his fellow New Yorker, **Alexander Hamilton**, to support him when the decision went to the House of Representatives. Hamilton did not. He thought Burr "a most unfit and dangerous man. . . ." The House was deadlocked for 35 rounds of voting. On the 36th ballot, due to Hamilton's influence, Burr lost. In accordance with the law at the time, Burr became vice president.

Jefferson and the other Democratic-Republicans did not want Aaron Burr on the 1804 presidential ticket. Burr decided to run for governor of New York instead. He had a secret plan: If elected, he would join Massachusetts, and the two states would secede from the union to form their own country. Hamilton got wind of the idea and was outraged. He wrote political and personal attacks that helped defeat Burr. Burr

Aaron Burr, a distinguished veteran of the American Revolution, served only one term as vice president.

challenged Hamilton to a duel to defend his honor. The duel took place on July 11, 1804. Hamilton lost the duel—and his life. Burr was accused but not convicted of murder.

Three years later, Burr was arrested for treason. He was plotting to take over the Louisiana Territory and secede. John Marshall presided over the groundbreaking trial. Burr, once again, was acquitted. He fled to Europe.

are never small." —GEORGE W. BUSH

After Operation Desert Storm (1991), President Bush's popularity shot up to 89% in the polls.

George Bush
41st president ★ 1924—

George Bush came to the Oval Office a decorated World War II pilot, a savvy oil company millionaire, a seasoned diplomat, a former CIA director, and an experienced vice president under **Ronald Reagan**.

President Bush navigated U.S. foreign relations through the end of the Cold War with the Soviet Union, which was in a state of collapse. In 1989, he ordered U.S. troops into Panama to arrest Panamanian dictator and drug trafficker Manuel Noriega. Then, in 1990, Bush led the U.S. and allied forces in the Persian Gulf War against Saddam Hussein, whose Iraqi army had invaded oil-rich Kuwait. Relentless air strikes started on January 16, 1991. Ground troops rushed in about a month later, and within 100 hours Kuwait was liberated—and Bush was a hero.

But postwar economic realities quickly caught up with the president. The deficit was out of control. Bush had already gone back on his most vocal campaign promise—"Read my lips: no new taxes." The country was headed for a recession. Bush served only one term (1989–1993).

George W. Bush
43rd president ★ 1946—

George W. Bush's presidency has been defined by two dates: December 12, 2000, the day the U.S. Supreme Court halted the disputed ballot count in Florida, and September 11, 2001, the day terrorists attacked the World Trade Center and the Pentagon.

The former governor of Texas was inaugurated after the topsy-turvy election of 2000. Democratic vice president Al Gore won the popular vote. Bush, a Republican, carried the electoral college vote after a series of court cases, reversals, and finally a Supreme Court ruling.

President Bush came into office with a conservative tax, energy, and defense agenda, which has been hotly debated.

But nothing was as tough as what came next.

President Bush had to respond to the deadly attacks in New York City and Washington, D.C. He declared war on terrorism and ordered the bombing of Afghanistan to break up the deadly al-Qaeda terrorist network.

*President George W. Bush at the Ground Zero attack site in New York City. He is the son of President **George Bush** and former first lady Barbara Bush.*

35

Richard Byrd
explorer ★ 1888–1957

Richard Byrd could be very persuasive. He talked his parents into letting him visit a family friend. That trip took him from his Virginia home halfway around the world to the Philippines—when he was 12!

Byrd graduated from the U.S. Naval Academy in 1912.

In 1925, he raised $140,000 for an expedition to the North Pole. On May 26, 1926, Byrd and his copilot Floyd Bennett took off from a base camp on a remote Arctic island. They flew about 1,750 miles to the North Pole, despite a dangerous oil leak. When they returned from their record-setting flight, Byrd had new scientific information. There was no continent up there. The North Pole was surrounded by an icy ocean.

Three years later, Byrd took off for another frozen unknown. On November 29, 1928, he became the first person to fly over the South Pole. From 1933 to 1956, Byrd led four more expeditions to Antarctica. He gathered important scientific, mapping, and geographic information, and helped determine that Antarctica *is* a continent.

In 1934, Richard Byrd lived alone for several dark winter months in Antarctica. Outside his shack, temperatures could drop to -80°F. He was nearly killed by carbon monoxide poisoning from his stove.

Calamity Jane
frontierswoman ★ c.1852–1903

When 24-year-old Martha Jane Burke Cannary sidled up to the bar and ordered drinks all around, she was a character even for the Wild West. Dressed in men's clothing, "Calamity Jane" boasted about her exploits as a gold miner, a mule skinner, a Sioux fighter, a wagoneer, a Pony Express rider, and an Army scout for General **George Custer**. Some of that might even have been true.

Details about Cannary's life are sketchy. Jane and the authors of the dime novels that made her famous went for action over accuracy. Cannary was probably orphaned at 14 when her family headed west. A good shot and sure rider, she took to wearing pants and got a job working on the Union Pacific Railroad.

Calamity Jane drifted around the West and Northwest, drinking, bragging, and possibly working some of the jobs she claimed. She may have married some dozen times before her hard life caught up with her. Calamity Jane died in a room above a saloon in Deadwood in the Dakota Territory.

The Life and Adventures of Calamity Jane: By Herself (c.1900) is one source of the many colorful stories that made its author a frontier legend.

John C. Calhoun
senator, vice president ★ 1782—1850

John C. Calhoun of South Carolina held many positions in his lifetime. He was secretary of war under **James Monroe** (1817–1825) and vice president under **John Quincy Adams** (1825–1829). Though he served in the federal government, Calhoun believed that states' rights should come first.

In 1832, Calhoun resigned as **Andrew Jackson**'s vice president and accepted a seat in the Senate. Senator Calhoun supported the proposed Act of Nullification. This would have allowed a state to nullify or ignore any federal law it felt was unconstitutional or not in the state's interest. Nullification was a serious threat to the authority of the federal government.

Three men dominated national politics from the 1820s to the early 1850s: John Calhoun, Henry Clay, and Daniel Webster.

Calhoun urged South Carolina to ignore federal law and refuse to pay import taxes imposed in 1828 and 1832. President Jackson sent federal troops to the state's border. Calhoun worked with **Henry Clay** to come up with a compromise in time to avoid a conflict.

Calhoun was just as adamant about the right to own slaves. This "peculiar institution," as he called slavery, was a "positive good." He argued in Congress that slaveholding states should not be restricted by the "tyranny of the majority." This was an important issue at a time when territories like California, Oregon, and Texas were trying to join the union.

George, Cecilius, and Leonard Calvert
founders of Maryland ★ c. 1580—1632 (George);
1605—1675 (Cecilius); 1606—1647 (Leonard)

In the 17th century, the political climate in Protestant England was not favorable for Catholics. So English nobleman George Calvert took himself off to Ireland, where he became baron of Baltimore. In 1623, he bought part of Newfoundland and sailed there in 1627. The climate in Newfoundland was pretty harsh, literally!

Calvert wanted a more hospitable site to establish a colony that would welcome Catholics. King Charles I granted Calvert land between the 40th parallel and the south side of the Potomac River. Unfortunately, Calvert died before this charter became official in 1634. His son Cecilius (Cecil) Calvert then founded the colony of Maryland on the land granted by the king. Cecil never actually set foot on the 12 million acres he inherited, but he governed wisely from England. His brother, Leonard Calvert, went to Maryland and served as the colony's first governor. Maryland became a prosperous colony and a fairly tolerant one. Maryland's Toleration Act of 1649 permitted freedom of religion for all Christians in the colony, fulfilling George Calvert's dream.

George Calvert (shown here) got the land for Maryland; his son Cecilius Calvert inherited it.

"If you've been

Ben Nighthorse Campbell

senator ★ 1933—

Ben Nighthorse Campbell is a member of two governing bodies: the U.S. Senate and the Council of 44 Chiefs of the Northern Cheyenne Tribe.

Campbell is currently the only Native American in the Senate. He was elected senator from Colorado in 1992 and reelected in 1998. Campbell had served in the state legislature before that.

He grew up in a poor, troubled family in California. He credits two things with helping him straighten out his life: the military and sports. Campbell served in the U.S. Air Force from 1951 to 1953. He became interested in judo and took that interest all the way up to black-belt level. Campbell won the U.S. Judo championships three times and was captain of the 1964 Olympic judo team.

Senator Ben Nighthorse Campbell poses with his patriotic Harley-Davidson motorcycle.

The Harley-riding senator is the first Native American to chair the Indian Affairs Committee. He serves on the powerful Appropriations Committee and has been involved in hotly debated issues as a member of the Energy and Natural Resources Committee. Senator Campbell was also, as he put it, "hammered on awfully hard" for switching from the Democratic to the Republican party in 1995.

Al Capone

gangster ★ 1899—1947

Alphonse "Scarface" Capone carried a business card that read "antiques dealer." He was a dealer all right. Capone was making millions by the time he was 30—none of it legally.

In the 1920s, Al Capone headed a crime ring of 1,000 gangsters in Chicago, Illinois. He made his fortune in criminal businesses, such as illegal gambling and bootlegging. Bootlegging was the sale and distribution of liquor during Prohibition (1920–1929), when alcohol was banned. Capone paid off judges, cops, and politicians. He organized rival gangs to work together. When that fell apart, his henchmen wiped out his opponents.

On February 14, 1929, Capone ordered the infamous St. Valentine's Day Massacre. Seven rival gang members were lined up in a garage and riddled with 100 bullets. After years of notorious crimes and bribes, this act proved too much. The FBI couldn't get him—but the IRS did. In 1931, he was convicted of not paying income tax and sentenced to 11 years in prison.

Al Capone's life of crime inspired 30 films. The Public Enemy (1931) included a moral warning about the evils of gangsterism.

hungry... it gives you a perspective."

Frank Capra
film director ★ 1897–1991

— BEN NIGHTHORSE CAMPBELL

Frank Capra on the set of It's A Wonderful Life.

Frank Capra had a degree in chemical engineering. He'd been a lieutenant in the army. In the 1920s, he was knocking around, doing odd jobs, looking for work. He found it when he talked his way into a film company. Capra got paid $75 to direct his first film. In 1928, he got a break when he signed a director's contract with Columbia Pictures.

Capra believed in the "American Dream." His sentimental comedies reflect this. Capra's trademark hero is the common man who triumphs over corruption and greed. **Clark Gable**'s tough-talking but bighearted reporter in *It Happened One Night* (1934) was one. That movie made Capra a star director when it won five Academy Awards, all of the major categories. Capra took home two more Oscars for directing *Mr. Deeds Goes to Town* (1936) and *You Can't Take It with You* (1938). Ironically, Capra is best remembered for his now-classic film *It's a Wonderful Life* (1947), which wasn't a big hit at the box office when it opened.

Andrew Carnegie
industrialist ★ 1835–1919

Andrew Carnegie gave away nearly $351 million before he died. Only about 1% of it went to his own workers' pension and relief funds.

At age 13, Andrew Carnegie worked six long days a week in a Pittsburgh, Pennsylvania, cotton mill and earned $1.20. By the turn of the century, he was the richest man in the world.

Carnegie, a native of Scotland, taught himself **Morse** code and got a telegraph job in the U.S. as a teenager. Then he worked for the Pennsylvania Railroad, rising from secretary to superintendent. He wisely bought company stock along the way.

In the 1860s, he went into the iron bridge–building business and made a fortune. But Carnegie realized the real money was in steel. He formed the Carnegie Steel Corporation in 1873 and controlled production and distribution. He ruthlessly drove competitors out of business and broke up labor unions. One of the bloodiest labor battles of the industrial age was an 1892 strike at the Carnegie steel mill in Homestead, Pennsylvania. Sixteen men died, 163 people were injured. The mill reopened with cheaper labor. Then in 1901, Carnegie sold his steel company to **J. P. Morgan** for $400 million.

Carnegie believed that rich people had an obligation to donate money for the public good. He built more than 2,500 libraries in the English-speaking world. He funded the Carnegie Institute and endowed other colleges for the working class.

"It is simply service

Rachel Carson
scientist ★ 1907—1964

The New York Times *called Rachel Carson a "physical scientist with literary genius."*

Biologist Rachel Carson's research showed that widespread use of toxic chemicals was poisoning the earth. She was outraged that governments and chemical industries encouraged the use of pesticides like DDT. They didn't want to hear about Carson's findings. So she went to a broader audience: the public.

In 1962, Carson published *Silent Spring*. In it, she documented the deadly effect of many chemicals on plants and animals, including people. The book sold more than 100,000 copies in four months and helped launch the modern environmental movement.

When *Silent Spring* also became a huge best-seller, the chemical companies went on the defensive. They attacked Carson's ideas. Carson testified before Congressional committees. President **John F. Kennedy** ordered a study of the issue. Many of Carson's findings were found to be true. Government policy began to change. Rachel Carson received the 1963 Conservationist of the Year award from the National Wildlife Federation for her brave and tireless work.

Jimmy Carter
39th president ★ 1924—

Foreign affairs provided the greatest triumph and biggest tragedy for Democratic president Jimmy Carter. Runaway inflation, high unemployment, and an energy crisis helped make him a one-term president (1977–1981).

Carter served as state senator and Georgia governor before winning the presidency in 1976. Once elected, he had a hard time getting bills passed through Congress. The economy didn't improve. International oil sellers raised their prices. And Carter signed a controversial agreement in 1977 returning the U.S.-built Panama Canal to Panama. Many voters were unhappy.

Public opinion improved in 1978 when Carter mediated the historic Camp David peace accords between Egypt and Israel. Then Iranian militants seized the U.S. embassy's staff in 1979. President Carter tried everything to free them: international diplomacy, economic sanctions, and finally a failed military rescue. Carter's popularity sank. He was defeated by **Ronald Reagan** in a landslide in 1980. On the last day of his presidency, Carter finally got the hostages home, after 444 days of captivity.

Jimmy Carter is still a respected and active mediator in global politics. He was awarded the Nobel Peace Prize in 2002.

that measures success."

— GEORGE WASHINGTON CARVER

George Washington Carver
scientist ★ 1864–1943

George Washington Carver did not believe in wasting anything. His pioneering work in botany and soil conservation helped save farming in the South and the Midwest.

Carver was born into slavery in Diamond Grove, Missouri. (Slavery was outlawed when he was a year old.) When he was 10 years old, he set off on his own to get an education. It took nearly 16 years for him to get to college. He worked all over the Midwest and went to school wherever they'd admit an African American.

In 1890, Carver enrolled in Simpson College in Iowa. He studied art and was a talented painter. Because he'd always been keenly interested in plants, he enrolled in Iowa State College in Ames. Carver graduated with a master's degree in agriculture. He became the first African American on the college's staff. Then **Booker T. Washington** came calling.

In 1896, Washington invited Carver to head the agricultural school at Tuskegee Institute, the African-American college he'd founded in Alabama.

Carver accepted and set up his Experiment Station, a farm at Tuskegee where he could study plants and improve agricultural methods. He realized that his fellow African Americans were trapped in a cycle of poor harvests and mounting debt. Growing cotton, a big cash crop, was partly to blame. Carver knew that cotton plants absorbed nitrogen and wore out the soil. Farmers should sometimes grow peanuts, sweet potatoes, soybeans, and other legumes instead of cotton, he said. Rotating crops would replenish the soil. Carver also suggested mixing in discarded plant material and manure. It would decompose and enrich the farm fields.

George Washington Carver received many awards and two honorary degrees.

Carver spread his message through his classes at Tuskegee. He also lectured and wrote pamphlets and articles. But most important, he developed his "mobile school." Carver and his students loaded up a wagon with tools, seeds, and samples from the Tuskegee Experiment Station. Then they'd go out into the fields. They'd talk to illiterate farmers and demonstrate new farming techniques. Carver also discussed nutrition and home gardens with his audience.

Always practical, Carver realized that there had to be a market for crops other than cotton if the farmers were to succeed. In his laboratory at Tuskegee, he developed more than 325 uses for the peanut, from ink to ice cream.

George Washington Carver became known worldwide. **Thomas Edison** offered him a $100,000 salary to come work at his lab. Carver declined. He stayed at Tuskegee for 47 years and never personally profited from his research.

Mary Cassatt
painter ★ 1844–1926

Mary Cassatt painted The Bath *from 1891 to 1892. It is one of her most famous works.*

In 1988, Mary Cassatt's painting, *The Conversation* (1896), sold for $4.1 million, the highest price ever paid for a painting by a woman.

Mary Cassatt broke with tradition in her art. Before the 19th century, portraits were usually posed, formal pictures of wealthy people. The people in Cassatt's portraits are warm, lively, and emotional. Cassatt used her own family members as models. Her most famous works explored the deep, loving relationship between mother and child.

Although it was unusual for a young girl at the time, Mary Cassatt was determined to become an artist. She studied at the Pennsylvania Academy of the Fine Arts and moved to Paris, France, in 1866. Cassatt's work attracted the attention of Edgar Degas, a well-known French painter. In 1879, he invited her to exhibit her work with a new group of painters called the Impressionists. The Impressionists caused a sensation with their innovative style of painting. Cassatt was the first and only American artist to hang work in the French Impressionist exhibitions. She started showing her work in the U.S. in 1876 and introduced American art audiences to Impressionism.

Willa Cather
author ★ 1873–1947

Willa Cather is considered a master writer of the American frontier and is known for creating strong women characters. Much of her inspiration came from the wide-open spaces and hardworking immigrants in Nebraska's Great Plains, where she grew up. Many of her novels have similar themes: the spirit and values of the pioneers, the relationship between achievement and satisfaction, and the tension between the immigrants' old world customs and their new frontier experiences.

Cather attended the University of Nebraska in Lincoln. An independent young woman, she cut her hair short and liked to be called "William." After graduating in 1895, she worked as a journalist. She published a few collections of poetry and short stories, then moved to New York in 1906. After the success of her first novel, *Alexander's Bridge* (1912), Cather followed with *O Pioneers!* (1913); *My Ántonia* (1918); and the Pulitzer prize–winning *One of Ours* (1922). *Death Comes for the Archbishop*, published in 1927, is considered Cather's finest novel.

This photo of Willa Cather was taken by Carl Van Vechten (1880–1964), known for his portraits of artists and writers.

"We come and go, but the

Carrie Chapman Catt
suffragist ★ 1859–1947

Carrie Chapman Catt was an experienced campaigner for women's right to vote by the time she was elected to her second term as president of the National American Woman Suffrage Association (NAWSA) in 1915. Five years later, her Winning Plan helped secure passage of the 19th Amendment, giving women the vote.

Catt's plan focused NAWSA efforts on two fronts: getting state legislatures to give women the right to vote and then using that state-level voting power to elect members of Congress who would pass a federal amendment giving all U.S. women the vote. NAWSA membership ballooned from 100,000 to more than two million by 1917.

Carrie Chapman Catt cast her hard-won ballot for the first time in 1920.

During World War I, Catt encouraged women to be part of the war effort at home. She thought this would make women look patriotic and help the suffrage movement. Catt herself served on the Woman's Committee of the Council of National Defense. Still, she didn't stop what she called her "red-hot never-ceasing campaign" to get women the vote. On August 26, 1920, Catt got what she wanted. The (**Susan B. Anthony**) 19th amendment passed.

Catt didn't rest there. She helped transform NAWSA into the League of Women Voters. The league's goal was to make sure women were active, informed voters.

Wilt Chamberlain
basketball player ★ 1936–1999

When "The Big Dipper" hit the court, he scored.

In 1959, Wilt Chamberlain signed with the Philadelphia Warriors. As the team's center, he blew out eight rookie records and was named both Rookie of the Year and Most Valuable Player (MVP).

Chamberlain *averaged* an astonishing 50.4 points per game during 1961–1962. In one amazing match with the New York Knicks that season, he shattered all records with 100 points! Chamberlain was the NBA's top scorer for his first seven seasons and the only NBA player to score 4,000 points in a season.

In his 14 seasons as a pro basketball player, Chamberlain also signed with the Philadelphia 76ers (1965–1968) and the Los Angeles Lakers (1968–1973). Chamberlain led both the 76ers and the Lakers to four NBA finals. The 76ers took the title in 1967; the Lakers in 1972.

During his career, Chamberlain won four MVP awards (1960, 1966–1968) and the Finals MVP in 1972. At 30.1 points per game, he has the second-highest career average in the NBA.

*Fierce competitors, Wilt Chamberlain (top) and Celtics center **Bill Russell** (bottom) faced each other in the NBA playoffs eight times, including this game in the 1967 division finals.*

land is always here." — WILLA CATHER

Charlie Chaplin
actor, director, producer ★ 1889—1977

He wore baggy pants, worn-out shoes, and a beat-up hat. He sported a quirky mustache and twirled a bamboo cane. His on-screen antics made Charlie Chaplin the most famous actor in movie history.

Chaplin came to America from England in 1912 and acted in silent slapstick comedies, many of which he wrote and directed. He introduced his famous hobo character in 1914, perfecting it in *The Tramp* (1915). Chaplin's hobo had empty pockets but a heart of gold. He was clumsy but classy. He was the underdog who stood up to the big dog. Chaplin's pantomimes and comic clowning raised the artistry of silent films. Audiences loved the Little Tramp in *The Kid* (1921), *The Gold Rush* (1925), *Modern Times* (1936), and *The Great Dictator* (1940), a funny, but sharp jab at Adolf Hitler.

Seeking as much control over his films as possible, Chaplin joined **Mary Pickford**, **D. W. Griffith**, and Douglas Fairbanks and formed the United Artists Corporation in 1919. During his career, Chaplin appeared in 82 films. He exiled himself to Switzerland in 1952 because of political disagreements with the U.S. Twenty years later he returned to receive a special Academy Award for his movie genius. Chaplin got the longest ovation in Oscar history.

Ray Charles
singer, composer ★ 1930—

Ray Charles lost his eyesight to glaucoma when he was six years old. At a school for the blind in St. Augustine, Florida, he found his true calling: music. He studied piano and saxophone. He composed music in Braille. When he was 17, Charles set out on his own for Seattle, Washington. There he played lounge music in nightclubs. In 1952, he signed with Atlantic Records. He began to develop his own unique style of music, one that married the soulfulness of rhythm and blues to the joy of gospel. And pulling it all together was Ray Charles's energetic piano playing and his gruff baritone.

His first big hit was "I Got a Woman" (1955). Many people consider this the first song of a new musical genre, soul. Four years later, Charles followed with the best-selling "What'd I Say." He now had his own band, which included a horn section and the Raelettes, a female trio, who added a call-and-response sound to his music. His famous recordings include "Georgia on My Mind" (1960), "I Can't Stop Loving You" (1962), and "Crying Time" (1967). The Grammys recognized Ray Charles's important contributions with a Lifetime Achievement Award in 1988.

agricultural implements, or rented slaves; we are men."

— CESAR CHAVEZ

Cesar Chavez
labor organizer ★ 1927–1993

Huelga! Strike! This was Cesar Chavez's rallying cry. It was soon taken up by thousands of unionized farmworkers.

Chavez and his family were Mexican-American migrant farmworkers in California. He knew all about the long, backbreaking hours in the fields, the exposure to deadly pesticides, the low wages, the crowded, miserable, unsanitary housing, the abusive overseers, and the discrimination. And he knew he had to do something about it.

Chavez, along with **Dolores Huerta**, established the National Farm Workers Association in 1962. The NFWA soon called for a strike against grape growers in the Delano, California, area. The NFWA demanded the farmworkers' right to organize unions.

The NFWA merged with a Filipino workers' union and became the United Farm Workers (UFW). The strike continued. Chavez called for a grape boycott. Seventeen million people stopped buying the fruit. By 1970, most table-grape growers in California had signed contracts with the UFW. The farmworkers' union itself was now 50,000 members strong. By 1975, their wages had tripled.

During the 1970s and 1980s, Chavez worked tirelessly to gain support from political, religious, and civil right leaders and the public for agricultural labor issues.

Shirley Chisholm
U.S. Representative ★ 1924–

"Service is the rent you pay for room on this earth," Shirley Chisholm once said. And she was willing to pay.

During the 1950s, Chisholm worked in child welfare. New York City's problems then led her into the world of politics. In 1969, she became the first black woman from Brooklyn elected to the New York state assembly. Four years later, Chisholm was elected to the U.S. House of Representatives. She was the first African-American woman to sit in Congress. Chisholm was a champion of equal rights and of government support for city programs. She was reelected five times, holding her seat in Congress from 1969 to 1983. She also helped found the National Women's Political Caucus in 1971.

In 1972, she entered the presidential primaries. Although she lost the Democratic nomination Chisholm paved the way for other African Americans, such as **Jesse Jackson**.

Henry Clay
politician ★ 1777—1852

Henry Clay had a vision of an economically sound, politically stable, strong, unified nation. In his 40 years of political office, he did everything he could to make his "American System" work.

Clay was Speaker of the House five times and secretary of state under **John Quincy Adams**. Clay and **John C. Calhoun** proposed tariff money be used to build roads, highways, and canals to improve business in the West and the South. Both of these "War Hawks" also urged Congress into the War of 1812 against the British. The British had been harassing American ships at sea and encouraging rebellion among the Native Americans on the northwestern U.S. frontier.

Clay represented Kentucky in the U.S. Senate (1806–1807; 1810–1811; 1831–1842; 1849–1852). He proposed the Missouri Compromise (1820–1821). Missouri joined the union as a slave state, Maine as a free state. This meant that there was a balance between the number of pro-slavery and antislavery members of the Senate. To avoid civil war, Clay helped draw up the Compromise of 1850. It admitted California as a free state and created new territories that could decide on slavery for themselves. It also included the Fugitive Slave Act, which meant that runaway slaves caught in free states had to be returned. Debate over the compromise was fierce, but in the end it passed.

Roberto Clemente
baseball player ★ 1934—1972

As a child in Puerto Rico, Roberto Clemente batted with guava tree sticks and broomstick handles. As an adult, he became one of the few Major League Baseball players to get 3,000 hits at bat.

Clemente was signed up by the Pittsburgh Pirates in 1954. They were the worst ball club in the National League. Clemente changed all that. He played right field, making stupendous catches. His throwing arm was legendary. His batting average often topped .300. With Clemente on the roster, the Pittsburgh Pirates won the World Series in 1960—for the first time in 33 years! They won the World Series again in 1971. Clemente stayed with the team for 18 years.

"The Great One" was *the* star baseball player of the 1960s. He was a great humanitarian, too, especially in his hometown, San Juan, where he worked to build a sports center for poor children.

On New Year's Eve, 1972, just a few months after his famous 3,000th career hit, Roberto Clemente was headed for Nicaragua with supplies for earthquake victims. He died when his plane crashed shortly after takeoff.

Roberto Clemente felt the sports press overlooked Hispanic players like himself. He had won consecutive Gold Glove awards and led the National League in batting, but wasn't named Most Valuable Player (MVP) until 1966.

than be President." — HENRY CLAY

DeWitt Clinton dumped water from Lake Erie into the Atlantic Ocean in a "Wedding of the Waters."

DeWitt Clinton
governor ★ 1769—1828

The first stretch of the Erie Canal opened near Rome, New York, in 1819. Only 15 miles of the great 363-mile waterway were finished and ready for use. People scoffed at "Clinton's Ditch."

DeWitt Clinton was the energetic, three-time mayor of New York City. In 1810, he saw the potential of backing an ambitious transportation idea: the Erie Canal. This inland canal would link Buffalo on Lake Erie with Albany on the Hudson River. Connecting the Great Lake to the river would open up important trade routes between the eastern and western U.S.

Clinton was appointed New York's canal commissioner (1810–1824). In 1817, he ran for governor on a pro-canal platform. He was elected by a landslide. But building the canal became a political—and an engineering—nightmare. Support for "Clinton's Ditch" wavered. Governor Clinton lost his 1822 bid for reelection. There was talk of not finishing the canal. Then money from the canal tolls started rolling in. Clinton was reelected governor in 1824. On October 26, 1825, he was triumphant. The Erie Canal was officially, fully open.

Hillary Rodham Clinton
senator, first lady ★ 1947—

On November 7, 2000, Hillary Clinton became the first sitting first lady elected to political office. She won the third-highest vote total ever gathered in a New York Senate race.

Before becoming first lady in 1993, Clinton had practiced law. The *National Law Journal* named her one of the 100 most powerful lawyers in America in 1988 and in 1991. She also emerged as a strong advocate on family, health, and education issues.

President **William Clinton** appointed Hillary head of his National Health Care Task Force. When the plan it proposed was rejected, the first lady took the brunt of the blame. She was also in legal trouble about her involvement in the Whitewater scandal, a series of shady real-estate deals in Arkansas. (The Clintons were later found innocent.) Then the Monica Lewinsky scandal broke. But Clinton was still tough enough to launch her own successful political career.

In her first 100 days as U.S. senator from New York, Clinton introduced 10 Congressional bills and cosponsored 66 others. She serves on several powerful Senate committees, including Budget; Environment and Public Works; and Health, Education, Labor, and Pensions (HELP).

William Clinton
42nd president ★ 1946—

He was the amazing "Comeback Kid" who never quit until he reached his goal. He was "Slick Willie," who could turn words inside out to suit his purpose. Bill Clinton's Democratic presidency (1993–2001) reflected both these sides of his personality.

Two-time governor of Arkansas, Bill Clinton took office in 1993. The new, young president and his staff were enthusiastically energetic, and couldn't deliver on earlier promises, such as health care reform and backing the rights of people in the military to be openly gay. To offset the bulging national debt, President Clinton also introduced a middle-class tax increase—it was not popular!

But the prosperous economy was.

During Clinton's first term, inflation, interest rates, and unemployment all dropped. In 1993, he negotiated the controversial North American Free Trade Agreement (NAFTA), which increased trade with Mexico and Canada. He slashed the budget deficit in half. On the foreign front, Clinton worked hard to end Haiti's dictatorship and to bring about a Middle East peace treaty. He got longtime adversaries Yasser Arafat of Palestine and Israeli prime minister Yitzhak Rabin to shake hands after 1993 peace negotiations. President Clinton also appointed the first woman attorney general, **Janet Reno**, during his first term. (Later he appointed the first woman secretary of state, **Madeleine Albright**.)

In the 1994 elections, Republicans won control of the House and Senate for the first time in 40 years. Clinton and Congress clashed over the 1995 budget. The president refused to accept the 1995 budget that Congress sent him. He thought the Republicans' cuts in social programs were too severe. It was a showdown—and the government shut down twice.

Even though Congress took the heat for the budget problems, President Clinton realized he had to stay in touch with the more conservative mood of U.S. voters. Clinton began to talk about welfare reform and a modest tax cut. Throughout his presidency, he was a brilliant public speaker who won over listeners with his warmth and intelligence. But the president's political life was about to be overshadowed by his personal life.

Independent Counsel Kenneth Starr investigated Bill and **Hillary Rodham Clinton** in connection with questionable business deals in Arkansas. Starr's work on this Whitewater investigation eventually led to the discovery of the president's extramarital relationship with White House intern Monica Lewinsky. Clinton very publicly denied everything at first, but he changed his story when called before the grand jury. On August 17, 1998, in a television speech watched by 67 million Americans, the president confessed to an "inappropriate sexual relationship" with Lewinsky.

The country was thrown into political turmoil. Despite a Gallup poll that indicated that Americans were against it 2 to 1, the House of Representatives voted for Clinton's impeachment in January 1999, on charges of perjury and obstruction of justice. In February, he was acquitted in the Senate. Though Clinton's personal ratings fell with voters, opinion of his job performance remained high.

"Opportunity for all,

Ty Cobb
baseball player ★ 1886–1961

His lifetime batting average was .367, the highest ever in Major League Baseball. In fact, some people call "The Georgia Peach" the greatest batter ever.

Georgia-born Ty Cobb signed with the Detroit Tigers in 1905. He played 24 seasons in the American League (1905–1928). Cobb got off to a slow start, both at bat and as an outfielder. But by 1907, he was hitting .350 and winning the first of his nine consecutive batting championships. Two years later, he won the Triple Crown: Cobb was top of the league at batting, RBIs (runs batted in), and home runs. And, as a base runner, he was legendary. Cobb stole bases 892 times, including 35 dashes home. Fans cheered his famous side slide, an exciting upright run, followed by a last-minute drop to his side, feet flying into the base mat.

Ty Cobb was a great, but gritty ballplayer. He argued and fought with rivals, umpires, fans, and even his own teammates.

Cobb helped the Tigers take their league pennant from 1907 to 1909, though they never won the World Series. In 1911, he batted .420, set several major league records of the time, and was chosen Most Valuable Player. By 1921, he was also managing the Tigers.

Cochise
Chiricahua Apache leader ★ c.1815–1874

A skilled fighter and respected leader, Cochise was extremely hostile toward white settlers. They were continually building forts and postal and trade routes through Apache land. When Cochise had gone to meet with U.S. officers, bringing his family as a sign of peace, the officers seized them all. Cochise boldly escaped; most of the others did not. Nor did his beloved father-in-law, who was killed after a white-flag request for a truce. Cochise sought revenge.

Throughout the 1860s, Cochise was the most feared chief in what is now Arizona and New Mexico. The U.S. Army couldn't capture him. They often couldn't even *find* him. Meanwhile, Apache parties raided and killed at will.

After the Civil War, the Army devoted more supplies and soldiers to "Indian Wars" in the Southwest. Some Apaches became guides and helped track Cochise. By 1872, Cochise had been at war for nearly

There are no known photos of Cochise, but artists have drawn the great Apache chief.

50 years. His people had sickened, suffered, and starved. Cochise negotiated the first Apache reservation ever set up in the tribe's homeland. He believed he had found a peaceful home for his people. But in 1876, two years after Cochise's death, the Apache were forcibly relocated.

responsibility for all." —BILL CLINTON

"I might have been born in a hovel, with the wind

Jackie Cochran won the prestigious aviation award, the Harmon trophy, 15 times.

Jackie Cochran
aviator ★ c.1910–1980

Boom! The loud sound *followed* the trail of the F-86 Sabre. That could only mean one thing: The jet's pilot, Jackie Cochran, had just become the first woman to break the sound barrier.

Cochran's record, set in 1953, was one of many in a soaring aviation career. In 1938, Jackie won the Bendix Cross-Country Air Race, flying from California to Ohio in just over eight hours. Two years later, she flew 332 miles per hour—faster than any woman or man had flown.

During World War II, Cochran flew U.S. bombers to Great Britain. U.S. president **Franklin D. Roosevelt** asked her how women pilots could help the war effort. Their talk led to the founding of the Women Airforce Service Pilots (WASP). Under Cochran as WASP director, 1,078 women flew planes during the war. They were not allowed to fly in combat. So they trained student pilots, towed targets for gunner training, and delivered bombers within the U.S. and Canada. Cochran was awarded the Distinguished Service Medal.

On May 4, 1964, Cochran became the fastest woman alive when she flew 1,429 miles per hour in a Super Star jet.

Buffalo Bill Cody
showman ★ 1846–1917

William Cody had worked as an Army scout, a buffalo hunter, and a hunting guide. But he figured out that the real money was in selling the romance of the Old West.

Cody earned his nickname when he worked as a hunter, providing meat for workers on the Kansas Pacific Railroad. In 1868, he beat a fellow hunter in a competition, killing 69 buffalo in one day. The legend of "Buffalo Bill" was born.

Soon "true" accounts of Cody's daring deeds were written up as sensational magazine stories and dime novels. By 1883, the tall, handsome, long-haired legend was starring in his own *Buffalo Bill's Wild West Show.* The cast included cowboys, Native Americans, all kinds of animals, and specialty acts like **Annie Oakley**. Performed outside, the show recreated the "Wild West" with its stagecoach holdups, Indian attacks, and shooting, roping, and riding displays. The extravaganza entertained thousands of people from Omaha and Brooklyn to London and Paris. Six million people enjoyed Buffalo Bill's

*Buffalo Bill Cody (r.) with **Sitting Bull**, who appeared in Cody's Wild West show in the 1880s.*

show when it played at the Chicago World's Fair in 1893. "Buffalo Bill's Wild West Show" ran for almost three decades, long after the real American West had been tamed.

but I was determined to travel and the stars." — JACKIE COCHRAN

Bessie Coleman
aviator ★ 1892—1926

Bessie Coleman was the world's first licensed African-American woman pilot.

Bessie Coleman was barred from aviation schools because she was an African American. She didn't let that ground her dreams of learning to fly.

Coleman was the 12th of 13 children in a sharecropper family in Atlanta, Texas. She picked cotton and did laundry to help the family and tried to save enough money for college. Eventually, she moved to Chicago and worked as a manicurist. Coleman was inspired by stories she heard about Eugene Jacques Bullard, an African American who had flown with the French army during World War I. Coleman's own flying adventures began in France, too. Toward the end of the war, she traveled there with a unit of the Red Cross. She started taking flying lessons. Within 10 months, she became a licensed pilot in 1921.

The following year, Coleman returned to the U.S. She worked in air shows, performing daredevil flying stunts like loops, twirls, and figure eights. Now that she was a pilot, her new dream was to open a flight school for African Americans. Before she could make this happen, Coleman died in an airplane crash in a Florida exhibition in 1926.

Samuel Colt
gunsmith ★ 1814—1862

Samuel Colt's "Peacemaker" was sometimes called the "gun that tamed the West" because it was the most popular firearm on the frontier.

Samuel Colt's legacy was the "Peacemaker," a single-action, six-shot revolver. The gun got its nickname because using it scared off (or killed off) enemies, thereby keeping the peace.

In 1836, Colt patented his revolutionary pistol. It was a more efficient handheld gun because its cylinder held six bullets. All six could be fired before the gun needed reloading. Still, his Paterson, New Jersey, factory went out of business because people weren't ready to give up their more traditional weapons.

With the onset of the Mexican War, the U.S. government ordered 1,000 guns from Colt. He produced them in a factory in New Haven, Connecticut. When the shipment went out in 1847, Colt's company began to thrive.

Colt's Patent Fire Arms Manufacturing Company turned out more than a half million guns from 1856 to 1865. Colt was a leader in new techniques in marketing and assembly-line production. His "Peacemaker" was one of the most important modern weapons used during the Civil War. Samuel Colt became one of the 10 wealthiest businesspeople in the country.

James Fenimore Cooper
author ★ 1789—1851

His popular 19th-century adventure stories were uniquely American. So were his frontier heroes. James Fenimore Cooper created a new body of literature for a new nation.

He grew up on the frontier himself, in his father's settlement of Cooperstown, New York. James attended Yale briefly and then shipped out as a sailor for six years. He didn't write his first novel until he was in his 30s.

Cooper then went on to write 32 novels, 12 works of nonfiction, a play, and numerous articles. His most famous works are the Leatherstocking Tales. This series of five best-selling books included *The Pioneers* (1823), *The Last of the Mohicans* (1826), *The Prairie* (1827), *The Pathfinder* (1840), and *The Deerslayer* (1841). American and European audiences loved Cooper's characters like the fearless scout Natty Bummpo (also called Hawkeye and Leatherstocking) and the noble Native

Ralph Waldo Emerson called James Fenimore Cooper's book The Pioneers *"our first national novel."*

Americans he met. They were fascinated by Cooper's descriptions of the beauty and danger of the untamed wilderness. In the Leatherstocking Tales, Cooper dealt with both the issues of his time and the recent past: war, colonization, and conflicts about America's westward expansion. He also celebrated (and romanticized) the rugged individualism people think of as "American."

A memorial at the site of the battle of Fort Washington honors Margaret Corbin. She is the only veteran of the American Revolution buried at West Point Military Academy.

Margaret Corbin
American Revolution patriot ★ 1751—1800

Margaret Corbin lived a full colonial experience, from surviving a Native American raid to getting caught up in a bloody American Revolution battle.

Corbin's parents disappeared during the 1756 raid on her childhood home in Pennsylvania. Margaret was raised by an uncle until she married. Then war broke out.

Like many soldiers' wives, Corbin followed her husband as the Continental army traveled. When John Corbin was killed at the battle of Fort Washington, New York, in 1776, "Captain Molly" took his place. She kept his cannon booming against the British, until grapeshot, the small iron balls fired by the enemy's cannon, tore up her left arm.

On July 6, 1779, Corbin became the first woman in the United States to receive a pension. The Continental Congress gave her a lifetime pension: one half of a soldier's pay and a clothing allowance. Captain Molly petitioned for, and won, the rest of the pension: an annual ration of rum or whiskey.

"One does not sell the land

Bill Cosby
entertainer ★ 1937—

Bill Cosby uses his comic genius to educate, promote social change, and, of course, make people laugh!

Cosby grew up in a Philadelphia housing project. Always a natural comedian, he started working comedy gigs in Philadelphia and New York City and then on the national comedy club circuit in the early 1960s. He cut a record, *I Started Out as a Child* (1964), and won the first of his six Grammys for comedy albums. A producer spotted him and cast him in a new TV show, *I Spy* (1965–1968). Cosby became the first African-American lead in a dramatic series. He won three Emmy Awards.

The cast of The Cosby Show. Bill Cosby was awarded a Kennedy Center Honor in 1998.

In the 1970s, Cosby created the popular Saturday morning cartoon, *Fat Albert and the Cosby Kids.* He acted in several movies, increased his visibility by becoming spokesman for products like Jell-O, and on top of everything else, earned a Ph.D. in education.

Cosby made media history in 1984 when *The Cosby Show* debuted. This warmhearted, funny show featured the joys and struggles of Dr. Cliff Huxtable, his lawyer wife, and their children. It was a whole new television portrayal of African Americans. The top-rated show aired until 1992.

Crazy Horse
Oglala Lakota Sioux leader ★ c. 1849—1877

When Crazy Horse rode into battle, he wore a hawk feather in his light brown hair, a small, smooth stone tied around his ear, and a lightning bolt painted on his cheek. He had seen these signs on his vision quest, the solitary spiritual retreat that made a Native American boy a man.

Crazy Horse (Tashunka Witko) was a skilled strategist and fearless fighter who was determined to preserve tribal territories and traditions. From 1865 to 1868, he and **Red Cloud** led attacks against the U.S. Army, which was building forts along the Bozeman Trail from Wyoming to Montana. Eight years later, Crazy Horse joined forces with **Sitting Bull** when the U.S. government wanted to open up sacred Sioux land in South Dakota to greedy gold seekers. The Lakota War of 1876–1877 began.

In 1876, Crazy Horse and his Sioux warriors surrounded and killed General **George Custer**'s troops at Little Big Horn. Their triumph was short-lived. The army pursued Crazy Horse and the Oglala. After a hard winter when buffalo and other food were scarce, they surrendered at Fort Robinson, Nebraska, in 1877. Still, officials feared Crazy Horse, and during an attempt to jail him, he was killed.

upon which the people walk."
— CRAZY HORSE

Davy Crockett
pioneer-statesman ★ 1786–1836

Davy Crockett, the man in the coonskin cap, and his rifle, Betsy, inspired popular books and, later, movies and a TV show.

"... half-horse, half-alligator, a little touched with the snapping turtle ... I can whip my weight in wild cats—and, if any gentleman pleases, for a ten dollar bill, he can throw in a panther." The tall tales told about this backwoods congressman from Tennessee transformed David Crockett, pioneer, hunter, and farmer into Davy Crockett, the living legend of the American frontier. And Crockett, famous for his sense of humor, added a few of his own colorful stories to his autobiography.

After serving two terms in his state's legislature, Crockett was elected to Congress in 1827 and again in 1829. Congressman Crockett was a hardworking, sincere politician. He opposed an act aimed at forcing Native Americans to live west of the Mississippi River. He supported a bill to sell federal lands in Tennessee to poor settlers for low prices. Powerful fellow Democrats opposed him on both these fronts.

Crockett lost his bid for reelection in 1835. He left for Texas, possibly in search of a new place to homestead. In early February 1836, Crockett arrived in San Antonio. He planned to join the Texans there in their fight for independence from Mexico. By the end of February, the Texas militia, including Crockett, was under siege by the Mexican army. He joined the fight. Crockett either died during San Antonio's famous Battle of the Alamo or was taken prisoner and executed by the Mexicans.

Walter Cronkite
television journalist ★ 1916—

He's called "the most trusted man in America" with good reason. That reason? Integrity.

Cronkite worked for United Press (UP) from 1937 to 1948. As a World War II correspondent, he saw plenty of action. After the war, he headed UP bureaus in Europe.

In 1950, Cronkite signed on as a correspondent with CBS in Washington, D.C. In 1962, he helped created the *CBS Evening News*. Cronkite became one of television's first anchormen. He defined the job. For 19 years, millions of Americans tuned in nightly to hear his steady, unbiased, insightful news reports.

Walter Cronkite covered some of the 20th century's most newsworthy events, from the Vietnam War to the *Apollo* moon landing, and every major international headline in between. Since his retirement from CBS News in 1981, the Emmy-winning journalist has hosted or produced television specials and documentaries.

"And that's the way it is." — WALTER CRONKITE

Celia Cruz
salsa singer ★ c.1929—

Celia Cruz is a powerful singer. She's a glamorous dresser and a wild dancer. No wonder she's been crowned the Queen of Salsa.

Born in Havana, Cuba, Cruz was the lead singer for La Sonora Matancera, a popular orchestra. In the 1950s, she played on radio shows, in films, and in Havana's famous nightclubs. When Fidel Castro came to power in 1959, Cruz and the other band members defected to the United States. She started touring with the legendary musician **Tito Puente** in the late 1960s. Cruz and Puente helped build a new young audience for salsa, a popular form of Latin-American dance music that combines jazz, blues, and other music forms with a lively, Afro-Caribbean beat.

Cruz has recorded more than 70 albums; 20 of them have gone gold. She's a popular concert headliner and has influenced many younger musicians, including **Gloria Estefan**.

Celia Cruz has won three Grammys.

Merce Cunningham
dancer-choreographer ★ 1919—

Merce Cunningham redefines space, time, and motion. "Wherever you are is the center, as well as where everybody else is," he said. For more than 50 years, he's created modern, abstract dances that reflect this idea. He's used both ancient tools, like the *I Ching*, the great Chinese book of spiritual symbols, and high-tech computer software to develop his work. He's worked with musicians, most often the famous minimalist composer, John Cage. Cunningham was one of the first choreographers to use electronic music. He's also worked with artists such as **Robert Rauschenberg** and **Isamu Noguchi**. Cunningham has a unique way of collaborating. He choreographs his dance work independently of the music or sets. In his piece *Ocean* (1994), the dancers didn't even hear the music until the night before the performance.

Cunningham came to the attention of the dance world when he danced as a soloist with the **Martha Graham** Company from 1939 to 1945. In 1954, he choreographed his first solo concert, with music by Cage. Nine years later, he founded the Merce Cunningham Dance Company. The company has presented more than 150 works. Cunningham has also created dance pieces for ballet companies in New York, Boston, Paris, and London, among others. In 1990, Cunningham was awarded the National Medal of Arts.

George Armstrong Custer
cavalry officer ★ 1839–1876

With his long, curly hair, red scarf, and fancy uniform, George Custer cut a fine military figure. But his bold recklessness cost him his life.

After the Civil War, Custer was given command of the Seventh Cavalry. He was supposed to stop skilled Native American warriors from attacking settlers on the western frontier.

In 1874, Custer willfully ignored a U.S. treaty and led 1,000 men on a gold-hunting mission on the Sioux Reservation. This set off a gold rush in the Black Hills in what is now South Dakota and Wyoming. The Sioux refused to sell their sacred land, so the U.S. declared war on them.

The Seventh Cavalry went after **Sitting Bull**'s and **Crazy Horse**'s warriors, who had joined forces. On June 25, 1876, they found them at the Little Bighorn River. Custer thought there were about 800 warriors. He divided his troop of 600, and took 225 men with him down into a bluff to surprise the tribes—which actually numbered 3,000 strong. Custer was trapped. In less than an hour, every soldier was dead. It was "Custer's last stand."

George Armstrong Custer was called "Long Hair" by Native Americans.

Benjamin O. Davis, Jr.
Air Force general ★ 1912–2002

Benjamin O. Davis, Sr., (r.), the first African-American army general, pins a medal on his hero son, Benjamin O. Davis, Jr. (l.)

Benjamin O. Davis, Jr., a four-star Air Force general and decorated pilot, had to fight for the right to serve his country.

Davis joined the military when it, like much of U.S. society, was segregated. In 1936, Davis became the first African American to graduate from the West Point military academy.

During World War II, Davis, and his all-black 99th Squadron, the Tuskegee Airmen, fought valiantly over North Africa and Italy. In 1944, he took charge of the African-American 332d Fighter Group. The 332d escorted bomber planes. They flew in more than 10,000 missions against often superior German aircraft in heavily defended areas. The Tuskegee Airmen never lost a plane they were protecting. Davis was awarded the Distinguished Flying Cross. Their success helped change the military's attitude toward segregated units. In 1948, President **Harry Truman** signed an order to integrate all of the U.S. armed forces.

After the war, Davis served in several key commands, including the chief of the Air Defense Branch of Air Force operations.

Bette Davis
actress ★ 1908—1989

As a child, Bette Davis went to the theater only twice. But those two times were enough to make her want to be an actress.

Davis moved from her hometown of Lowell, Massachusetts, to New York in 1928. She enrolled in acting school and made her stage debut the following year. By 1930, Davis had gone Hollywood. She failed her first screen test. Eventually, she signed with Warner Brothers. After five years of making movies, often second-rate ones, Davis broke out. She won an Academy Award in 1935 for her role in *Dangerous*. But it was her second Oscar, for *Jezebel* (1938), that changed her career. Once considered droopy-eyed and unsexy, Davis was now top dollar at the box office.

In 1941, Bette Davis became the first woman to head the Academy of Motion Arts and Sciences, the professional organization that awards the Oscars. In 1977, she was the first woman to receive the prestigious American Film Institute Life Achievement Award. Just hours before she died in Spain, she received a lifetime achievement award at the San Sebastian Film Festival in 1989.

Bette Davis's role in All About Eve *(1951), a classic film about ruthless actresses, won her a third Oscar.*

Jefferson Davis
Confederate president ★ 1808—1889

After the fall of the Confederacy in 1865, Jefferson Davis was tried for treason and imprisoned for two years.

In 1861, two men were inaugurated: **Abraham Lincoln** and Jefferson Davis, president of the Confederate States of America.

A graduate of West Point military academy and a hero of the Mexican War, Davis represented Mississippi in the U.S. Senate from 1847 to 1851 and from 1857 to 1861. In between, he was appointed secretary of war by President Franklin Pierce. Davis staunchly supported states' rights. He opposed any law that blocked the spread of slavery through the territories. When Mississippi seceded from the Union in 1861, he went with it.

The Confederate presidency was a tough job. Davis had to run a war without federal taxes or laws to support it. He headed a group of states that put their individual rights first. Davis was a military man at heart and an intellectual. He was also a man of integrity. But he was not a great administrator.

President Davis fought with his exceptional generals and his unexceptional cabinet. He and other Confederate leaders miscalculated how much help they'd get from France and England. Increasingly, Davis found himself heading a confederacy whose cities were occupied by Union forces and whose armies were shoeless, starving, and out of supplies.

"All we ask is to be left alone." —JEFFERSON DAVIS

Miles Davis
jazz musician ★ 1926—1991

He was just like the jazz he played: moody, cool, surprising.

Miles Davis started playing trumpet when he was 10. He studied classical music at the prestigious Juilliard Music School. But it was New York City's hot jazz clubs that really interested Davis. By 1945, he was playing with his idol, **Charlie Parker**, in Parker's quintet.

Davis constantly reinvented himself musically. In the late 1940s, he formed a band and played his own brand of "cool jazz." Cool jazz was softer, sparer, and more melodic than bebop. Davis's classic album *Birth of the Cool* (1949) defined this new form of jazz. His haunting album *Kind of Blue* (1959) reached new heights in jazz improvisation. And when the 1960s ushered in rock music, Davis kept his mind and ears open. He introduced rock rhythms and electronic instruments to jazz improvisations and helped create a new form of jazz called fusion. Davis also experimented with avant-garde and funk elements in his music. His various bands included some of the great names in jazz, such as saxophonists Cannonball Adderly and John Coltrane and pianist Herbie Hancock.

Dorothy Day (l.) has been nominated for sainthood in the Catholic Church.

Dorothy Day
social worker ★ 1897—1980

Left-wing journalist Dorothy Day was 30, pregnant, unmarried, and had just become a Catholic. She was looking for a way to balance her radical social ideas with her religious faith. She found it when she started the Catholic Worker movement with Peter Maurin.

Day and Maurin started a newspaper, called *The Catholic Worker*. In it, they wrote about social and labor changes they felt were needed in America. Day urged readers to fight poverty and injustice. She believed that spirituality meant responsibility for others. The first issue came out on May 1, 1933. By December, 100,000 copies a month were being printed. Day next set up "houses of hospitality," where poor and homeless people got food, shelter, and comfort. She started communes where the rural poor farmed together.

Day built the Catholic Worker program into a national movement that drew in thousands of volunteers. She supported the civil rights struggle. She marched in anti-Vietnam War demonstrations. She picketed with **Cesar Chavez** and striking farmworkers. She was jailed and even shot at. But to many people, Dorothy Day was a "living saint."

"*Without faith in each other,*

Eugene V. Debs
activist ★ 1855–1926

Socialist Eugene V. Debs ran for president five times (1900, 1904, 1908, 1912, 1920). He ran his last campaign from a jail cell.

Debs organized the American Railway Union in 1892. The ARU was embroiled in a bitter, 27-state labor strike against the Pullman company in 1894. Debs was jailed. He realized that if workers' lives were to improve, laws would have to change. He threw himself into politics when he was released.

Debs founded the Social Democrat party in 1897 (which evolved into the Socialist party). He hit the presidential campaign trail. Debs supported women's right to vote and workers' right to organize unions. He called for laws to limit child labor and improve job safety. He cofounded the Industrial Workers of the World (IWW), an international labor union, in 1905. Thousands rallied to hear Debs's ringing speeches. But Debs's ideas were just too radical for other people.

During World War I, Debs told an Ohio crowd that "you are fit for something better than slavery and cannon fodder." He was convicted of treason under a wartime espionage law. Debs was sentenced to 10 years. Even though he was stripped of voting privileges, he still ran for president in 1920. Convict 9653 got 919,799 votes, nearly 6% of those cast. Public outrage resulted in Debs' pardon the following year.

Emily Dickinson
poet ★ 1830–1886

"You cannot put a fire out;/A thing that can ignite/Can go, itself, without a fan/Upon the slowest night." The soul of Emily Dickinson, one of America's finest poets, burned with such a fire. Her 1,775 untitled poems explore the great mysteries of life: nature, love, longing, death. Her metaphors, rhythm, even punctuation were unusual and modern for the 19th century.

Dickinson came from an upper-class New England family. She attended Amherst Academy and then Mount Holyoke Female Seminary. These were among the few times Dickinson ever left home. She lived her life mostly as a recluse, writing and gardening.

In 1862, Dickinson sent some of her poems to the editor of *The Atlantic Monthly*, Thomas Wentworth Higginson. He

This daguerreotype is the only known photo of Emily Dickinson, the "Belle of Amherst."

discouraged her from publishing her work because it was "too delicate." Though the two became close friends, Dickinson took Higginson's advice and did not publish her work. Instead, she sewed her poems into little booklets and hid them in trunks and closets. Her sister Lavinia found the poems after Emily's death, and published them in the book *Poems* (1890).

we cannot go on. — DOROTHY DAY

Joe DiMaggio
baseball player ★ 1914–1999

In 1954, Joe DiMaggio married movie star **Marilyn Monroe**.

Twenty-nine homers, a .323 batting average, 15 triples, a World Series victory—and that was just Joe DiMaggio's *first* year with the Yankees!

"The Yankee Clipper" was one of baseball's most popular players. DiMaggio was a smooth center fielder and a sensational slugger. The New York Yankees signed him in 1934 for the then huge sum of $25,000. In his first four years in a Yankees uniform, DiMaggio helped the team win four World Series championships. In 1939, he was the American League's Most Valuable Player (MVP). Two years later, DiMaggio went on his famous hitting streak. In 1941, he smacked at least one hit in game after game—for a record-breaking 56 games in a row! Even Congress had a page who kept members posted daily on how DiMaggio was doing. Once again, "Joltin' Joe" was MVP and the Yanks won the World Series.

DiMaggio served in the Army during World War II and returned to baseball in 1946. By the time he retired in 1952, he had picked up another MVP (1947) and had a lifetime batting average of .325. Out of respect, the Yankees retired his uniform, too. Number 5 is forever Joltin' Joe's.

Walt Disney
media entrepreneur ★ 1901–1966

In 1928, animator Walt Disney released "Steamboat Willie." It was the first cartoon with synchronized sound. It starred a cocky little creature with Disney's own voice . . . Mickey Mouse!

Mickey was a financial gold mine for Disney. He assembled a Hollywood studio of animators. He wrote and edited story lines and helped create more lovable cartoon characters. In 1937, Disney produced *Snow White and the Seven Dwarfs*, the first animated feature film ever made. It was a box-office smash. His studio followed with other film classics, some of which combined animation, live action, and music. (Disney won 32 Academy Awards for his work.) When television arrived, he embraced that medium, too. *The Wonderful World of Disney* premiered in 1954. Disney studios produced the cartoons, nature shows, and dramas that aired on the TV program. Walt was the show's host.

Walt Disney with Pinocchio.

Then, in 1955, Disney opened the country's first real theme park in Anaheim, California. The media king supervised the planning and design of Disneyland's "Magic Kingdom" himself. Walt Disney helped define our modern entertainment culture.

"...Dream, diversify, and

Dorothea Dix
social reformer ★ 1802—1887

In the 1840s, the treatment of the mentally ill was horrific. Disturbed women were jailed with male criminals. Naked prisoners stood roped and chained in their cells. Dorothea Dix went on a crusade to change all this. By 1847, she had traveled more than 30,000 miles across the country, investigating and lobbying on behalf of neglected prisoners.

Dix had a direct role in founding 32 new mental hospitals throughout the country. Partly because of her efforts, the number of mental asylums rose from 13 in 1843 to 123 in 1880. In 1845, she cowrote *Remarks on Prisons and Prison Discipline in the United States.* Many institutions eventually adopted some of the reforms suggested in this book.

During the Civil War, Dix was named chief of nurses for the Union Army. She then formed the Army Nursing Corps and, along with Dr. **Elizabeth Blackwell** in New York, trained volunteer nurses like **Louisa May Alcott** for the war effort. After the war, Dix continued her hospital and asylum reform work. Her life's efforts helped lay the groundwork for modern and humane treatment of institutionalized people.

Stephen A. Douglas
senator ★ 1813—1861

The "Little Giant" swung a mighty political club.

Stephen A. Douglas was a U.S. senator from Illinois from 1847 to 1861. He believed the federal government should encourage the nation's growth, particularly in the western territories. However, he thought decisions about slavery should be left up to the people in a state or territory. This is called "popular sovereignty." Douglas's two viewpoints led to the controversial Kansas-Nebraska Act of 1854.

At that time, Douglas was trying to get the government to build a transcontinental railroad. Railroads brought new opportunities for business development along their routes. Douglas wanted the railroad to go through Chicago, which would be profitable for his state.

Douglas had to get the support of Southern senators who wanted the railroad to go through their states. They also wouldn't vote for routing the railroad through places where slavery was illegal. To appeal to these Southerners, Douglas proposed the Kansas-Nebraska Act, which divided the Nebraska Territory into two new territories. These territories, Kansas and Nebraska, were granted popular sovereignty. This overrode the Missouri Compromise (1820), which banned slavery in these new territories. Thousands of pro-slavery supporters and antislavery abolitionists rushed into Kansas. Murder and violence broke out. The country lurched closer to civil war.

*Senator Stephen A. Douglas and newcomer **Abraham Lincoln** ran against each other for Illinois's seat in the U.S. Senate in 1858. Their famous debates reflected the complicated politics of slavery, abolition, and equality.*

Frederick Douglass
abolitionist ★ 1818–1895

Frederick Augustus Washington Bailey was born sometime in February 1818 on a Tuckahoe, Maryland, plantation. From an early age, he was consumed by a burning question: Why am I a slave? Asking that question changed his life—and the course of the nation.

Frederick Douglass's image appeared on sheet music; in newspapers and etchings; as paintings and statues; and even on dolls.

When he was seven, Frederick was sent to Baltimore, Maryland, where he tricked others into doing the illegal: teaching a slave to read. Disguised as a sailor, Frederick eventually escaped to New York City and then Bedford Falls, Massachusetts, in 1838. He changed his last name to Douglass to fool slave hunters. He also married a freed woman, Anna Murray, with whom he eventually had five children.

Three years later, Douglass attended an abolitionist convention in Nantucket, Massachusetts. Douglass brought his audience to tears by simply telling his own life story. **William Lloyd Garrison** was in that audience and encouraged Douglass to join his American Anti-Slavery Society. Douglass became one of the group's most famous speakers, delivering more than 100 powerful speeches around the country.

Douglass was so eloquent that people began to doubt his story. They said that no true slave could possibly be that intelligent or well-spoken. To prove them wrong, Douglass wrote *Narrative of the Life of Frederick Douglass* in 1845. It was a best-seller. It also told his master where he could now find his runaway slave. Douglass fled to England, where slavery was illegal. He lectured there for two years, while his friends back home raised $700 to buy his freedom.

When Douglass returned, he moved his family to Rochester, New York. His home became an important stop on the Underground Railroad. Douglass also started publishing *The North Star*, a newspaper devoted to stories by and about African Americans. Its motto was "All rights for all!"

During the Civil War, Frederick Douglass campaigned for freedom for slaves and for African Americans to be allowed in the Union army. When black regiments were recruited but given low pay and highly dangerous missions, Douglass met with President **Lincoln** about the problem. He was the first African American ever to attend a White House reception.

The war freed the slaves, but didn't make them equal. So Douglass did not give up the struggle. For three more decades, he wrote, lectured, and lobbied politicians on behalf of African Americans' rights. He supported **Ida B. Well**'s anti-lynching campaign. Influenced by **Elizabeth Cady Stanton**, Douglass became a key figure in the women's rights movement. He was appointed U.S. marshal of the District of Columbia (1877–1881) and minister to Haiti (1889–1891), the first African American to hold these government positions.

On the morning of February 20, 1895, Frederick Douglass, now 77 years old, went to the National Council of Women meeting in Washington, D. C. He died that night of a heart attack; 25,000 people attended his funeral.

"The only way you get something is to fight for it." — FREDERICK DOUGLASS

W.E.B. Du Bois

scholar, civil rights leader ★ 1868–1963

William Edward Burghardt Du Bois was a brilliant author and intellectual. He studied African-American sociology (how people live together in a society) and, in 1897, introduced it as an academic field. Then a wave of lynchings at the turn of the century turned the scholar into a radical.

W. E. B. Du Bois called for immediate protest and political action by blacks. This differed from African-American leader **Booker T. Washington**'s emphasis on economics over equal rights. Du Bois gave voice to his activist views in his acclaimed book *The Souls of Black Folks* (1903). He declared, "The problem with the 20th century is the color line." Booker T. Washington wasn't willing to cross that line. Du Bois wanted to erase it.

In 1909, Du Bois helped found the National Association for the Advancement of Colored People (NAACP). Du Bois was

W.E.B. Du Bois was the first African American to earn a Ph.D. from prestigious Harvard University.

the only black person on the NAACP's first board. From 1910 to 1934, he served as NAACP director of publicity and research. Du Bois also edited the *Crisis*. The militant journal publicized NAACP fights against racial injustice. It printed Du Bois's rousing editorials and critical essays. It featured the work of black artists and writers and profiles of notable African Americans.

Throughout his lifetime, Du Bois remained a strong voice in the black protest movement.

Isadora Duncan

dancer, choreographer ★ 1877–1927

Isadora Duncan was banned in Boston in 1922. Her bare feet, flowing robes, and loose-limbed dancing were just too shocking!

Duncan rejected ballet's hard toe shoes and corseted costumes—too deforming. She rejected ballet's precision—not enough expression. Duncan created her own free style, based on natural and spontaneous movement. She was one of the first to develop what is now called modern dance.

Born in San Francisco, California, Duncan danced with a company in New York in 1896. At the turn of the century, she toured Europe. Her innovative style was a sensation in England, France, Hungary, and Germany. However, when she returned to the United States in 1908, she did not receive ovations. Some people dismissed her expressive gliding and swaying form of dance.

Duncan returned to more appreciative audiences in Europe. She also started dancing schools for children there, and in the U. S. In 1927, Isadora Duncan got into a sports car. She was killed instantly when the car sped off and her flowing scarf got caught in its wheels.

Bob Dylan

singer, composer ★ 1941—

Bob Dylan makes poetry musical and music poetic. Over a career that's spanned four decades, he's reinvented himself and his music many times. There's been Dylan the folk singer, Dylan the protest singer, Dylan the rocker. He's gone electric, gone country, and gone deep inside himself and back out again. And Dylan's artistic journey has changed the course of American music.

Robert Zimmerman was born into a middle-class Jewish family in Duluth, Minnesota. He renamed himself after the poet Dylan Thomas and moved to New York City in 1960 to be closer to his hero, folk singer **Woody Guthrie**.

Dylan started singing and playing guitar and harmonica in the folk and blues clubs that popped up all over Greenwich Village. He was scruffy, his voice was gravelly, but he was writing some powerful songs. People started listening. Popular folk trio Peter, Paul,

Bob Dylan, shown here in 1992, has written more than 500 songs and released more than 43 albums.

and Mary's version of Dylan's song "Blowin' in the Wind" got lots of radio airplay. Folk star **Joan Baez** promoted him at the 1963 Newport Folk Festival. Best of all, Dylan had a record contract.

Dylan's early albums, *The Freewheelin' Bob Dylan* (1963) and *The Times They Are A' Changin'* (1964), provided the sound track for the turbulent 1960s. Songs like "A Hard Rain's a-Gonna Fall," "Masters of War," and "The Times They Are A' Changin'" captured the spirit of social unrest and political protest.

Dylan was changing, too. He stunned his folk fans by plugging in an electric guitar. Dylan's *Bringing It All Back Home* (1965) did have an acoustic side. But the album's electric blues and the surreal lyrics of songs like "Subterranean Homesick Blues" showed a whole new side to the singer-songwriter. He was just as electric and eclectic in *Highway 61 Revisited* (1965) and *Blonde on Blonde* (1966). And Dylan was finally reaching commercial audiences. The folk-rock group The Byrds made Dylan's song "Mr. Tambourine Man" a number one single. Dylan's own recordings of "Like a Rolling Stone" and "Rainy Day Women Nos. 12 & 35" also hit the charts.

In the 1970s and 1980s, Dylan toured with various artists, including The Band, Joan Baez, and **Jerry Garcia** and the Grateful Dead. He released 25 live, studio, or collection albums, including *Blood on the Tracks* (1975), *Slow Train Coming* (1979), and *Oh Mercy* (1989).

The 1990s brought all kinds of kudos and awards. The Grammys gave Dylan a Lifetime Achievement Award in 1991. He became the first rock star ever to receive the Kennedy Center Honor (1997). He dominated the 1997 Grammys when *Time Out of Mind* won three awards, including Album of the Year. Dylan picked up an Oscar in 2000 for a sound-track single "Things Have Changed." His 2001 release *Love and Theft* got rave reviews.

"You don't need a weatherman to tell which way the wind blows." — BOB DYLAN

Amelia Earhart

aviator ★ 1897– c.1937

Amelia Earhart left a note for her mother in the event of her death. Part of it read: ". . . even though I have lost, the adventure was worth the while." That line sums up Earhart's approach to flying . . . and life!

In the 1920s, Earhart flew in air shows and air races. In 1928, she was the first woman aboard a transatlantic flight. The following year, Earhart helped organize the Ninety-Nines, a female pilots' organization with 99 members. She served as the group's first president.

Earhart was the first woman to fly solo across the Atlantic Ocean (1932). Much of the 2,026-mile flight from Newfoundland to Ireland was through dangerous thunderstorms and fog. Earhart still set a transatlantic record, crossing in 14 hours and 16 minutes. Three years later, she became the first person to fly solo from Hawaii to California, a 2,400-mile trip over the Pacific Ocean.

Amelia Earhart, shown here in 1928.

Earhart's last flight was her most ambitious. In 1937, she and her copilot, Fred Noonan, took off from Miami, Florida, in a twin-engine Lockheed Electra. They were headed on a 27,000-mile trip around the world at the equator. On July 2, the plane disappeared over the Pacific Ocean. Earhart and Noonan were never seen again.

George Eastman

inventor ★ 1854–1932

In the 1870s, photography was a complicated, expensive art. It required almost 50 pounds of equipment, from heavy cameras to breakable glass plates to burning, acidic chemicals. Therefore, most photographs were taken in studios—until George Eastman came along.

In 1885, Eastman revolutionized the field: He invented film. Eastman's lightweight strip of emulsion-covered paper was wound on a roll. Three years later, he invented his little, square, wooden handheld camera, the Kodak. It was loaded with film for 100 photos. The user just clicked a button to take a "snapshot."

In 1889, Eastman applied for a patent for celluloid film, which would soon be transformed into one of the world's most popular forms of photography—movies!

George Eastman, in 1890, holding one of his inexpensive Kodak No. 2 cameras.

Eastman introduced his famous Brownie camera in 1900 (it cost $1) and his Eastman Kodak Company thrived. Eastman, who'd grown up in poverty and dropped out of school at age 14, donated more than $75 million to medical centers and universities in his lifetime.

Mary Baker Eddy
religious leader ★ 1821–1910

Mary Baker Eddy is the founder of Christian Science. She established the Mother Church—the First Church of Christ, Scientist—in Boston, Massachusetts, in 1879. After intense study of the Bible's New Testament, Eddy believed she understood the method by which Jesus Christ healed people. She felt her mission was to share this knowledge.

Eddy traveled around the country holding classes and tutoring students about her beliefs. She started working on *Science and Health*, a book about her Christian Science philosophy. In her book, Eddy explained her belief that good health depends upon spiritual understanding, rather than just upon standard medical practices.

Mary Baker Eddy's book, Science and Health *(1875), is still in print, and has sold more than 10 million copies.*

Mary Baker Eddy personally taught hundreds of students, many of whom became teachers themselves. By 1890, there was a National Christian Scientist Association, which included 33 teaching centers.

The press was sometimes full of bad publicity about church teachings and personal attacks on Eddy. There were also church members who questioned her methods and authority. Nonetheless, she maintained her leadership of the Mother Church in Boston. In 1908, Eddy established the *Christian Scientist Monitor*, a respected, award-winning newspaper that is still published. There are now several thousand Christian Science branches worldwide.

Marian Wright Edelman
children's rights advocate ★ 1939–

In 2000, Marian Wright Edelman was given the Presidential Medal of Freedom. The award honored her passionate crusade to improve the lives of the nation's children.

Edelman is a lawyer and the founding president of the Children's Defense Fund (CDF). Under her leadership, CDF has developed into a powerful advocacy group for better child care, health care, education, and employment opportunities for young people.

Educated at Yale Law School, Edelman became the first African-American woman to pass Mississippi's bar exam. She trained with the National Association for the Advancement of Colored People (NAACP), and then set up a private practice. As a lawyer, Edelman fought against school segregation and helped get civil rights protesters out of jail during the 1960s.

She was jailed and threatened by attack dogs for her civil rights activities. She decided that the best way to improve things was to change federal government policies. In 1968, Edelman moved to Washington, D.C., and started an organization called the Washington Research Project, which represented the rights of poor people and people of color. Five years later, she founded CDF.

"Genius is one percent inspiration, ninety-nine percent perspiration."

— THOMAS ALVA EDISON

Thomas Alva Edison

inventor ★ 1847—1931

Imagine a world without lightbulbs. Or recorded sound. Or movies. That's the world that Thomas Alva Edison was born into. That's not the world he left behind.

His was a classic American success story. Edison was born in Ohio. His large family wasn't that well off. As a boy, Thomas was home-schooled and self-taught. He was also partially deaf. Edison worked all kinds of odd jobs. One of those jobs, telegrapher, took him out of Ohio, and into the world of inventions.

Always a tinker, Edison looked for ways to improve the telegraph system. But it was another invention that gave him his start. In 1869, Edison was living in New York City. He invented a ticker-tape machine, the "Universal Stock Printer." Edison sold his invention for $40,000. He set up a small laboratory in Newark, New Jersey, with the money. There he manufactured more sophisticated telegraph inventions, including one that could handle several messages at once.

Edison believed inventions had to sell in order to be successful. He was the first person to set up an industrial research and design center. In 1876, Edison opened his "invention factory" in Menlo Park, New Jersey.

Thomas Alva Edison holds an incandescent lamp (a lightbulb). The date of this photo is unknown.

In 1877, the "Wizard of Menlo Park" stunned the world with his latest invention, the phonograph. The tinfoil-covered cylinder played "Mary Had a Little Lamb" when you turned the crank. It was the first time sound had been recorded and reproduced. That same year, Edison improved **Alexander Bell**'s telephone by developing his own carbon phone transmitter.

Edison then turned his inventive mind from sound to light. Others had made electric lighting possible. Edison wanted to make it practical. It took more than a year of experiments, but Edison finally perfected an incandescent lamp. In December 1879, Menlo Park was lit up by Edison's latest invention. By 1882, a whole square mile of lower Manhattan was glowing, powered by Edison's generator on Pearl Street. Edison created a utility system to electrify the world.

Edison built a new, larger laboratory in West Orange, New Jersey, in 1887. This lab had everything from a power plant to a physics lab. Within a few years, it also had a strange-looking shed covered in black tar paper. This was where the Edison company produced its latest invention—"motion pictures." Edison and his staff, particularly William Dickson, had been experimenting with **George Eastman's** new celluloid film for several years. They developed the Kinetograph, a motion picture camera, in 1891 and the Kinetoscope, a machine that allowed a single viewer to watch a short movie reel, in 1894.

"Imagination is more important than knowledge."

Albert Einstein
physicist ★ 1879–1955

— ALBERT EINSTEIN

Albert Einstein calculated some of physics' most fundamental equations and changed the world of science.

Born in Germany, Einstein got off to a slow start. He didn't talk much and wasn't really a fluent speaker until he was nine years old. He hated school and was a poor student. But he was passionate about physics and mathematics.

Albert Einstein moved to Switzerland. He got a degree at a prestigious engineering school, and then he went to work in a patent office in 1902. Einstein said the job left him plenty of time to think about physics. And think he did.

Einstein published three revolutionary scientific theories when he was only 26 years old. In March 1905, he explained photoelectric theory, saying that light was made up of individual particles or photons, not just waves. In June, he wrote his theory of relativity, stating that the speed of light is a constant (186,000 miles per second) and that all other motion is relative. In September, Einstein argued that matter and energy are the same thing in two different states. He published his famous $E = mc^2$ equation, which means that mass could be converted into energy . . . lots of it! Einstein's theory is the basis of atomic energy.

Albert Einstein willed his brain to science after his death.

In 1908, Einstein gave up patents for professorships, first at universities in Switzerland and then in Germany. He continued working on his radical ideas about the universe. One of them, Einstein's unified theory of gravitation (1915), turned Isaac Newton's time-honored laws of gravity upside down. In March 1919, observations by a group of British astronomers proved that Einstein's theory was correct. Einstein was awarded the Nobel Prize for physics a few months later.

When the Nazis rose to power in the 1930s, they didn't care about Einstein's scientific reputation. They attacked his work because he was a pacifist, a humanitarian, and a Jew. The physicist and his family emigrated to the U.S. in 1933. (He became a citizen in 1940.) Einstein was appointed head of the new Institute for Advanced Study at Princeton University in New Jersey. In 1939, he added his name to a letter from prominent scientists urging President **Franklin Roosevelt** to fund a nuclear bomb project before the Nazis produced one.

After World War II, Einstein joined his peers on the Emergency Committee of Atomic Scientists, a group that lobbied for international nuclear arms control. Toward the end of his life, Einstein tried to develop a unified field theory, one that would pull together principles of gravity, electromagnetism, and nuclear force.

Dwight Eisenhower
34th president ★ 1890—1969

Dwight Eisenhower wasn't a star at West Point military academy. Nobody expected him to become a general—or president!

Eisenhower led successful World War II campaigns in North Africa, Sicily, and Italy. He quickly rose through the ranks. In 1943, as supreme Allied commander, Eisenhower planned one of the most daring, dangerous, and crucial maneuvers of the war: the D-Day invasion of Normandy, France, on June 6, 1944.

After the war ended, "Ike" was a national hero. In 1952, Eisenhower ran for president and won as Republican candidate.

Eisenhower served two terms (1953–1961). He was an easygoing president, a symbol of prosperous times—but not everything was as peaceful as it seemed. Eisenhower was forced to send federal troops to Arkansas to enforce new laws about desegregating public schools. Senator **Joseph McCarthy** was unjustly attacking people for being Communists. And the Soviet Union's *Sputnik* satellite launched the space race.

President Eisenhower promoted international peace efforts. He helped negotiate an end to the Korean War and agreed to cultural exchanges with the Soviets. But he also believed in building up the U.S. nuclear warhead arsenal. Eisenhower thought the threat of "massive retaliation" would keep the country's enemies at bay.

T. S. Eliot
author ★ 1888—1965

Though he wrote literary criticism and plays, T. S. Eliot is most famous for his poems. Eliot's poems are deep, difficult, disturbing, and often dark. He explored the isolation and complexity of civilization. And he had a profound effect on modern poetry.

Thomas Stearns Eliot was born in St. Louis, Missouri. He moved to England in 1914 and spent the rest of his life there. Eliot worked in a London bank while he wrote poetry and essays. He founded a literary journal, *Criterion*. In 1917, he published his first major collection, *Prufrock and Other Observations*. It included one of his most famous poems, "The Love Song of J. Alfred Prufrock."

Five years later his masterpiece, *The Waste Land* (1922), was published. It reflects the chaos and horror of a world that had just witnessed World War I.

T. S. Eliot wrote a book of light verse, Old Possum's Book of Practical Cats, *for his godchildren. It became the hit musical* Cats *in 1981*

Eliot followed with *The Hollow Men* (1925) and *Four Quartets* (1943). He was awarded the Nobel Prize for literature in 1948.

"I'm trying to play the

Gordon Parks took this photo of Duke Ellington in 1943.

Duke Ellington

composer, musician ★ 1899—1974

Duke Ellington reigned in nightclubs, on stages, and in symphony and opera halls around the world. He was one of America's top composers and one of jazz's legendary bandleaders. When people heard his signature call, "Get out of the way, 'cause here comes the Duke!" they cheered.

Edward Kennedy Ellington was born into a middle-class African-American family in Washington, D.C. He was an athletic child and a talented student who intended to study art. (A classmate gave him the nickname Duke because Ellington was such a sharp dresser.) Along the way, his mother steered him into piano lessons. Ellington applied himself more seriously to the instrument in high school. He also started composing music.

In the early 1920s, Ellington joined a band called The Washingtonians. Ellington eventually took over as bandleader. He added innovative jazz musicians like Bubber Miley, who wailed on his trumpet and even used a bathroom plunger over the end of it to create a whole new sound. Ellington found other musicians with unique sounds. His band grew to 10 members. By 1927, Duke and his band were the headliners at the famous Cotton Club in Harlem, New York.

Ellington "played" his band like it was an instrument itself. He composed music that let each of his band members shine. He layered his pieces with unusual instrumentals and shifting solos. He wrote cool, thoughtful, "mood" pieces. He was influenced by ragtime and blues, but his band's "swing" and growling "jungle" jazz was a whole new thing. Audiences loved it! Ellington's fame spread all across the country when his Cotton Club appearances were broadcast on the radio. He became the first nationally known African-American bandleader.

Ellington expanded the band and continued to write musical hits such as "Mood Indigo" (1930), "It Don't Mean a Thing If It Ain't Got That Swing" (1932), and "Black and Tan Fantasy" (1938). Throughout the 1940s, Ellington toured the United States. For several years, he played an annual concert at Carnegie Hall. These shows featured his ongoing composition, "Black, Brown, and Beige." This ambitious work debuted in 1943 and told the history of African Americans through music. During this decade, he recorded Billy Strayhorn's "Take the A Train" (1941), a piece that became a theme song for Duke Ellington and his band.

Interest in big bands waned in the 1950s. Jazz took a turn in another direction. Ellington and his orchestra kept playing, mainly in Europe. But at the late-night, closing set of the 1956 Newport Jazz Festival in Rhode Island, Ellington and his band brought a screaming, cheering audience to its feet.

Duke Ellington continued to lead bands and compose music throughout his life. His later work included sacred music. In 1969, he was awarded the Presidential Medal of Freedom.

natural feelings of a people." —DUKE ELLINGTON

Ralph Waldo Emerson coined the phrase "the shot heard 'round the world" in "Concord Hymn," his poem about the first battle of the American Revolution.

Ralph Waldo Emerson
philosopher ★ 1803—1882

On January 25, 1820, Emerson, then a 17-year-old Harvard student, wrote the first entry in his personal journal. For the next 50 years, he kept track of his thoughts on spirituality and nature. He also became one of the greatest thinkers and teachers of his time.

By the 1830s, Emerson had found a broad audience for his ideas. He became a popular speaker in the "lyceum" movement. Americans flocked to their local lyceum (lecture hall) to hear talks on the important issues of the day. For Emerson, those issues often centered on nature. He believed that if people closely observed nature, they'd uncover truths about *human* nature. He said it was possible to "transcend" the limits of daily life and thought by exploring one's unique inner soul and emotions. This philosophy was called transcendentalism. Emerson's speeches, essays, and poems encouraged self-reliance and quiet reflection. His work joyfully celebrated harmony with nature.

Emerson's writings, such as *Nature* (1836) and his *Essays* series (1841 and 1844), were enormously popular in America and Europe. He was an active abolitionist and the intellectual leader of the Concord Group of transcendentalists that included **Henry David Thoreau**.

Gloria Estefan
singer ★ 1958—

Cuban-born Gloria Estefan was one of the first Spanish-speaking pop artists to cross over into English-speaking markets. In 1975, she started singing with Emilio Estefan and his band. The band became the Miami Sound Machine, and had big hits in Spanish-speaking countries. Then in 1985, they blew open the U.S. market with "Conga," a song from the band's album *Primitive Love*. "Conga" became the first single in recording history to make *Billboard*'s dance, pop, Latin, and soul music charts.

Gloria Estefan's popularity in the United States grew as she toured, cut more albums, and made music videos. After a long, painful recovery following a serious accident, Estefan astonished fans with not only a new album, *Into the Light* (1991), but also a comeback tour. She won the American Music Award and BMI Songwriter of the Year in 1989 and Grammys in 1993, 1995, and 2000. She cowrote "Reach," the official song of the 1996 Olympics, and sang at the 2002 Olympics. She took home the 2000 American Music Award of Merit.

Gloria Estefan hosted the first Latin Grammy Awards, held in 2000.

"The past is not dead. It is not even past."

— WILLIAM FAULKNER

William Faulkner
author ★ 1897—1962

In his Nobel Prize speech, William Faulkner (r.) said that the only subjects worth writing about were the "universal truths": pity, pride, honor, love.

William Faulkner used his own world, Oxford, Mississippi, to create a prize-winning fictional world, Yoknapatawpha County.

His novels *Sartoris* (1929), *The Sound and the Fury* (1929), *As I Lay Dying* (1930), *Light in August* (1932), and *Absalom, Absalom!* (1936) described the fortunes and misfortunes of several generations of Yoknapatawpha families. Through their stories, Faulkner exposed the impoverished gentility, greed, passion, strength, and racism of Southern culture. He showed the corrupt aristocracy of the Old South in decline.

Faulkner often wrote in a stream-of-consciousness style. Words flowed on the page like thoughts flit through the brain. Many of his novels told the main story from more than one point of view and sometimes in dialect.

Critics usually liked Faulkner's bold new style—but that didn't sell a lot of books. Faulkner went to Hollywood and wrote screenplays to help support his family. He even sold one of his own books, *Intruder in the Dust* (1948), to MGM Studios. This brought him more financial security. Winning the Nobel Prize for literature the following year brought him more fame.

Enrico Fermi
physicist ★ 1901—1954

Italian physicist Enrico Fermi split a uranium atom in 1934. He didn't realize the full impact of this experiment yet, but it and World War II would affect the scientist's next moves.

Fermi was awarded the Nobel Prize for physics in 1938 for his studies in radioactivity. He and his family then used the award as an opportunity to emigrate to the U.S. to escape the rising tides of Fascism and Nazism in Europe.

Based on his own work and that of other scientists, Fermi proposed the theory of atomic chain reactions. He believed that splitting a uranium atom would produce neutrons that spontaneously keep splitting more uranium atoms. This would release a tremendous amount of energy. Fermi thought he had figured out a way to safely harness that energy. In 1942, he tested his hypothesis.

Physicist Enrico Fermi calculated that a subatomic particle, the neutrino, existed.

Fermi and his team built a 26-foot-high "atomic pile" of uranium and graphite in a squash court at the University of Chicago. On December 2, 1942, they set off the first nuclear chain reaction, which successfully unleashed and controlled atomic energy. By 1944, Fermi was working with **Robert Oppenheimer**'s team, building the atom bomb.

Ella Fitzgerald
jazz singer ★ 1917–1996

Jazz great Ella Fitzgerald won 13 Grammys, including a 1967 Lifetime Achievement Award. From 1953 through the mid-1970s, she was voted best female vocalist by *Down Beat*, the influential jazz magazine. Fitzgerald was awarded the Presidential Medal of Freedom in 1992. In six decades of singing, she recorded more than 2,000 songs on 70 albums, which sold 40 million copies. She's the undisputed "first lady of Song."

Fitzgerald's big break came at the famous Apollo Theater in Harlem, New York. The crowd at amateur night applauded wildly after 15-year-old Ella's performance. Bandleader Chick Webb "discovered" her and signed her on as a singer with his big band. Fitzgerald and Webb had their first hit together, "A Tisket a Tasket," a new and jazzy version of an old nursery rhyme.

In 1942, Fitzgerald struck out on her own. She covered everything from blues to ballads to scat—the improvised, spontaneous syllable singing she helped make famous. Fitzgerald toured with **Dizzy Gillespie**. In 1946, she started singing in Norman Granz's "Jazz at the Philharmonics" tours. She continued touring heavily until she was nearly 70.

F. Scott Fitzgerald
author ★ 1896–1940

F. Scott Fitzgerald dubbed the 1920s the "Jazz Age." He and his beautiful wife, Zelda, were the era's fun-loving, wild-partying, golden couple. Their antics and anxieties inspired some of Fitzgerald's greatest works.

His first novel, *This Side of Paradise* (1920), was a thinly disguised account of his college years at Princeton University. It brought him fame and fortune. In 1920, Scott married Zelda Sayre.

The Fitzgeralds drank heavily, spent lavishly, and lived glamorously. Scott wrote short stories to pay the bills. The couple moved from New York to the French Riviera where Scott wrote his most famous novel, *The Great Gatsby* (1925).

The Fitzgeralds' extravagant lifestyle eventually caught up with them. Zelda had a nervous breakdown. Scott was an alcoholic. He finished one more novel, *Tender Is the Night* (1934), but sales were poor. By the time Fitzgerald died of a heart attack at 44, all his books were out of print. It was years before his work was again fully recognized and appreciated.

Henry Ford
industrialist ★ 1863—1947

He was a man with a mission: mass-produce cars and make it possible for the middle class to afford them. In doing so, Henry Ford revolutionized American industry.

Ford produced his first car in 1896. It had an internal combustion engine, bicycle wheels, and a tiller. Seven years later, he opened up the Ford Motor Company near Detroit, Michigan. Ford's Model T car was introduced in 1908. The world's first automatic conveyor moved the car through stations where workers were responsible for one part of its assembly. In 1913, it took 12 hours to make a Model T. By 1914, the Ford plant was doing it in 93 minutes. Because of this streamlined production, Ford was able to drop his car prices from $850 (1908) to $360 (1916). And at a time when American workers made about $11 a week, Ford paid $5 *a day*. He wanted his workers to be able to afford the cars they were building.

Car manufacturing opened up thousands of new jobs, fueled the gas station business, spurred the need for highway construction, and made Henry Ford a very rich man. The Ford Motor Company is now the largest producer of trucks and the second-largest producer of cars in the world.

Dian Fossey
zoologist ★ 1932—1985

The subjects of Dian Fossey's scientific research were six feet tall and weighed hundreds of pounds. They growled and grunted. Not surprising—they were gorillas.

Sponsored in part by the National Geographic Society, Fossey set up the Karisoke Research Centre in the Parc National des Volcans in Rwanda, Africa. There she studied the lifestyles and communication skills of 51 gorillas. She discovered that gorillas were peaceful vegetarians who lived in family groups. They used more than 12 different sounds to communicate. She also discovered that the gorilla population was shrinking because hunters and farmers were invading their habitats. Fossey started an international campaign to save the gorillas. Still, the poaching continued. In 1978, several of Fossey's gorillas were killed. Her fight against this slaughter made world headlines. Fossey wrote a best-selling book about her work, *Gorillas in the Mist*. (It later became a popular movie.) In 1985, Fossey was murdered in her cabin in Rwanda. Many people think poachers killed the zoologist, but no one was ever charged with her death.

Stephen Foster

composer ★ 1826—1864

Stephen Foster wrote more than 200 songs, including the state songs of Florida ("Swanee River") and Kentucky ("My Old Kentucky Home").

Many people consider Stephen Foster America's first real composer. Born near Pittsburgh, Pennsylvania, Foster played flute, guitar, and piano as a child. He was working as a bookkeeper in Cincinnati when he wrote "Oh! Susanna." Foster sold the song for $100 in 1848. It became a huge hit the next year when prospectors in the California gold rush adopted it as their anthem. His next popular piece, "I Dream of Jeannie with the Light Brown Hair" (1850) was a love song to his new wife.

The Fosters moved to New York to be closer to Stephen's publisher. His work was widely performed by Christy's Minstrels, the most famous minstrel troupe of its time. Minstrel music was sung and played by white people in black-face makeup pretending to be slaves. Foster realized that minstrel singing would bring his music to a wide audience. But he intended his "plantation songs," as he called them, to be nostalgic and compassionate, not mocking.

Foster's later years were troubled by financial and health worries. He drank heavily and was ill with tuberculosis. Though he composed 46 new songs during his last year of life, most were forgotten, except for one masterpiece, "Beautiful Dreamer."

Aretha Franklin

soul singer ★ 1942—

Aretha Franklin was the first woman ever inducted into the Rock and Roll Hall of Fame. Now that's *respect*.

The Queen of Soul has been singing for more than 40 years. She cut her first gospel album when she was 15. By 1960, she had signed with Columbia Records. Franklin started singing jazz, rhythm and blues, and pop music. In 1967, she had a big hit single, "I Never Loved a Man." "Respect" hit the charts the following year and earned Franklin her first of 17 Grammy Awards. Many people thought of this song as an anthem for African Americans and feminists since it was released when the struggles for civil rights and equal rights were gaining ground.

Aretha Franklin continues to be one of music's great rhythm and blues and gospel singers. She's even experimented with hip-hop music on her 1998 album, *A Rose Is Still a Rose*. Franklin has recorded more than 51 albums. Twenty of them have gone gold. In 1994, Franklin was honored with a Lifetime Achievement Award at the Grammys.

Benjamin Franklin
statesman, scientist, publisher ★ 1706—1790

At an early age, Ben Franklin devoted himself to "arriving at moral Perfection" by mastering 13 virtues. He clearly practiced virtue number six, Industry: "Lose no time; be always employ'd in something useful."

Boston-born Franklin ran away from his printing job and arrived in Philadelphia as a penniless teenager in 1723. Seven years later, he had his own print shop and his own newspaper, the *Pennsylvania Gazette*. But what first brought Franklin fortune and fame was his publication, *Poor Richard's Almanac*. His booklet full of farming and weather information, historical facts, and witty sayings like "the early bird catches the worm," was published from 1732 to 1757. It sold nearly 10,000 copies a year.

Franklin was a civic-minded intellectual. He founded the first colonial lending library, a volunteer fire department, a hospital, and the American Philosophical Society. He also established a postal system that linked the colonies. He was even more devoted to scientific studies. Among his many inventions were swimming flippers, bifocal glasses, and an efficient stove heater. On one famous stormy day in 1752, Franklin used a kite and a key to prove that lightning was electricity.

A well-known public figure, Franklin was very involved in the politics of his day. At that time, there was growing friction between the American colonies and Great Britain, often over taxes. Franklin was one of the first to see that the colonies would be more powerful if they united. But Franklin also tried to help keep peace with Great Britain at first. From 1757 to 1762 and again in 1764, he sailed to England to argue for colonists' rights.

When the American Revolution broke out, Benjamin Franklin became a leader in the struggle to build a new country. He represented Pennsylvania in the Continental Congress, where he served on a committee with **Thomas Jefferson** and **John Adams**. The committee's task was to write a declaration of independence. When he was 70 years old and in failing health, he traveled to France to ask for help with the war effort. Franklin, in his big fur hat and homemade bifocals, was the toast of Paris. In 1777, the French signed an alliance treaty that Franklin helped draw up. Within six years, he helped negotiate the Treaty of Paris (1783) with England, which granted full independence to the American colonies.

"If you would not be forgotten,
As soon as you are dead and rotten,
Either write things worth reading,
Or do things worth the writing."

— BENJAMIN FRANKLIN

In 1785, Franklin returned to Philadelphia. He was elected head of Pennsylvania. Two years later, he represented his state at the Constitutional Convention. His clever good humor and diplomatic skills calmed many heated debates about how to govern the new nation.

John C. Frémont
explorer ★ 1813—1890

John C. Frémont's nickname was "The Pathfinder." Reading about his adventures encouraged many Americans to pack up and head west.

Lieutenant Frémont of the U.S. Army led an expedition in 1842 through uncharted lands in what is now Oregon and Wyoming. His mission was to find a route for a transcontinental railroad through the Rocky Mountains. Frémont and his wife, Jessie Benton Frémont, wrote exciting, colorful reports of the expedition. They fired the imagination of the American public. They championed the cause of "manifest destiny," the idea that the United States had a divine right to expand westward.

Frémont continued exploring through the 1840s. He saw the rich potential of California. This area, however, was controlled by Mexico. Frémont helped change that. He took part in the Bear Flag Revolt (1846), when California settlers challenged the Mexican government. The following year, he led his troops in a full-scale battle to turn California into a U.S. territory. Frémont later became one of California's first senators.

Betty Friedan
feminist leader, author ★ 1921—

Betty Friedan in 1963. In 2000, she published her memoir, Life So Far. Clearly from the title, she expects to accomplish still more.

In the 1950s, women were expected to give up their careers when they married and had children. Betty Friedan found that being a wife and mother was just not enough. She wasn't alone.

Friedan's best-seller, *The Feminine Mystique* (1963), exploded the myth that all women were "happy housewives" and helped launch the modern women's movement. In 1966, Friedan and several other feminists founded the National Organization for Women (NOW), which became the strongest women's rights group in the country. Friedan served as NOW's president until 1970. The following year, she joined **Shirley Chisholm**, **Fannie Lou Hamer**, and **Gloria Steinem** in founding the National Women's Political Caucus to bring more women and women's issues into politics. In 1973, she helped establish the First Women's Bank and Trust Company.

In the 1970s, Friedan fought for women's reproductive rights, equal pay for women, child care, and the Equal Rights Amendment. She also found time to write. In *The Second Stage* (1981), she looked at love, personal freedom, and families. In *The Fountain of Age* (1993), she challenged society's ideas about aging. Four years later, her book *Beyond Gender: The New Politics of Work and Family* (1997) called for women and men to put aside "identity politics" and find new ways to balance careers, families, and time.

"To be a poet is a condition,

Robert Frost
poet ★ 1874—1963

In his 30s, Robert Frost was a farmer by day and a poet by night. He eventually reaped more from poetry: four Pulitzer prizes, 44 honorary degrees, a professorship at Harvard, and a lasting reputation as one of America's most beloved and widely read poets.

Frost was born in California, but his ancestors were staunch New Englanders. After his father's death, Robert's mother moved the family to Massachusetts. New England's scenery and sensibility would be a profound influence on Frost's poems. So would the plainspoken rhythms of New England speech.

In 1912, Frost sold his farm and moved his family to England. He thought his poetry might be appreciated there. He was right. An English press published two collections of his poems, *A Boy's Will* and *North of Boston*, in 1913. They were both literary sensations— and the news spread back across the ocean. The unknown farmer who'd left the U.S. in 1912 returned as a famous poet in 1915.

Frost spent the rest of his life writing poems, such as the famous and often-quoted "Stopping by Woods on a Snowy Evening" and "The Road Not Taken." He was a popular lecturer and teacher, and won many literary awards.

Robert Fulton
inventor ★ 1765—1815

The 133-foot boat chugged out of New York Harbor in 1807 and headed up the Hudson River. A black cloud billowed out of its smokestack. Thirty-two hours later, the *Clermont* docked in Albany, New York. Some people jeered at "Fulton's Folly." But Robert Fulton was on his way to developing the first commercial steamship.

Fulton came from a Pennsylvania farming family. He was a talented artist who went to England in 1786 to study painting. But he soon found engineering more absorbing. He designed a submarine and convinced Napoleon Bonaparte to pay for it. In 1800, Fulton launched his submarine—with himself in it. The *Nautilus* could dive 25 feet.

Fulton invented many things, including a powered shovel for canal digging and a "sighting mechanism" for his submarine.

When he couldn't keep the French, and later the British, interested in his naval designs, Fulton turned to the commercial steamboat. Fulton figured out how to improve steam engines and how to make steamboats competitive with sailing ships. He built 15 of these boats. Fulton's steamboats were the first on the Mississippi River and the first used by the U.S. Navy.

not a profession." — ROBERT FROST

Clark Gable in Gone With The Wind.

Clark Gable
actor ★ 1901—1960

Clark Gable was rejected at his first movie screen test because his ears were too big. He still became one of Hollywood's hottest leading men . . . jug ears and all!

Gable, a former oil driller from the Midwest, landed a contract with MGM in 1930. Nicknamed "The King," he ruled the decade! Gable's acting with stars like Norma Shearer (*A Free Soul*, 1931) and Jean Harlow (*Red Dust*, 1932; *China Seas*, 1935) was electrifying. His performance in **Frank Capra**'s screwball comedy *It Happened One Night* (1934) won him an Oscar. "The King" was box-office gold. But his crowning role was yet to come.

Oddly enough, Gable wasn't originally interested in the part that became his most famous legacy. Now, it's impossible to imagine anyone *but* Gable in the all-time classic *Gone with the Wind*. He brought passion, wit, and a touch of rascal to the role of Rhett Butler, the dashing hero of the Civil War epic. *Gone with the Wind* opened in 1939 and held the all-time box-office record for 30 years!

Gable made 69 films in a career that spanned four decades.

Jerry Garcia
rock 'n' roll artist ★ 1942—1995

There are 23 Grateful Dead albums. But it was the group's live shows before thousands of devoted "Deadheads" that made them one of the most popular rock 'n' roll bands ever.

Jerry Garcia formed The Grateful Dead (first called The Warlocks) in San Francisco in 1965. Garcia played guitar, wrote songs, and led the band. The Dead quickly became part of the exploding psychedelic, acid-rock scene. Their unique sound fused many musical styles: rock, acid rock, jazz, folk, blues, and bluegrass. In concert, Garcia's creative guitar-playing was legendary, as was the band's famously long improvisations. The Grateful Dead rejected the commercialism of rock 'n' roll and let their fans tape-record or "bootleg" their concerts. In the studio, Garcia and the rest of the band produced best-selling albums like *Workingman's Dead* (1970) with its hit, "Casey Jones," and the signature song, "Truckin'" from *American Beauty* (1970).

In the 1980s, Jerry Garcia's drug use nearly killed him. Grateful to be alive, Garcia pulled the band together and produced their best-selling album *In the Dark* (1987).

This psychedelic poster for a Grateful Dead concert dates from 1967. The band broke up after Jerry Garcia's death in 1995.

Judy Garland (l.) won a special Academy Award for her role in The Wizard of Oz.

Judy Garland
actress, singer ★ 1922—1969

A star *was* born when Judy Garland made her stage debut at three. She sang and danced in vaudeville shows for 10 more years. Then **Louis B. Mayer** himself signed her to MGM studios in 1936. Like audiences to come, he was bowled over by her voice.

The starlet made several popular films with Mickey Rooney. When Judy was a teenager, she landed the role that would make her an international star: the lead in *The Wizard of Oz* (1939). Garland played Dorothy, the tornado-tossed heroine. When she sang "Over the Rainbow," she melted hearts in movie theaters all over the world.

Garland made 32 movies over the course of her career, including *Meet Me in St. Louis* (1944) and *A Star Is Born* (1954), for which she received an Oscar nomination. Her 12 albums were best-sellers; *Judy at Carnegie Hall* (1961) won five Grammys. She appeared in sold-out concerts on Broadway and at London's Palladium. A talented but troubled artist, Garland suffered from depression and dependency on pills and alcohol. Her career moved in fits and starts and included several comebacks.

William Lloyd Garrison
abolitionist ★ 1805—1879

In calling for an end to slavery, William Lloyd Garrison was ahead of his time. Decades before the Civil War, he started his abolitionist newspaper, *The Liberator* (1831), and organized the New England Anti-Slavery Society (1832) and the American Anti-Slavery Society (1833).

Garrison's editorials and speeches loudly denounced slave owners and traders. Southerners were outraged; there were bounties offered for Garrison's arrest and even a $3,000 reward for his ears. Many Northerners were also angered by Garrison's attacks. In 1835, a Boston mob seized Garrison at an antislavery meeting and hung a noose around his neck. The mayor stepped in and threw Garrison in jail, to keep him from being hanged. None of these threats stopped the abolitionist. He continued to expose the evils of slavery in his newspaper. During the Civil War, Garrison kept the pressure on President Abraham Lincoln to deal with the slavery issue.

In 1865, the last issue of Garrison's *The Liberator* was published. It contained the words of the newly ratified 13th Amendment—which outlawed slavery.

Bill Gates

computer entrepreneur ★ 1955—

Computer genius Bill Gates predicted he'd make a million dollars by the time he turned 30. As it turned out he was a *billionaire* by 31.

Gates wrote his first software program when he was 13. He and his friend Paul Allen worked for a computer company finding "bugs," or problems. Their own high school paid the teens to develop a class scheduling program. Gates dropped out of Harvard University to form Microsoft with Allen in 1975. The rest is high-tech history.

Microsoft's first success was a version of the programming language BASIC for Altair, the first microcomputer. In 1980, the corporate giant IBM wanted Gates to create an operating system for its new line of personal computers (PCs). In a brilliant financial move, Gates agreed to lease, not sell, his new MS-DOS (Microsoft Disc Operating System) to IBM. Leasing means Microsoft collects fees when other companies use their software. IBM's personal computers were best-sellers. Microsoft got rich, too.

Fortune *magazine lists Bill Gates as the wealthiest person in America.*

Much of Bill Gates's genius lies in figuring out what's the hottest new technology trend and how Microsoft can shape it into a marketable—and profitable—product. Microsoft software like Word, which replaced complicated DOS commands with simple menus and the now universal point-and-click devices, was enormously successful. In 1990, Gates brought out the first of many Microsoft Windows programs. This product made PCs just as user-friendly and accessible as **Steve Jobs**'s Macs.

Still, other, smaller companies beat Gates to the punch when it came to the Internet. But by 1995, Gates had made Internet products a priority at his company. Microsoft Explorer quickly became one of the world's most widely used Internet browsers. Maybe too quickly. In 1995, the U.S. Justice Department started investigating Microsoft. They were concerned that Bill Gates was running a monopoly and that Microsoft used unfair business practices to squash its competition.

"Pick good people, use small teams, give them excellent tools." — BILL GATES

Complicated lawsuits followed. The legal cases are still being settled.

Meanwhile, Bill Gates remains the most powerful man in the technology field. As of 2001, nearly 85% of all PCs used Microsoft systems. The company has 44,000 employees worldwide and revenues of more than $25 billion a year. Gates and his wife, Melinda, created a foundation to promote education and global health. They have donated more than $21 billion to the foundation, which funds libraries, scholarships, and international vaccine campaigns.

Lou Gehrig
baseball player ★ 1903–1941

Lou Gehrig batted behind **Babe Ruth** in the Yankees' famous "Murderers' Row" of powerhouse hitters. That often left him in Ruth's shadow. Gehrig didn't need the spotlight, though. He just needed to play ball.

The Bronx-born first baseman helped make the Yankees the dominant team in baseball during the late 1920s and early 1930s. Gehrig was an outstanding fielder, and his batting average topped .300 for 12 seasons in a row. He took home the American League's Most Valuable Player award three times (1927, 1931, 1934). He once hit four consecutive home runs in a single game (1931) and won the 1924 American League's Triple Crown for best in batting, home runs, and RBIs (runs batted in). Gehrig had a career batting average of .340, smacked out 493 home runs, and smashed in a record 23 grand slams.

Fans and sports writers called Gehrig the "Iron Horse" because he always played ball despite injuries or illness. But in 1939, Gehrig realized there was something affecting his game. He was diagnosed with ALS (amyotrophic lateral sclerosis), a rare spinal condition now often called "Lou Gehrig's disease." Gehrig dropped out of the Yankee lineup. Two years later, the pride of the Yankees was dead.

Frank Gehry
architect ★ 1929—

What makes Frank Gehry's architecture so edgy is that it doesn't seem to have edges. His buildings flow, they ripple, they arch, they curve, they seem to ignore straight lines.

Frank Gehry's Guggenheim Museum in Bilbao, Spain.

Gehry and his family moved from Canada to Los Angeles in 1947. He studied art and architecture at the University of Southern California. In 1962, he opened his own studio in Los Angeles He designed shopping centers, museums, offices, and furniture.

Gehry is famous for expanding the relationship between the inside and the outside of a building and its surroundings. In his award-winning designs, he's used common construction materials like chain-link fencing and interesting ones like high-tech, expensive titanium. Gehry's Chiat/Day Headquarters in Los Angeles has a middle building that's a giant pair of binoculars. His apartment building in Prague, in the Czech Republic, is nicknamed the "Fred and Ginger." Its glass tower swoons into a concrete one, suggesting the famous dancing couple, **Fred Astaire** and **Ginger Rogers**. Gehry's innovative design for the Guggenheim Museum in Bilbao, Spain, helped establish him as one of the world's most famous modern architects.

"Life is chaotic, dangerous, and surprising.

Geronimo
Chiricahua Apache leader ★ c.1829—1909

Geronimo (Goyathlay), the great Apache chief, fought two enemies: the Mexicans, who were the Apaches' traditional foes, and the U.S. settlers and soldiers, the new threat.

In 1850, Mexican troops killed Geronimo's mother, wife, and three children. He joined forces with **Cochise** and other Apache leaders to seek revenge. For years, Geronimo led raids into Mexico. By the 1860s, he and his warriors were attacking U.S. citizens, too. The Apache were trying to drive the gold-hungry pioneers out of their sacred land. The U.S. Army galloped in to protect them and tried to track down the wily chief.

By 1876, the U.S. government forced all the Apache to leave their homelands and move to a hot, barren reservation in Arizona. They lured Geronimo in through trickery. But they couldn't keep him there. For nine years, the chief and his warriors would escape, be pursued, surrender, and escape again. The final surrender came in 1886. The "Indian Wars" were officially declared over. Geronimo was held as a prisoner of war for 14 years in Florida, Alabama, and Oklahoma.

The Apache chief Geronimo's name now stands for bravery and perseverance. During World War II, soldiers parachuting into enemy lines yelled "Geronimo" as they jumped.

George Gershwin
composer ★ 1898—1937

George Gershwin grew up in a Russian-Jewish immigrant household in Brooklyn, New York. He studied classical music, but he sought his fortune in popular music. In 1920, Gershwin wrote a song called "Swanee." A famous vaudeville star, Al Jolson, sang it. Hundreds of thousands of record and sheet music sales followed. Gershwin became a very famous, very rich young man.

In 1924, he was commissioned to do an orchestral piece. Gershwin was too busy writing Broadway musicals to give it much thought. But on a train ride, the rhythm of the train wheels got him thinking. In three weeks, Gershwin composed his groundbreaking jazz symphony, *Rhapsody in Blue*.

For the next two decades, Gershwin's music was everywhere. His orchestral works, *Concerto in F* (1925) and *An American in Paris* (1928) were applauded in concert halls. He collaborated with his lyric-writing brother, Ira, on hit stage musicals like *Funny Face* (1927), *Girl Crazy* (1929), and the Pulitzer prize-winning *Of Thee I Sing* (1931).

In 1935, Gershwin's full-length opera, *Porgy and Bess*, opened on Broadway. It had an all-black cast included the now classic song, "Summertime."

Buildings should reflect it." — FRANK GEHRY

J. Paul Getty
oil entrepreneur ★ 1892–1976

John Paul Getty was a shrewd oilman and a modern one, too. He hired geologists and used science to help him locate oil sites. He made a million dollars as an independent oil producer in Oklahoma in 1916. During the 1930s and 1940s, he aggressively bought other oil companies and leases. He turned the 1929 stock market crash into an opportunity by scooping up oil company stocks at bargain-basement prices. He legally wrangled with his mother to gain controlling interest in his late father's company in 1933. He was a greedy and ruthless financial high-roller. But he also amassed a major art collection, which became the Getty Museum in California.

One of Getty's smartest moves was far from the Midwestern and Western oil fields. In 1948, Getty signed a $9.5 million cash deal with the king of Saudi Arabia. Getty got the rights to drill for oil on an unseen site between Saudi Arabia and Kuwait. He even had to pay a steep royalty to the Saudis on whatever oil he did find . . . *if* he found it. Four years and a $30 million investment later, Getty Oil struck a gusher of "black gold" in the Middle East.

Althea Gibson
tennis player ★ 1927–

Growing up in New York's Harlem, Althea Gibson played all kinds of sports. She was particularly good at paddle tennis, a kind of street tennis. A local coach noticed and gave Gibson her first tennis racket. Within five years, Gibson won the 1947 national Negro women's title from the American Tennis Association (ATA), a black sports organization. It was the first of her 11 ATA championships.

Gibson then fought for the right to play in U.S. Lawn Tennis Association (USLTA) and Grand Slam tournaments, which were segregated events. In 1950, Gibson broke through the USLTA's color barrier. When she stepped onto the court at the prestigious Forest Hills tennis tournament in New York, she became the first African American to play in the U.S. Open. The following year, Gibson broke the same barrier at Wimbledon, England's world-famous international tennis competition.

Gibson's strength, stamina, and determination took her to the top. She was the first African American to win a Grand Slam. She won the singles and doubles championships at Wimbledon, and the U.S. singles at Forest Hills, the first African American to do so.

In 1958, she did it all over again. In three seasons, Gibson won 11 major titles. She retired from amateur tennis in 1958.

"No matter what accomplishments you

Josh Gibson
baseball player ★ 1911—1947

When he rolled up his sleeves, stepped up to the plate, and assumed his powerful, confident stance, baseball fans got ready to watch the ball rip.

Right-hander Josh Gibson was a mighty slugger. He spent 17 years in the Negro Leagues from 1930 to 1946, playing primarily with the Homestead Grays and the Pittsburgh Crawfords. At that time, baseball was a segregated sport. Accurate statistics for the Negro Leagues weren't always kept. Still, Gibson's estimated stats were impressive for *any* league: a .391 batting average and 962 home runs, including 75 runs in one season (1931). He was the top batter in the Negro Leagues four times. He was also chosen for the East-West All Star team nine times. When not walloping home runs, he was a skilled catcher for his Pittsburgh-based teams.

Josh Gibson, the "black Babe Ruth," once hit an astounding 575-foot home run.

Sadly, Josh Gibson died a few months before **Jackie Robinson** integrated Major League Baseball, opening up new possibilities for African-American players. Gibson was inducted into the Baseball Hall of Fame in 1972.

Dizzy Gillespie
composer, musician ★ 1917—1993

John Birks Gillespie changed the rhythms and harmonies of jazz. He added a Latin flavor and an Afro-Cuban beat, and he played bebop like nobody else.

Nicknamed "Dizzy" for his constant clowning, Gillespie played trumpet with the big names in music during the 1930s and 1940s—Cab Calloway, Fletcher Henderson, and Earl "Fatha" Hines. But Dizzy wanted to break out of their traditional big band sound. He sat in on jam sessions with jazz players like **Charlie Parker**. His music took on more of a bebop sound. Bebop is a jazz style marked by fast tempos and ever-changing, unusual chords. Gillespie was one of bebop's most innovative composers, arrangers, and players. He wrote classics like "A Night in Tunisia" and "Salt Peanuts" (both 1942). He started a quintet and played regularly

His trumpet, with its unusual, upturned bell, was a sign of Dizzy Gillespie's originality and unique jazz style.

at The Onyx Club on New York's 52nd Street, the capital of bebop music. Gillespie also toured with small jazz groups that included other legendary performers like Max Roach on drums and Charles Mingus on bass. Gillespie was a headliner at the first Newport Jazz Festival in 1954.

Dizzy Gillespie won many awards in his life, including a Lifetime Achievement Award at the 1989 Grammys and the National Medal of Arts (also 1989). For more than three decades, he topped jazz polls of the music industry.

make, somebody helped you." —ALTHEA GIBSON

"Zero-G and I feel fine."

— JOHN GLENN, JR.

John Glenn, Jr. walks to the launch pad of the space shuttle Discovery.

John Glenn, Jr.
astronaut, senator ★ 1921—

In February 1962, John Glenn, Jr.'s paycheck was $245 higher. It was extra pay for a recent flight . . . around the earth!

Glenn was a major in the Marines and a navy test pilot when NASA selected him in 1959. He became one of the Mercury 7, the nation's first astronauts. The U.S. was in a "space race" with the Soviet Union. The Soviets launched the first satellite, *Sputnik* (1957), and put the first person in space (1961).

On February 20, 1962, Glenn climbed into the 36-cubic foot space capsule he called *Friendship 7*, after his fellow astronauts. Glenn became the first American to orbit the planet. He traveled 81,000 miles and circled the earth three times.

Glenn became a national hero. After retiring from NASA in 1964, he served as an executive with several businesses. He also launched a political career. Senator Glenn of Ohio, a Democrat, served four terms (1974–1992).

In 1998, Glenn convinced NASA they should study the effects of space travel and weightlessness on the aged. On October 29, 1998, John Glenn joined the crew of the space shuttle *Discovery*. He was 77 years old, the oldest person ever to blast off into space.

Emma Goldman
anarchist ★ 1869—1940

J. Edgar Hoover handled Emma Goldman's deportation and called her "the most dangerous woman in America."

Emma Goldman was one of the most famous radical speakers of her time. She attacked capitalism, war, and discrimination. Her speeches were so fiery that she was jailed several times for making them.

Goldman supported the anarchist movement, which rejected all forms of government. At the turn of the century, anarchists, Socialists, and Communists were considered suspicious and dangerous. Goldman's enemies called her "Red Emma," linking her to Russian communism and to socialism.

Goldman was often followed by the police as she traveled around the country lecturing on labor issues, women's rights, and birth control.

From 1906 to 1917, Goldman published *Mother Earth*, a magazine that promoted ideas on women's liberation. In 1917, she was sentenced to two years in jail for speaking out against drafting soldiers for World War I. In 1919, Red Emma and 248 other "subversives" were deported to the Soviet Union.

Samuel Goldwyn
film producer ★ 1882—1974

Schmuel Gelbfisz left his native Poland alone and penniless as a teenager. In America, he became Samuel Goldwyn, legendary Hollywood producer and star-maker.

Goldwyn formed a partnership with his brother-in-law and Cecil B. DeMille, a film director, in 1913. Their first movie, *The Squaw Man,* was a big hit. It was also the first feature-length film made in an emerging new film center: Hollywood.

Since his first film company was a big success, Goldwyn formed (and later broke up) mergers with other film partners. By the time his film company became part of Metro-Goldwyn-**Mayer** (MGM) in 1922, Samuel was no longer part of it. In fact, as of 1923, he was the sole boss of his own independent studio, Samuel Goldwyn Productions. He brought the "Goldwyn touch" with him. The producer was famous for recognizing top talent in

Samuel Goldwyn was famous for "Goldwynisms," or mixed-up phrases like: "Include me out" or "I don't think anybody should write his autobiography until after he's dead."

screenwriters, directors, and upcoming stars, like **Lucille Ball**. Two of the most important films to come out of Goldwyn Productions were the sensational post-World War II drama, *The Best Years of Our Lives* (1947), and the Academy Award-winning *Porgy and Bess* (1959).

Samuel Gompers
labor leader ★ 1850—1924

The late-19th century was a period of upheaval in the U.S. as it shifted from an agricultural nation to an industrial one. The clashes between big business and its laborers gave rise to leaders like Samuel Gompers.

Gompers was a Jewish immigrant from London who worked as a cigar maker in New York. He became president of a cigar makers' union and was banned from future factory jobs because of his organizing work. Gompers was broke—but not broken.

It was clear to him that the only way to

This memorial to Samuel Gompers, one of the most famous labor leaders in America, is in Washington, D.C.

force business to improve jobs and salaries was to form a union of skilled workers in different trades. Gompers cofounded what became the American Federation of Labor (AFL) in 1886 and served as its president until 1924. He traveled across the country convincing skilled workers and other craftsmen's unions to join the AFL. Millions of people did. The AFL fought successfully for an eight-hour day, higher wages, pensions, workers' insurance, and child labor laws. Gompers's union was criticized for being too conservative and for representing only skilled workers. The AFL eventually merged with **John L. Lewis**'s union for unskilled workers.

Berry Gordy, Jr.
Motown founder ★ 1929—

Berry Gordy, Jr., borrowed $800 in 1959 to start a record label in his hometown, Detroit, Michigan. By the 1970s, Motown had become a music empire that earned $40 million a year.

Gordy had a head for business and an ear for music. He signed local talent, like Smokey Robinson and the Miracles, and Mary Wells, to Motown. The Miracles' "Shop Around" hit big in 1961, selling a million copies. Wells's "My Guy" topped the charts in 1964. Eventually, Motown stars would include **Diana Ross** and the Supremes, The Four Tops, Marvin Gaye, **Stevie Wonder**, The Temptations, Gladys Knight and the Pips, and the Jackson Five.

Motown's success was based on creativity and Gordy's keen business sense. Gordy promoted the "Motown Sound" as the "Sound of Young America," and in the 1960s and 1970s, young America listened!

Berry Gordy, Jr., wins a Rock and Roll Hall of Fame Award in 1988. He sold his company to RCA for $61 million that same year.

Katharine Graham
newspaper publisher ★ 1917—2001

Katharine Graham took over her family's newspaper business in 1963 after her husband committed suicide. She taught herself how to be a publisher and turned the *Washington Post* into a first-class newspaper.

Graham hired legendary editor Ben Bradlee, brought on more staff, and built the *Post*'s reputation for hard-hitting investigative reporting. She made two decisions that had a big impact on American history. In 1971, Graham defied a court order and published the Pentagon Papers. These classified documents showed secret decisions the U.S. government had made about the controversial Vietnam War. Graham felt the court order was an attack on freedom of the press.

In 1972, *Post* reporters Carl Bernstein and Robert Woodward linked a burglary at the Democratic National Committee

Katharine Graham won a Pulitzer prize in 1998 for her acclaimed memoir, Personal History.

Headquarters in the Watergate building in Washington, D.C., to President **Richard Nixon**. For a long time, the *Post* was the only paper reporting the story. The Nixon administration threatened Graham. She refused to back down. The full Watergate scandal was exposed, which led to Nixon's resignation. The *Post* won a 1973 Pulitzer prize for this coverage.

Katharine Graham headed a media empire that included the award-winning *Washington Post, Newsweek* magazine, and several radio, cable, and television stations.

Martha Graham
dancer, choreographer ★ 1894—1991

Martha Graham, the "Mother of Modern Dance," was fascinated with the way movement communicates truth beyond words. She founded the Martha Graham School of Contemporary Dance in New York in 1929. Graham's style was new and daring. She rejected the pointed toe of classical ballet for a more modern dance that acknowledged the body, breathing, and gravity. She used movement to explore mood, emotion, and expression far beyond what was common at the time.

Graham choreographed and danced in nearly 200 works, including pieces that were inspired by politics (*Revolt*, 1927); religion (*Primitive Mysteries*, 1931); and history (*Appalachian Spring*, 1944). She created dance works about great women, such as **Emily Dickinson** and Joan of Arc. She was nearly 65 when she danced the title role in *Clytemnestra* (1958), the greatest one of her pieces inspired by Greek myths.

Graham received the 1976 Medal of Freedom and the 1985 National Medal for the Arts.

Ulysses S. Grant
18th president ★ 1822—1885

Ulysses S. Grant's leadership brought the Union army victory in the Civil War. His lack of leadership brought scandal to the presidency afterward.

Grant, a former career soldier, was working as a store clerk when the Civil War broke out. He volunteered in 1861. Three years later, President **Abraham Lincoln** promoted him to commander of all the Northern armies.

Grant was a dogged military leader. He never gave up, and he accepted only "unconditional and immediate surrender." Though losses were heavy on both sides, Grant's campaign broke the Confederate army. He was a national hero and was easily elected to two terms as president (1869–1877).

President Grant was an honest man, but his administration was rocked by scandals, among them the attempt to corner the gold market, which set off a national economic depression. Grant had no part in the scams—but members of his cabinet, and even his vice president did.

After leaving the White House, Grant eventually moved to New York. Bad personal investments left him penniless. He was ill with cancer and worried about family finances, so he began writing his memoirs. He finished several days before his death. **Mark Twain** published Grant's book. It sold 500,000 copies and earned $450,000 for his family.

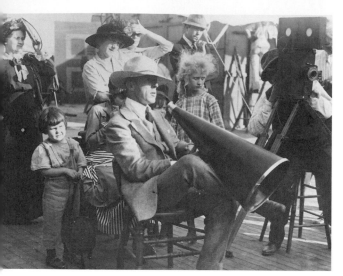

D. W. Griffith

film director ★ 1875—1948

David Wark Griffith was one of the most influential people in the history of filmmaking. He was among the first to see the possibilities of the medium and the power of moviemaking.

Between 1908 and 1913, Griffith directed 450 silent films for the Biograph Film Company. He pioneered the use of now common film techniques such as different camera angles, crosscuts, close-ups, fade-outs, and flashbacks.

In 1915, Griffith released one of the world's first film masterpieces, *The Birth of a Nation*. Audiences were blown away by Griffith's sweeping, violent epic about the post-Civil War South. No one had ever

D. W. Griffith on the set of Intolerance. *The set was a mile wide and 90 feet high in places. The film used 4,000 extras, three orchestras, and hundreds of dancers.*

seen anything like the innovative editing and incredible camera work in Griffith's silent film. But its social message and portrayal of the Ku Klux Klan enraged African Americans and others. As if in response, he released another spectacle, *Intolerance*, in 1916. This ambitious silent film told four stories of inhumanity and injustice set in different ages.

In 1919, Griffith, **Mary Pickford**, **Charlie Chaplin**, and Douglas Fairbanks formed United Artists Corporation to gain control over their work. Griffith released several films under United Artists and made nearly 40 feature films during his career.

Florence Griffith-Joyner

Olympian ★ 1959—1998

As a girl, Florence Griffith-Joyner raced against jackrabbits in California's Mojave Desert. It was her earliest sprint training.

During her years at California State and the University of California, Los Angeles, Griffith-Joyner set championship records in the 200- and 400-meter races. She made the Olympic team in 1984 and took home a silver medal for the 200-meter dash. At the 1988 Olympics in Seoul, South Korea, she became a three-time gold medal winner (100- and 200-meter races; relay), and a silver medalist for the 1,600-meter relay. Olympic audiences were dazzled by her athletic talents, not to mention her polished six-inch fingernails and bright one-of-a-kind running outfits.

Olympic track-and-field events were a family affair for Flo-Jo. Her husband was world-class jumper Al Joyner, and her sister-in-law was gold medalist **Jackie Joyner-Kersee**. Griffith-Joyner served on the President's Council on Physical Fitness and Sports before tragically dying of a heart seizure at age 38.

Sarah Grimké (l.) and Angelina Grimké (r.)

Sarah and Angelina Grimké
abolitionists ★ 1792—1873 (Sarah);
1805—1879 (Angelina)

Sarah and Angelina Grimké witnessed the cruelty of slavery firsthand in South Carolina. They were born into one of the South's most aristocratic slaveholding families. Sarah Grimké joined the Quakers and left Charleston for Philadelphia in 1822. Seven years later, Angelina joined her.

In the mid-1830s, the Grimkés heard about the mobs that sometimes broke up meetings of the American Anti-Slavery Society. Angelina wrote to the society's leader, **William Lloyd Garrison**, saying abolition "is a cause worth dying for." Garrison printed Grimké's letter in his newspaper; readers were amazed at the powerful antislavery words of a slave owner's daughter. In 1836, the American Anti-Slavery Society invited the sisters to New York to speak.

For the next two years, the Grimkés toured New England and the East delivering their abolitionist message. In 1838, Angelina Grimké became the first woman to speak before a U.S. legislative body when she brought an antislavery petition signed by 20,000 women before the Massachusetts state legislature.

Matt Groening
cartoonist ★ 1954—

Who's got a domed head and loves doughnuts? Who's got a big heart and bigger hair? Whose name is a mixed-up spelling of *brat*? What second-grader plays a mean sax? What little baby has a pacifier for a mouth? Matt Groening's *The Simpsons!* D'oh!

Originally from Portland, Oregon, Groening moved to Los Angeles, California, in 1977. He didn't find work as a writer and thought L.A. was horrible. Groening took his frustrations out on paper. He created *Life in Hell*. People loved the comic strip's two bummed-out bunnies bumbling their way through life. Television producer James L. Brooks thought *Life in Hell* was funny, too. In 1985, he asked Groening to come up with something for television. One-minute Simpson cartoons aired on the Tracey Ullman show in 1987. The first full show of *The*

Matt Groening with a Bart Simpson doll.

Simpsons debuted on December 17, 1989. It's now the longest-running prime-time comedy. Groening oversees production of *The Simpsons* episodes and all licensing of Simpson products. He heads a billion-dollar media empire that also includes his other animated TV show, *Futurama*.

"Don't have a cow, man!" —BART SIMPSON

"This land is your land, this land is my land . . .

Musicians from Joan Baez to **Bob Dylan** to **Bruce Springsteen** have been influenced by Guthrie's work.

Woody Guthrie
folk singer, composer ★ 1912–1967

Woodrow Wilson Guthrie left his Oklahoma home when he was 16. His rambling life took him around the country. Woody left a musical record of his trip—nearly 1,000 folk songs. These "talking blues" tell the stories of people, politics, and the American landscape.

When he was hitchhiking and riding the rails, Guthrie saw how people in the Midwest and West suffered because of drought and the Great Depression. He saw how hardworked and ill-treated migrant workers were. Guthrie started singing about what he'd seen on a Los Angeles radio show in 1937. Three years later, folklorist Alan Lomax recorded Guthrie's *Dust Bowl Ballads* for the Library of Congress. That same year, Woody moved to New York. He started playing with Pete Seeger and others who shared his left-wing political ideas. Guthrie believed that music could change minds. He sang in bars, union halls, and migrant camps. He sang on picket lines, at strikes, and at protest marches.

Woody Guthrie helped make folk music popular in the 1940s and early 1950s. He wrote folk classics like "This Land Is Your Land," "So Long, It's Been Good to Know Ya," "Roll On Columbia," and "Pastures of Plenty." His likable, folksy songs are often musical calls for radical political and social change.

Nathan Hale
American Revolution leader ★ 1755–1776

Schoolteacher. Spy. Hero. Nathan Hale accomplished a lot in his 21 short years.

Hale, a soldier in the Continental army, volunteered to gather information about British movements in New York. He infiltrated British lines and mapped out their troop positions. On his way back to report to General **George Washington**, Hale was betrayed by a relative. The British captured him on Long Island. There was no trial. Sir William Howe ordered him hanged and refused to allow Hale a last visit with a clergyman, or even a bible. There is no record of Nathan Hale's supposed last words, "I only regret that I have but one life to lose for my country." But he was an important symbol of bravery for the patriots.

this land was made for you and me." — WOODY GUTHRIE

Civil rights activist Fannie Lou Hamer speaks out at the 1964 Democratic Convention.

Fannie Lou Hamer
civil rights activist ★ 1917–1977

Fannie Lou Hamer knew about injustice. Her grandparents were slaves and her parents sharecroppers. When she registered to vote, she was fired from the plantation job she'd held for 18 years. When she helped other African Americans register, she was arrested and severely beaten. Still, Hamer dreamed of justice—and worked for it.

In the early 1960s, Hamer became involved with the Southern Christian Leadership Conference (SCLC) and the Student Nonviolent Coordinating Committee (SNCC), two groups fighting for civil rights. Despite threats on her life, she helped lead a huge voter registration drive that turned into the Mississippi Freedom Democratic Party (MFDP). The MFDP protested the fact that all of Mississippi's delegates to the 1964 National Democratic Presidential Convention were white. Hamer's speech to the convention committee about her prison beatings and the way black people were cheated out of their rights as citizens was broadcast on national television. Hamer played an important role in raising public and political awareness about the unfair policies that kept African Americans from voting. Her efforts helped pass the 1965 Voting Rights Act, which bans literacy tests and other barriers set up to keep black people from registering to vote.

Dorothy Hamill
Olympic skater ★ 1956—

The "Hamill camel" is a figure-skating spiral spin to a sit spin. The "Hamill wedge" was a popular pixie haircut. And who's the Hamill behind this? Dorothy, the Olympic medalist, Ice Capades star, and one of America's favorite figure skaters.

As a child, Hamill trained seven hours a day, six days a week. It paid off. In 1974, she won the first of three consecutive national championships and a silver medal at the world championships. By 1976, Hamill was considered the best women's free skater in the world.

That same year, Hamill packed up her figure skates and headed for the 1976 Winter Olympics in Innsbruck, Austria. She brought along her lucky rag doll to calm her jitters before competitions. But on ice, Hamill seemed completely in command. Her outstanding performance earned her near-perfect scores and a gold medal.

Later that year, Hamill signed on as star skater with the Ice Capades. She thrilled audiences with her performances for seven years. Hamill also bought the failing Ice Capades in 1992. She revamped it into a world-class spectacle before selling it in 1994.

Alexander Hamilton
secretary of the treasury ★ 1757—1804

Alexander Hamilton fought bravely in the American Revolution. Then he faced the political and economic battles of a struggling new nation.

Hamilton, a Federalist, believed in a strong central government. He thought presidents and senators should rule for life.

In 1787, Hamilton represented New York at the Constitutional Convention. Hamilton, **James Madison**, and **John Jay** wrote 85 essays, collected as *The Federalist Papers* (1787–1788). These writings explained the main ideas of the new system of government proposed by the convention's delegates. *The Federalist* was instrumental in getting the U.S. Constitution ratified.

President **George Washington** appointed Hamilton secretary of the treasury in 1789. The states faced enormous debts from the American Revolution. They also used their own forms of money. In fact, many people didn't even use money, they bartered.

In 1790, Hamilton presented a plan to Congress. He argued that the federal government should assume the war debts. This would help unite the states. Hamilton also convinced Congress to charter the First Bank of the United States in 1791. The bank would hold the government's money, and issue and regulate paper currency. Hamilton's plans helped stabilize the economy.

Mia Hamm
soccer Olympian ★ 1972—

On July 10, 1999, 40 million people in the U.S. tuned into the Women's World Cup. They watched Mia Hamm and the rest of the women's soccer team run, pass, and kick their way to victory over China. It was the biggest women's sporting event in American history.

At age 15, she was the youngest member ever to play on the U.S. national team. The famous forward in the number 9 shirt has won numerous Most Valuable Player (MVP) awards and broken many goal and assists records. She has scored more than 109 career goals, won an Olympic gold medal (1996), and belonged to two Women's World Cup championship teams (1991, 1999). In 2001, FIFA, soccer's world governing body, gave Hamm its first woman player of the year award.

Now playing for the Washington Freedom team, Mia Hamm is the biggest audience draw in the Women's United Soccer Association.

at making proselytes by fire and sword." – ALEXANDER HAMILTON

John Hancock
American Revolution leader ★ 1737–1793

John Hancock scrawled his bold, now famous signature on the Declaration of Independence in 1776 and said, "The British ministry can read that signature without spectacles." The British already wanted to hang him for treason.

Hancock, who had inherited a fortune from his uncle, was one of the richest men in America. He put his wealth, his respectability, and his brains at the service of the revolution. Along with **Sam Adams**, Hancock was the leader of the Massachusetts Sons of Liberty, which carried out anti-British acts like the Boston Tea Party (1773). Two years later, he represented Massachusetts at the Second Continental Congress and was elected its president. Much to Hancock's disappointment, he was not chosen commander-in-chief of the newly formed Continental army. (That job went to **George Washington**.) Nonetheless, he continued to finance the war for independence.

John Hancock became Massachusetts's first governor in 1780. He was reelected several times after that. His support and influence helped get the U.S. Constitution and the Bill of Rights ratified.

Ruth Handler
toy entrepreneur ★ 1916–2002

Ruth Handler was executive vice president of Mattel, a company her husband had founded, from 1948 to 1967. She expanded the toy company by doing things that were revolutionary at the time, such as creating year-round television ads directed at children and toys that went with TV shows. But her biggest moneymaker was Barbie. Handler saw that her daughter liked playing imaginative games with paper dolls of adult women. She thought that girls would love a real doll that was grown up. Over the objections of other Mattel executives, Handler got her doll manufactured. Barbie debuted in 1959. Girls went crazy for this $3, molded plastic, "shapely teenage fashion model" doll with high heels and breasts. Mattel sold 351,000 Barbies the first year. Handler expanded the Barbie line to include clothes, houses, and cars. Barbie got a doll boyfriend, best friend, and siblings. Mattel became a very hot company.

Handler left Mattel in 1975 because of a legal and financial dispute over Mattel's stock. Due to cancer, she had had a breast removed (mastectomy). Handler formed the Nearly Me company in 1976, to create products for other women who had gone through mastectomies.

Lorraine Hansberry
playwright ★ 1930–1965

In 1938, Lorraine Hansberry's father moved the family into an all-white neighborhood in Chicago. Some neighbors hurled bricks through their windows. Twenty years later, Hansberry turned the painful racism of her childhood into a powerful, award-winning play.

A Raisin in the Sun opened at the Ethel Barrymore Theatre in 1959. It was the first play by an African-American woman to make it to Broadway. The family in *Raisin* struggles with the decision about whether or not to move into a white neighborhood. Hansberry's drama challenged many stereotypes about African-American family life. It portrayed the different responses black people had to racism. The Broadway version was produced and directed by African Americans. It was a smash! Hansberry was awarded the New York Drama Critics Circle Award for Best Play. Two years after the stage show, *Raisin* was made into a prize-winning film (1961). Hansberry's second play, *The Sign in Sidney Brustein's Window*, opened on Broadway in 1964. She died of cancer shortly thereafter.

*Lorraine Hansberry got her play's title from a **Langston Hughes** poem: "What happens to a dream deferred?/ Does it dry up like a raisin in the sun,/ Or does it explode?"*

Keith Haring sometimes drew 40 subway murals in a day!

Keith Haring
pop artist ★ 1958–1990

New York City subway riders were the first to see the art that made Keith Haring famous. In fact, they could watch the artist at work, too. Haring drew on the big, blank, black paper panels saved for advertising posters in the stations. Using white chalk, he scrawled crawling babies, barking dogs, dancing people, grinning TV sets, and flying saucers. His lines were simple and fluid. The effect was startling and funny.

Haring moved from Kutztown, Pennsylvania, to New York City to attend art school in 1978. New York was energized: graffiti art, punk rock, and hip-hop were bursting out. Haring jumped right into this whole scene. In 1982, a show of Haring's work drew 4,000 people to a New York art gallery.

Haring experimented with electric colors in bold combinations. He added patterns and complicated backgrounds to his symbollike drawings. He did set designs, clothing designs, and sculptures. He painted large-scale murals. Haring's work often carried a social-political message, like his "Free South Africa" posters, 20,000 of which were distributed in 1985. He also created art to promote AIDS awareness and discourage drug use. Haring himself died of AIDS when he was only 31.

 "You furnish the pictures and

Nathaniel Hawthorne
author ★ 1804—1864

His ancestors included sea captains and a judge at the infamous Salem witch trials. His childhood included periods of solitude, with only books or the woods for company. Sometimes he wrote, sometimes he worked as a civil servant.

Hawthorne's first novel, *Fanshawe*, was published in 1828. It didn't get much notice and not even the author liked it. Hawthorne continued publishing short stories in magazines in the 1830s. In 1837, his collection *Twice-Told Tales* got good reviews, but didn't earn much. Hawthorne took a dull job at the Boston Customs House so he could earn a living and get married. Hawthorne kept writing. When money was short, he secured jobs through political friends. When political administrations changed, he would be out of a job. But unemployment left more time for writing.

By 1850, Hawthorne had finished a novel set in the Puritan past of his birthplace, Salem, Massachusetts. *The Scarlet Letter* seethed with secrecy, sin, hypocrisy, and guilt. It was a great success. His other masterpiece, the eerie *House of Seven Gables* (1851), is also set in Salem.

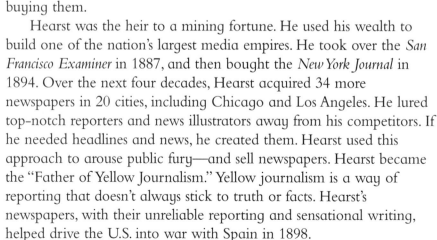

*Nathaniel Hawthorne and his wife, Sophia Peabody, lived in Concord, Massachusetts, from 1842 to 1845. They were among the intellectuals surrounding **Ralph Waldo Emerson** and **Henry David Thoreau**.*

William Randolph Hearst (c.)

William Randolph Hearst
newspaper publisher ★ 1863—1951

Scandal, sports, and comics. William Randolph Hearst knew how to sell his newspapers. And by the 1920s, one out of four Americans was buying them.

Hearst was the heir to a mining fortune. He used his wealth to build one of the nation's largest media empires. He took over the *San Francisco Examiner* in 1887, and then bought the *New York Journal* in 1894. Over the next four decades, Hearst acquired 34 more newspapers in 20 cities, including Chicago and Los Angeles. He lured top-notch reporters and news illustrators away from his competitors. If he needed headlines and news, he created them. Hearst used this approach to arouse public fury—and sell newspapers. Hearst became the "Father of Yellow Journalism." Yellow journalism is a way of reporting that doesn't always stick to truth or facts. Hearst's newspapers, with their unreliable reporting and sensational writing, helped drive the U.S. into war with Spain in 1898.

Hearst moved on to movies, radio, magazines, and syndication. He assembled the world's largest private art collection, and he built his dream home, the grandiose Hearst Castle in San Simeon, California.

I'll furnish the war." — WILLIAM RANDOLPH HEARST.

Ernest Hemingway
author ★ 1899—1961

When he was 18, Ernest Hemingway got a job as a reporter at the *Kansas City Star*. His short, lively newspaper writing later influenced the spare writing style he became famous for as a novelist.

Hemingway always craved action. In World War I, he drove a Red Cross ambulance and was badly wounded by shrapnel. During the 1920s, Hemingway lived in Paris and frequently visited Spain. He was a big bullfighting fan. His first novel, *The Sun Also Rises* (1926), was set in this world of macho bravery and post-war sadness. It was a best-seller. While the Spanish Civil War and World War II raged, Hemingway was there with his reporter's notebook. His front-line observations inspired some of his finest novels, such as *A Farewell to Arms* (1929) and *For Whom the Bell Tolls* (1940).

Hemingway later moved to Florida, and then Cuba, and continued to write acclaimed short stories, nonfiction, and novels. His 1953 book *The Old Man and the Sea* won the Pulitzer prize. Readers bought more than five million copies in two days. Hemingway was awarded the Nobel Prize for literature in 1954.

Jimi Hendrix
rock 'n' roll artist ★ 1942—1970

In his lifetime, he released only four albums. Yet his influence on rock 'n' roll, jazz, funk, punk, pop, and hip-hop lives on. That's why many people call Jimi Hendrix the greatest guitarist of all time.

Seattle-born James Marshall Hendrix formed the Jimi Hendrix Experience in England in 1966. The band's debut album, *Are You Experienced?* (1967), with its now classic "Purple Haze," sent shock waves through the rock world. Hendrix followed with an outrageous show at the Monterey Pop Festival in California. He whaled on his guitar, played it with his teeth, and set it on fire.

Hendrix's frenzied playing teased, stroked, and tore sounds out of the guitar that no one had ever heard before. Sometimes his notes floated off into the cosmos. Sometimes his guitar screamed. He used innovative recording effects on two more groundbreaking albums, *Axis Bold as Love* (1968); and *Electric Ladyland* (1968). His live album, *Band of Gypsys* (1970), was an electric blend of rhythm and blues. In 1970, Hendrix's bold experiments with music ended with his accidental drug-related death.

Jimi Hendrix's explosive version of "The Star-Spangled Banner" at the 1969 Woodstock Festival made it rock 'n' roll's anthem.

"Give me liberty or give me death." — PATRICK HENRY

This woodcut depicts Patrick Henry's fiery 1775 speech.

Patrick Henry
American Revolution leader ★ 1736—1799

"Give me liberty or give me death," Patrick Henry thundered to the Virginia Assembly in March 23, 1775. His words became the rallying cry of the American Revolution.

Henry was a famous and fiery speaker and an outspoken member of Virginia's elected governing body, the House of Burgesses. There, Henry loudly criticized the Stamp Act in 1765. Virginia's English governor dissolved the House of Burgesses in response. Henry joined other radical patriots in demanding an end to British tyranny. He supported boycotts and served as a delegate to both Continental Congresses (1774; 1775). Henry organized troops and overthrew Virginia's British governor. He was then elected to the job himself. Governor Henry served five terms.

Fearful that it would set up too powerful a central government, Henry did not support the 1787 Constitution. He argued for a Bill of Rights to be added. As always, Patrick Henry was *very* persuasive. Those first 10 amendments to the Constitution were ratified in 1791.

Jim Henson
puppeteer ★ 1936—1990

Jim Henson cut up a green coat and turned it into a frog. A frog puppet, that is. Well, actually, a Muppet.

In 1954, a Washington, D.C., station advertised for a puppeteer for a children's TV show. Henson, then in high school, got the job. Within a year, he had his own five-minute program, *Sam and Friends*. (Kermit was one of those friends!)

In the1960s, Henson and his Muppets appeared on other television shows. His big break came in 1969. Henson created Big Bird, Bert and Ernie, and a whole Muppet gang. They got a new television address: Sesame Street. *Sesame Street* made life and learning a lot more fun for millions of kids. And they became loyal viewers of Henson's own *The Muppet Show* (1976–1981). Every week, nearly 235 million people in 100 countries tuned in to the lively world of Miss Piggy, Gonzo the Great, Fozzie Bear, and Kermit. The Muppets also starred in movies. Their creator won several Emmys and a Grammy Award. In 1979, Henson founded Jim Henson's Creature Shop, which uses technology to create incredible mechanized puppets. Sadly, this pioneer of puppetry died suddenly from pneumonia when he was only 53.

"The lure of the Arctic is tugging at my heart."

— MATTHEW HENSON

Matthew Henson
explorer ★ 1866–1955

In 1887, Matthew Henson was working as a store clerk in Washington, D.C. Naval officer **Robert E. Peary** walked in and hired him as his servant. The two men spent the next 22 years on death-defying expeditions.

Peary and Henson made seven dangerous trips to the Arctic between 1891 and 1909. Henson built the base camps and the sledges for pulling loads across the ice and snow. He befriended the local Inuit guides, who taught him important survival skills. The explorers traveled uncharted paths through a treacherous landscape. The ice itself could suddenly crack underfoot, plunging them into

Matthew Henson in 1901. The media, U.S. government, and explorer organizations honored Robert Peary for the North Pole expedition. Henson was ignored because he was an African American.

water that was -15°F. There was always the danger of injury, food shortages, or just getting lost. But Henson and Peary were determined to become the first people to reach the North Pole.

In July 1908, they set sail on a powerful icebreaking ship, the *Roosevelt*, and landed within 413 miles of the North Pole. In the spring, they set off across the polar sea ice by dog sledge. By April, they were 174 miles from the North Pole. Henson blazed the way, using his keen sense of direction. Henson, Peary, four Inuit, and 40 dogs set out on the final leg. Five days later, Henson held the American flag over the North Pole. (In the 1980s, new research suggested that the Peary-Henson expedition had miscalculated and were about 50 miles away from the North Pole.)

Katharine Hepburn
actress ★ 1909—

During a film shoot, Katharine Hepburn broke the heel of her shoe. She didn't ask the cameras to stop rolling. She ad-libbed, "I was born on the side of a hill" to explain why she stood lopsided and continued with the scene. That's classic Hepburn: quick, witty, and determined to move ahead.

Hepburn began her Hollywood career in the 1930s. She won her first Academy Award for *Morning Glory* (1933), her third film. That same year, she created her popular portrayal of Jo March in a film of **Louisa May Alcott**'s *Little Women*. She then starred in several popular screwball comedies, such as *Bringing Up Baby* (1938).

In 1942, Hepburn and Spencer Tracy made *Woman of the Year*, their first movie together. They became one of Hollywood's most famous couples on-screen and off, making eight more films together.

Katharine Hepburn portrayed strong, spirited women in nearly every movie she made. She played a queen at war with her husband in *Lion in Winter* (1968) and won an Oscar. She also won Academy Awards for *Guess Who's Coming to Dinner?* (1967) and *On Golden Pond* (1981).

Milton Hershey

entrepreneur ★ 1857–1945

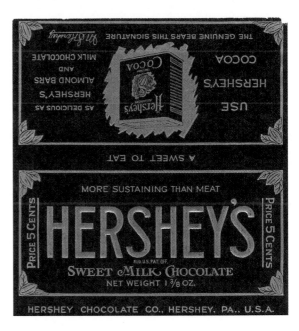

As a child, Milton Hershey had a sweet tooth. As an adult, he made a fortune on sweets.

Hershey came from a Pennsylvania Mennonite family. He had only a fourth-grade education, but continued another kind of schooling when he worked for candymakers in Philadelphia and Denver. Then he tried going into business himself. After several failures, Hershey finally achieved success with the Lancaster Caramel Company. In 1893, he went to the World's Columbian Exhibition in Chicago. He saw German chocolate-making machinery. At that time, chocolate was imported and expensive. Hershey saw a big business opportunity: mass-produced chocolate candy for the masses!

In 1894, he formed the Hershey Chocolate Company. He eventually sold the caramel business for $1 million, but kept the chocolate candy-making machines. Between 1903 and 1905 Hershey built the world's largest chocolate manufacturing plant. He chose a site in central Pennsylvania's dairy country. Lots of cows meant lots of fresh milk, the secret to Hershey's recipe for milk chocolate. The candy entrepreneur built the prosperous town of Hershey, Pennsylvania. Hershey himself became a millionaire. He was also known for his generosity, especially for funding the Milton Hershey School for disadvantaged children.

Ted Hoff's work with microprocessors built on the work previously done by **Jack Kilby** and Robert Noyce on integrated-circuit silicon chips.

Marcian E. Hoff

computer scientist ★ 1937—

Marcian "Ted" Hoff thought small and came up with a really big idea: the microprocessor chip.

Hoff, who holds a Ph.D. in electrical engineering, went to work at Intel, a new technology company founded by Robert Noyce in 1968. At that time, computers were big and bulky. They had to have a different integrated circuit for every application the computer performed.

In 1969, a Japanese company hired Intel to develop circuits for their new calculator. They figured it would take 12 chips to make their instrument work, and some of those chips had to have 5,000 transistors packed into them. Hoff went to work—on a better idea. By 1971, he had invented the microprocessor. Hoff's chip was the size of a thumbnail, but it ran all of a computer's central processing. This compact chip could be used as the "brains" of all kinds of computers and appliances. Hoff's microprocessor revolutionized the computer industry.

"The life of the law has not been logic:

Abbie Hoffman
activist ★ 1936—1989

He was the clown of radical politics in the 1960s. But Abbie Hoffman also turned on thousands of people to political activism and involvement.

Hoffman, a civil rights worker, cofounded the Youth International Party (YIP) in 1966. The Yippies, as members were called, became famous for outrageous protests. They once threw money around the New York Stock Exchange to expose corporate greed. Hoffman helped organize demonstrations protesting the Vietnam War. The FBI created a 4,101-page file on the radical leader because of his politics and actions.

Abbie Hoffman is arrested in Washington, D.C. in 1968 and, because of his shirt, charged with mutilating the U.S. flag.

In 1968, Hoffman and the Yippies held an antiwar demonstration/rock 'n' roll party during the Democratic National Convention in Chicago. More than 10,000 people came. So did more than 20,000 police and soldiers. The whole world *was* watching when a police riot broke out. Demonstrators, news reporters, even convention delegates were beaten. Hoffman and six other leaders were arrested and tried for conspiracy to start a riot at their "Chicago Seven" trial in 1969. Hoffman used every opportunity to air his views on what he saw as the injustice, inequality, and hypocrisy of American culture.

Hoffman went "underground" in 1973 to avoid jail after a drug bust. He eventually served a work-release sentence, and became involved in environmental activism.

Billie Holiday
singer ★ 1915—1959

She could bring an audience to tears with her singing. Her very heart and soul came out of her mouth.

Billie Holiday was born into a life of poverty and misery in Baltimore, Maryland. She moved to New York City in 1928 and started singing in nightclubs as a teenager. She brought all the loneliness and longing of her youth to her performances.

In the 1930s, Holiday toured with Count Basie's and Artie Shaw's big bands, among others. Saxophonist Lester Young nicknamed the elegant, gardenia-wearing singer "Lady Day." Jazz musicians loved playing with her because of Holiday's extraordinary vocal phrasing and timing. But Holiday tired of the grueling tour schedule and the racism she experienced on the road. She returned to New York in 1939.

There, Holiday became a glamorous nightclub celebrity. In the 1940s, she followed with many of her now classic hits, such as "God Bless the Child." Lady Day's personal life was less successful. Her beautiful voice was silenced when she died from liver and heart problems at 44.

It has been experience." — OLIVER WENDELL HOLMES, JR.

Oliver Wendell Holmes, Jr., was a Union soldier during the Civil War. His harsh, violent experiences convinced him that the law was a better way to resolve conflict.

Oliver Wendell Holmes, Jr.

U.S. Supreme Court justice ★ 1841—1935

Oliver Wendell Holmes, Jr., was a Massachusetts Supreme Court judge until 1902. That year, President **Theodore Roosevelt** appointed him to the U.S. Supreme Court. Holmes became known as the "Great Dissenter" because he presented the minority opinion on many cases. It was a position he had taken before.

As a young legal scholar, Holmes wrote a famous series of lectures and opinions, collected as *The Common Law* (1881). He looked at the history of unwritten laws. He argued that laws are affected by the moral, social, political, and economic ideas of any given time. This outlook shaped Holmes's rulings as a judge.

Justice Holmes sat on the Supreme Court for 30 years. He believed that the U.S. Constitution was purposefully written so that judges could deal with an ever-changing nation. He was a strong advocate of labor laws and freedom of speech. In one famous case, Holmes wrote that the government had to show "clear-and-present danger" before it could limit anyone's right to free speech. At the time, only one other Supreme Court justice agreed with Holmes's minority opinion. Since then, "clear-and-present danger" has become the legal standard for judging censorship.

Winslow Homer

painter ★ 1836—1910

Winslow Homer's oil paintings and watercolors are beautiful records of 19th-century life and landscape.

Homer, who was born in Boston, Massachusetts, was a self-taught artist. In 1859, he moved to New York and began illustrating for *Harper's Weekly* magazine. He covered **Abraham Lincoln**'s inauguration and the Civil War. Homer's wartime illustrations were

The Gulf Stream (1899) by Winslow Homer.

noted for their realism and their sensitive portrayal of people. One, *Prisoners of the Front* (1866), brought him national recognition after it was exhibited.

Homer's oil paintings celebrated American rural life. In the 1870s, Homer began working with watercolors. These paintings had a new intensity of color and light. They also sold.

Homer started painting what would become his most famous subject: the sea. Homer was inspired by the rugged life he had observed in a fishing port in England. He started painting seascapes, sailors, and fishermen and their wives. His work captured the beauty and power of the ocean and the dangerous struggles of men and women whose lives depended upon the sea.

J. Edgar Hoover

FBI head ★ 1895–1972

When J. Edgar Hoover took over the Federal Bureau of Investigation (FBI) in 1924, it was inefficient and corrupt. Hoover cleaned house and improved agent training and discipline. He installed modern crime-fighting techniques like standard crime statistics, central banks of fingerprints (1925), and a crime lab (1932). Then he ran the FBI with an iron fist for 48 years until his death in 1972.

Hoover and his "G-men" enjoyed enormous popularity in the 1930s. Movies, radio, and newspapers glorified the government agents' pursuit of lawless, violent gangsters. But Hoover himself wasn't above breaking the law. His policy was "act first, talk

J. Edgar Hoover was head of the FBI through eight presidential administrations.

afterward." Hoover encouraged bullying witnesses and illegal wiretaps. He was an intense anti-Communist and authorized FBI surveillance of groups he decided were un-American. He ordered investigations of the personal lives of people he suspected of being Communists or subversives. This list was very broad and included politicians, political activists, liberals, entertainers, labor leaders, and civil rights leaders. Sometimes Hoover honored requests from elected officials and secretly had their political opponents investigated. Meanwhile, up until the 1960s, the FBI, under Hoover's direction, virtually ignored big-city organized crime rings like the Mafia.

Bob Hope entertains troops on a 1983 Christmas tour.

Bob Hope

actor, comedian ★ 1903–

He's been on the road since he was a teenager. The road he has traveled has made Bob Hope rich, famous, and beloved.

Hope started out singing and dancing in vaudeville shows in the 1920s. He tossed in a bit of comic "patter" to liven things up. That comic style landed him a part in a Broadway musical, some comedy films, and a host spot on a popular radio show. In 1938, Hope headed for Hollywood.

Between 1938 and 1972, Hope appeared in 58 feature films. The most famous were the seven "Road" pictures he made with Bing Crosby and Dorothy Lamour. These comedies, like *Road to Singapore* (1940) and *Road to Utopia* (1946), proved that Hope was a master of clowning and the quick quip.

In addition to being a frequent host of the Oscars and producing television specials, Hope has traveled extensively overseas to entertain U.S. troops. In World War II, the Korean War, the Vietnam War, and in the Persian Gulf, Bob Hope was there with his annual holiday show. Hope has received five special Academy Awards for his humanitarian work. In 1985, he was awarded a Kennedy Center Honor.

"The whole answer is there on the canvas." — EDWARD HOPPER

Edward Hopper
painter ★ 1882—1967

Edward Hopper painted the real world, including all the mystery and loneliness in it.

Born in Nyack, New York, Hopper came to Manhattan in 1899 to study art. He was greatly influenced by Robert Henri. Henri was a leader of the "Ashcan" art movement, which held that everyday objects and real life were the best subjects for paintings.

It took nearly 20 years for Hopper to establish himself as an artist. During that time, he supported himself as a newspaper and magazine illustrator, a job he hated. But after a successful show of watercolors at the Brooklyn Museum in 1923, audiences began to appreciate—and buy—his work.

Edward Hopper was one of America's greatest realist painters. Automat *(1927) is one of his most well-known paintings.*

Hopper's oil and watercolor paintings are famous for the way he used solid shapes, shadow, and light to turn ordinary scenes of tenements, storefronts, motels, diners, or gas stations into their own private dramas. There was often a sense of solitude in the central images of his paintings, whether they were people or buildings. Hopper's work captured the changing landscape, physical and psychological, as America changed from a rural to an industrial nation.

Grace Murray Hopper received more than 50 medals and other awards for her achievements. Here, she checks out her invention, COBOL.

Grace Murray Hopper
scientist ★ 1906—1992

Grace Murray Hopper said she was "born with curiosity." She turned that into a career. By the time she retired at 79, "Amazing Grace" was a rear admiral in the U.S. Navy who had revolutionized computer programming.

Hopper earned a Ph.D. in mathematics from Yale University in 1934, a very rare accomplishment for a woman at that time. She became a math professor. When the United States entered World War II in 1941, she volunteered for military service. Her first assignment was at a military computation center at Harvard University. There, she helped develop and program the world's first large-scale digital computer, a 50-foot-long, 8-foot-high computer called the Mark I. She was the first to call computing errors "bugs."

In 1952, she invented the first computer compiler, a coding system that saved countless hours of programming. Hopper also developed COBOL, the first user-friendly computer language in the 1960s.

Harry Houdini
escape artist ★ 1874—1926

Houdini introduced the Milk Can Escape in St. Louis, Missouri, in 1908. The can was full of water and padlocked. Houdini's hands were chained.

Padlocks, chains, and handcuffs couldn't hold him. He broke out of jail cells, trunks, and crates nailed shut. Just like the posters said: "Nothing on Earth Can Hold Houdini a Prisoner."

Harry Houdini, born Ehrich Weiss, transformed himself from a small-time magician into the world's greatest escape artist. Through rigorous training and exercise, Houdini developed a flexible and muscular body. He practiced his escape routines over and over. By 1899, Houdini had a top-notch vaudeville act.

From 1900 until his death on Halloween, 1926, Houdini toured Europe and the U.S. In his Manacled Bridge Jump, he was chained, handcuffed, and submerged underwater—and escaped! In the daring Chinese Water-Torture Cell, Houdini was submerged upside down and locked into a tall glass vat. In minutes, he reappeared onstage. The vat was still locked and full. Thousands of people lined the streets to watch when Houdini introduced his amazing Suspended Straitjacket Escape. Some of Houdini's tricks remain a mystery to this day.

Sam Houston
soldier, statesman ★ 1793—1863

Sam Houston led the military battle for Texan independence, the political battle for its statehood, and the unsuccessful battle to keep Texas in the Union during the Civil War.

Houston, an experienced lawyer, politician, and soldier, headed west in 1829. Three years later, he was in Texas. That territory belonged to Mexico and was inhabited by Native Americans, but American settlers were streaming in. By 1835, those Americans wanted independence from Mexico. Sam Houston was appointed leader of the Texas army that was going to win it.

A few weeks after the Mexican army killed 183 Americans at the Battle of the Alamo (1836) in San Antonio, Houston and his men trounced the Mexican army at San Jacinto and formed the republic of Texas. Houston was elected governor. He worked hard to bring financial stability to Texas, to ensure basic rights for the Native Americans who lived there, to ease border tensions with Mexico.

Texas was admitted to the Union in 1845. By the 1860s, Texans were caught up in the slavery debate and voted to secede, along with the other Southern states. Rather than risk civil war in the state, Governor Houston resigned in 1861. He died two years later, whispering his last word: "Texas."

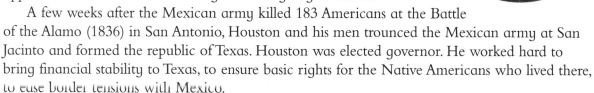
"Remember the Alamo!" —SAM HOUSTON

Edwin Hubble

astronomer ★ 1889–1953

Edwin Hubble wanted to solve the mystery of nebulae, the fuzzy, mysterious clouds of light in outer space. When he did, he opened up the whole universe.

In 1919, Hubble went to work at the prestigious Mount Wilson Observatory in southern California. There, he spent hours observing the skies through the brand-new 100-inch Hooker telescope. It was the most powerful one in existence. Hubble found proof of his radical new theory about nebulae. At the time, nebulae were thought to be clouds of glowing gas. Then Hubble spotted Cepheid, a variable star in the Andromeda Nebulae. He applied measurement techniques developed by astronomer Henrietta Swan Leavitt. On November 24, 1924, Hubble shocked the world with his findings: Our galaxy, the Milky Way, was *not* the whole universe! Andromeda lay beyond it. Nebulae were actually galaxies in a vast universe!

In 1925, the astronomer created the Hubble classification system for analyzing galaxies and studying their distances from Earth. Within four years, he had proven another startling idea—the universe is expanding! Hubble based his theory on studies he did on the quality of red light that came from nebulae. His book on space studies, *The Realm of the Nebulae* (1936), was a best-seller.

Dolores Huerta

labor leader ★ 1930–

"She was always out in front, and she would talk back. She wasn't scared of anything," a fellow organizer said of Dolores Huerta, cofounder of the United Farm Workers (UFW) union. She became a leadership model for Mexican Americans, particularly women.

In 1962, Huerta joined **Cesar Chavez** and created the National Farm Workers Association (which became the UFW in the 1970s). The National Farm Workers Association fought for farmworkers' rights to minimum wages, paid holidays, unemployment insurance, and pensions. When California grape-pickers went on strike for fair pay in 1965, Huerta helped lead a 300-mile march to the California state capitol in Sacramento to call attention to their struggle. She also helped to organize a successful boycott, convincing people not to buy grapes until the farm workers' demands were met. When the boycott succeeded, it was Dolores Huerta who negotiated the first contract between the farm workers' union and the landowners. She was elected vice president of the UFW in 1972.

"Literature is a big sea of many fish.

Langston Hughes
poet ★ 1902—1967

Langston Hughes grew up in the Midwest, but became a leading citizen of the literary world.

In 1919, Hughes wrote his famous, eloquent poem, "The Negro Speaks of Rivers." This ambitious work about the world heritage of African Americans was published in 1921. That same year, Hughes visited Harlem, New York, for the first time. He was inspired by the energy of the African-American artists and writers whose work sparked the Harlem Renaissance.

As a young man, Hughes worked on a ship's crew and sailed to Spain and Africa. He lived in Paris. He moved to Washington, D.C., and worked in a restaurant. And he kept writing poems. Poems that had a new, jazzy rhythm. Poems that used ordinary language to talk about the everyday hardships and strengths of African Americans. Poems that used humor and irony as weapons against bitterness.

Langston Hughes was a popular lecturer and social and civil rights activist.

In 1925, his work "The Weary Blues" won a literary competition. Hughes' literary career was launched. During his lifetime, 47 volumes of his work were published, including poetry, short stories, novels, plays, essays, an autobiography, and his famous columns for *The Chicago Defender*, the country's largest African-American newspaper.

Zora Neale Hurston and **Langston Hughes** wrote a comedy together called Mule Bone *(1930–1931)*.

Zora Neale Hurston
author ★ 1891—1960

Zora Neale Hurston loved to find out how people lived. But she didn't do so by just reading a book. She lived their lives with them.

Hurston grew up in Eatonville, Florida, the first incorporated, all-black town in the United States. She moved to New York and became the first African-American graduate of Barnard College. Hurston received a degree in anthropology, the study of human beings and the way they live. Hurston researched religious cults in Louisiana, Jamaica, and Haiti, and took part in rituals there. In Florida, Alabama, and the Bahamas, she worked in labor camps and learned from voodoo doctors. She collected the folklore, legends, and beliefs handed down through generations. Her books *Mules and Men* (1935) and *Tell My Horse* (1938) capture what she learned in her travels.

Hurston's most popular book was *Their Eyes Were Watching God* (1937). It is a novel about an African-American woman who follows her dreams and goes against what people expect her to do. The main characters of many of Hurston's books are women trying to create meaningful lives for themselves.

I let down my net and pulled." —LANGSTON HUGHES

Anne Hutchinson
religious leader ★ c.1591–1643

Anne Hutchinson believed salvation lay in a direct, personal relationship with God. The Puritans of the Massachusetts Bay Colony were not ready for such radical ideas.

Hutchinson and her family emigrated from England and arrived in Boston in 1634. Within three years, she was denounced as "a woman not fit for our society." Hutchinson's crime was to encourage people to make their own moral choices. She also dared to preach, something forbidden to women. Hutchinson had been holding religious meetings in her parlor. Sometimes as many as 80 men and women crowded in to hear her speak. Puritan leaders felt their authority was threatened. They banned her meetings.

In 1637 and again in 1638, Anne Hutchinson was brought before the Massachusetts Bay Colony General Court. The second time, she was 46 years old, pregnant, and ill. The General Court was made up of Puritan leaders; there was no jury. Hutchinson was thrown out of the church and banished. The Hutchinsons and 35 other families moved to Rhode Island.

Anne Hutchinson preached to people in her home.

Andrew Jackson
seventh president ★ 1767–1845

Andrew Jackson is the only president who retreated from his own inaugural celebration! Thousands of his supporters overran the White House, breaking windows, standing on the furniture, and spitting tobacco juice on the floor. Jackson fled to a hotel.

Jackson was the first president from a humble background. He was born in a log cabin in South Carolina. He became a lawyer and a war hero, driving the British from New Orleans during the War of 1812. Jackson believed in the political power of the "common man." He thought the nation shouldn't be controlled by the elite group of wealthy or educated politicians from the East Coast who had traditionally run the country. His "Jacksonian democracy" appealed to Americans, many of whom were frontier settlers, laborers, and immigrants. With their support, Jackson served two terms as president (1829–1837).

To get his way with Congress, President Jackson often took his case directly to the American people. He used the "spoils system" and rewarded his political supporters with government jobs. He vetoed any legislation that didn't fit his political goals.

He also backed the Indian Removal Act of 1830, which displaced thousands of Native Americans from their land in the South.

Jesse Jackson
civil rights leader ★ 1941—

The Reverend Jesse Jackson has inspired millions with his verve and vision. He's alienated others. But he forced the nation to listen when African Americans said, "I *am* somebody!"

After **Dr. Martin Luther King, Jr.**'s assassination in 1968, Jackson emerged as a leader of the civil rights movement. He founded Operation PUSH (People United to Serve Humanity) in Chicago in 1971 and PUSH-EXCEL (for students) in 1976. Jackson's rousing speeches spread the word: Self-respect, responsibility, education, and *action* would further the civil rights cause.

In 1984, Jesse Jackson became the first black man to run for the Democratic presidential nomination. He vowed to represent a "Rainbow Coalition" of "the disinherited, the disrespected, and the despised." He rolled out voter drives. He settled an international crisis by getting a U.S. naval pilot downed in Syria set free. But he didn't get the nomination. Jackson ran again in 1988. Seven million primary voters chose Jackson. He didn't win the candidacy, but he did force the Democratic party to take black political power seriously.

Jackson was awarded the Presidential Medal of Freedom in 2000. He continues to be an outspoken champion of equal rights and social justice.

Michael Jackson
singer, composer ★ 1958—

Michael Jackson has taken many strange turns. But one thing hasn't changed yet. He made the world's best-selling pop album . . . ever!

Thriller, released in 1982, has sold 51 million copies. Jackson supported it with slick, high-tech music videos that featured hit singles like, "Billie Jean" and "Beat It." These videos helped pave the way for music videos by other African-American artists.

Thriller won a record-breaking eight Grammys and made Jackson a superstar. But he had also been a child star. Michael started singing with his family's group, the Jackson 5, in 1963, when he was five years old. Michael's astonishing voice helped Jackson 5 songs like "The Love You Save" and "ABC" zoom to the top of the charts. The same thing happened when Jackson went solo in 1971. His albums *Off the Wall* and *Bad* joined *Thriller* as best-sellers. His performances were mind boggling. In 1993, Jackson received a Grammy Living Legend Award. He released several albums during the 1990s. *Invincible*, his first studio album in four years, was released in 2001.

Jesse James
outlaw ★ 1847—1882

Jesse James was a Confederate guerrilla who killed unarmed men and robbed trains. After the Civil War, he went into the same line of work.

The James gang is credited with the first daytime bank robbery during peacetime in America. They held up a bank in Liberty, Missouri, in 1866 in broad daylight and rode off with $60,000.

Over the next 15 years, Jesse James and his outlaws robbed 10 banks and seven trains, and held up four stagecoaches in Missouri, Kentucky, and other parts of the Midwest. Guards, engineers, and passengers often died in these crimes. Then, during an 1876 bank robbery attempt in Northfield, Minnesota, the townspeople fought back. All of the James gang, except Jesse and his brother, Frank, were killed or captured. Jesse moved to St. Louis, Missouri, with his family. He lived undercover, mainly retired. But in 1881, he masterminded one, maybe two violent train robberies in Missouri. The governor offered $5,000 each for Jesse and Frank's capture. On April 3, 1882, Jesse James was at home. He took off his guns, stood on a chair, and straightened and dusted a picture. A fellow outlaw, Robert Ford, shot him dead through the back of the head for the reward.

Photos of Jesse James were rare, so not many people knew what he actually looked like.

John Jay
diplomat, Supreme Court justice ★ 1745—1829

During the American Revolution and its aftermath, John Jay played an important role in defending the new nation. Jay was a lawyer and a skilled diplomat. He served in the first Continental Congress (1774) and became president of the second in 1778.

In 1782, Jay, along with **John Adams** and **Benjamin Franklin**, negotiated the settlement between Great Britain and the newly independent American colonies. Jay served as the U.S. secretary of foreign affairs from 1784 to 1790.

Jay had a reputation as an influential diplomat. But some of his negotiations were politically controversial. Jay's Treaty (1794) allowed British ships to inspect American ships suspected of carrying supplies to France, Britain's enemy. In exchange, the British withdrew their troops from the Northwest Territory. Many people thought Jay had betrayed America's independence and neutrality. Jay thought his agreements were necessary; the nation was ill-equipped to go to war with Spain or Great Britain.

In between diplomatic roles, John Jay served as the country's first Supreme Court justice. He was nominated to the court by President **George Washington**.

*John Jay contributed five essays to The Federalist Papers (1787–1788), which argued for ratification of the Constitution. His coauthors were **Alexander Hamilton** and **James Madison**.*

Thomas Jefferson
third president ★ 1743–1826

He wrote his own gravestone epitaph: "Here was buried Thomas Jefferson, Author of the Declaration of Independence, of the Statute of Virginia for Religious Freedom, and Father of the University of Virginia." The great but modest statesman left out so much more—including his presidency!

Jefferson, the philosophical scholar, self-taught architect, violinist, inventor, amateur naturalist, and Virginia farmer, had one of the most brilliant minds in American history. A poor public speaker, he was a great writer. Jefferson had already written several well-known essays when a Continental Congress committee appointed him to write their Declaration of Independence in 1776.

The Declaration of Independence reflected Jefferson's beliefs that the liberties of the people must be protected above all else. He was opposed to a powerful federal government and thought the individual states' rights had to come first. These were the ideas Jefferson supported when he ran for president in 1800. It was a messy, bitter campaign against his former ally, **John Adams**. Jefferson won and served two terms (1801–1809).

Thomas Jefferson's presidency was an era of tricky international diplomacy. President Jefferson sent out the Navy between 1801 and 1805 to defend American ships against pirates in the Mediterranean. Because of English and French attacks, he signed the Embargo Act in 1807. This act was unpopular because it drastically cut U.S. shipping trade with European countries; but it did keep the nation from being dragged into an ongoing European war.

Jefferson's work at home was even more dramatic. In 1803, he authorized the Louisiana Purchase. France, desperate to fund its war chest, sold the U.S. all its land from the Mississippi River to the Rockies for $15 million. The nation doubled in size—for three cents an acre! Jefferson sent **Meriwether Lewis** and **William Clark** out to map the new American frontier.

Toward the end of his second term, Jefferson succeeded in getting a bill passed that prohibited the importation of slaves as of January 1, 1808. (The slave trade continued, illegally.) Slavery presented a serious, troubling conflict to a human rights advocate like Jefferson. His original draft of the Declaration of Independence had included strong antislavery language, but several Southern colonies refused to sign until it was removed. Jefferson owned slaves, but freed some of them in his will. Most historians agree he had a deep, long-term relationship with an enslaved woman, Sally Hemings, who bore several of his children.

> ## "We hold these truths to be self-evident, that all men are created equal . . ."
> — THOMAS JEFFERSON

President Jefferson refused to run for a third term because he thought long-held offices were dangerous in a democracy. He retired to his home, Monticello, and then designed the buildings and set the curriculum of the University of Virginia.

Mae C. Jemison
astronaut ★ 1956—

Biomedical engineer Mae C. Jemison applied for the National Aeronautics and Space Administration's (NASA) astronaut program. NASA received 2,000 applications; 100 people were interviewed; in 1987, 15 astronaut trainees were chosen. Dr. Jemison was one of them.

On September 12, 1992, she and six other crew members boarded the space shuttle *Endeavour*. Jemison carried an **Alvin Ailey** Dance Company poster and a flag from the Organization of African Unity. The first African-American woman in space was taking symbols of her heritage with her. During the *Endeavour*'s eight-day space orbit, Jemison studied how weightlessness affects the development of frogs' eggs. Her other experiments included how to work with IV fluids in microgravity.

Six months after her shuttle mission ended, Jemison retired from NASA. She started her own technology consulting company, which specializes in social issues and technology design. She is an environmental studies professor at Dartmouth College in New Hampshire and created "The Earth We Share" space and science camp for children.

Steven Jobs and Stephen Wozniak
computer entrepreneurs ★ 1955—(Jobs); 1950—(Wozniak)

Steven Jobs and Stephen Wozniak founded Apple Computer, Inc., in 1976. Each Steve sold off a treasured belonging to fund the start-up. Jobs gave up his VW bus; "Woz," his calculator. The company was named after Jobs's favorite fruit; its office was in his garage. Within a year, they introduced Apple II, the first computer mass-marketed, or advertised, and aimed at all consumers. The two Steves had started a revolution.

From 1977 to 1982, Apple Computer, Inc., created and dominated the personal computer market. Woz was mainly interested in the technical aspects of computers. Jobs handled most of the business dealings and new product development. In 1984, he introduced the Macintosh. This computer had a simple point-and-click graphic interface and a mouse. Macs could be used at home or in the office. They changed the world of computer design.

By 1985, Wozniak had retired from Apple to pursue other interests. Jobs also left that year, after losing management struggles within the company. He founded a software company and bought Pixar Animation Studios. Jobs produced Pixar's computer-generated blockbuster movies *Toy Story* (1995), *Toy Story 2* (1999), and *Monsters, Inc.* (2001). Jobs returned to Apple in 1996 and helped turn the company around with new Mac product lines.

Apple's Steve Wozniak in 1993.

Andrew Johnson
17th president ★ 1808—1875

Abraham Lincoln's assassination put Vice President Johnson in the White House. Trying to follow Lincoln's ideas for Reconstruction after the Civil War almost put him out.

Andrew Johnson was known as the "Tennessee Tailor" because he had come from a poor frontier family and learned sewing to earn a living.

During Johnson's Democratic presidency, members of the Republican party called the Radical Republicans wanted to punish the South for the Civil War. These Radical Republicans also wanted to make sure that southern Democrats didn't rise to power again. President Johnson favored a more tolerant approach toward the former Confederacy. In 1868, Radical Republicans in the House of Representatives even went so far as to impeach Johnson, although they had no real constitutional grounds for doing so. The Senate voted on 11 articles of impeachment. Johnson was saved from conviction—by one vote.

*Andrew Johnson's impeachment trial was the first ever of an American president. This would not happen again until President **Bill Clinton**'s trial in 1999.*

Lyndon B. Johnson
36th president ★ 1908—1973

Lyndon Baines Johnson (LBJ) was the kind of large, loud, American politician who could shake hands—and twist arms. He took office within hours of President **John F. Kennedy**'s assassination in 1963. Because Johnson was caring *and* ruthless, folksy *and* powerful, he was able to push through groundbreaking legislation on civil rights, the environment, and his "War on Poverty." LBJ's programs like Head Start preschools (1964) and Medicare/Medicaid health plans (1965) helped thousands of poor Americans. He fought for passage of the Civil Rights Act (1964), which banned discrimination in jobs and public places. He pushed for the Voting Rights Act (1965), which banned literacy tests that had disqualified African-American voters and kept them from voting.

Still, the country became increasingly divided and violent in the 1960s. Race riots broke out, especially when **Dr. Martin Luther King, Jr.**, was assassinated in 1968. Congress passed the Gulf of Tonkin Resolution (1964), which gave Johnson open-ended powers to conduct the controversial war in Vietnam. In 1965, he sent in U.S. troops and started air raids. By 1968, there were 500,000 Americans in Vietnam—and thousands of body bags coming home. The antiwar movement exploded. Massive protests were common. LBJ became the enemy in many people's minds. On March 31, 1968, President Johnson said he would stop the bombing of North Vietnam. He then dropped a political bomb himself: He was not going to run for president again.

"The Great Society rests on abundance

"Magic" Earvin Johnson
basketball player ★ 1959—

On the court, Earvin Johnson's playing was pure magic. Without looking, he'd pass the ball front, side, back, off of a spin, over his shoulder, through his legs. He'd score as the buzzer sounded. He practically invented the triple-double (10 or more points, assists, and rebounds in a game). And his smile was as dazzling as his playing.

In 1979, Johnson signed with the Los Angeles Lakers. It was the only professional basketball uniform he ever wore. In his 13 seasons as the Lakers' point guard (1979–1991), Johnson helped bring the team to nine National Basketball Association (NBA) finals, where they won five of those championships. He was voted both Most Valuable Player (MVP) and playoff MVP three times, as well as NBA All-Star MVP twice. Johnson holds the record for most career assists (2,346) and steals (358). His championship playing, his famed rivalry with **Larry Bird**, and his

Magic Johnson played on the gold-medal winning Dream Team in the 1992 Olympics. In 1996, he came out of retirement for one more season with the Lakers.

dazzling smile and joyful style on court helped renew national interest in pro basketball.

In 1991, Johnson revealed that he was HIV-positive. He became active in promoting AIDS education and awareness.

Marion Jones
Olympian ★ 1975—

As a student at the University of North Carolina, Marion Jones led the Tar Heels to a National College Athletic Association (NCAA) basketball championship in 1994 *and* went on to become All-American in four college track events. But basketball is hard on the body. Jones broke her foot twice. She was unable to compete for a spot on the 1996 U.S. Olympic track-and-field team. Jones put on her running shoes again. She started training with a new coach. It paid off. In 1998, she lost only one out of 36 track-and-field competitions.

Jones's real goal was her famous "Drive for Five" gold medals at the 2000 Olympics in Sydney, Australia. Gold medal one: Jones whooshes through 100 meters in 10.75 seconds. Gold medal two: Marion Jones burns up the track, winning the 200-meter race by a record-breaking 13 feet. Gold medal three: Jones, running third in the 4x100 relay, leaves the other runners in the dust. She scored bronze medals for the long jump and for the 4x400 relay. Although her medals weren't all gold as she'd hoped, Marion Jones became the first woman to win five track-and-field medals in a single Olympics.

and liberty for all." —LYNDON B. JOHNSON

Mother Jones
labor leader ★ 1830–1930

In 1871, Mary Harris Jones, a widowed dressmaker, stopped in at a Knights of Labor meeting in Chicago. She found her life's work: labor reform.

For more than 50 years, Jones goaded workers to strike for better working conditions and living wages. Railroad workers, coal and copper miners, and textile and streetcar workers called this tough Irish-American woman "Mother." She joined them in the dangerous, violent labor battles that were fought across the United States. Jones helped convince workers in West Virginia and Pennsylvania to join the United Mine Workers union. She organized miners' wives into "mop-and-broom brigades" to keep strikebreakers out of the mines. In 1903, Mother Jones organized the Crusade of the Mill Children and marched with them from Pennsylvania to President **Theodore Roosevelt**'s summer home on Long Island. He refused to see Mother Jones, but the publicity brought national attention to child labor. Union officials did not always approve, but Mother Jones's sensational acts helped keep labor struggles in the headlines and in the public eye.

Janis Joplin helped open up the world of rock 'n' roll to women.

Janis Joplin
singer ★ 1943–1970

No one at the 1967 Monterey Pop Festival had ever seen or heard anything like this—hair flying, body shaking, and a three-octave voice that reached sultry lows and howling highs. And the singer was a woman!

Janis Joplin was rock 'n' roll's first female superstar. Joplin, who hailed from Port Arthur, Texas, became part of the 1960s hippie scene in California. From 1966 to 1968, she sang with a band called Big Brother and the Holding Company. They appeared with her in Monterey for her legendary performance of "Ball and Chain." Joplin and Big Brother's first album, *Cheap Thrills* (1968), rocketed to number one on the charts and went gold. That same year, Joplin went solo. Rock audiences were blown away by her incredible performances of songs like "Piece of My Heart." Joplin's raw, soul-baring singing style was heavily influenced by the blues. She was at work on an album with her new Full Tilt Boogie Band in 1970 when she died of an accidental drug overdose. That album, *Pearl* (1971), featured two Joplin classics: the heart-wrenching "Cry Baby" and the wistful "Me and Bobby McGee."

"The stakes are too high for

Scott Joplin
composer, musician ★ 1868—1917

The "Father of Ragtime" taught himself piano as a child. He continued his education as a piano player in smoky St. Louis saloons. Scott Joplin didn't get to study music formally in college until he was 28. Three years later, he was famous.

In 1899, Joplin published "Maple Leaf Rag." It was the first sheet music to sell more than a million copies. Ragtime, an early form of jazz, became *the* musical craze. It has a syncopated rhythm and Afro-Caribbean roots, with a bit of European marching music thrown in. Joplin published more than 50 ragtime pieces, including another famous work, "The Entertainer" (1902).

Joplin, a gifted pianist, wanted to incorporate ragtime into other musical forms, particularly opera. He wrote two operas. One work, *A Guest of Honor* (1903), was lost, possibly at a copyright office. The other, *Treemonisha*, was staged in Harlem, New York, in 1915. Joplin paid for the theater and the cast himself. He also played the piano during the performance. The whole show was ignored by critics. This was a huge blow to Joplin, who died two years later. In 1976, Joplin's opera was staged again and won the Pulitzer prize.

Barbara Jordan
U.S. Representative ★ 1936—1996

Barbara Jordan grew up in Houston, Texas, in the 1930s, when the South was still segregated. She believed that the best way to fight discrimination was to forge new laws—and have more African Americans involved in making those laws.

Jordan went to law school and then entered politics. In 1966, she was elected to the Texas state senate. She was the first African-American member since 1883, and the first woman member ever.

In 1972, Texan voters sent her to the U. S. House of Representatives. During her six years in Congress, Jordan helped create laws that made life better for poor people and people of color. In 1973, she authored a bill banning racial discrimination at schools and companies that receive federal monies. Jordan was also a member of the House Judiciary Committee. During the 1974 Watergate hearings, she made a powerful speech. She called for President **Nixon**'s impeachment because he had disregarded the U.S. Constitution.

Barbara Jordan addresses the Democratic National Covention in 1992.

Jordan gave the keynote address at the 1976 and the 1992 Democratic national conventions. After she retired from Congress in 1978, she became a university professor. In 1994, Barbara Jordan was awarded the Presidential Medal of Freedom.

government to be a spectator sport." —BARBARA JORDAN

"Talent wins games, but teamwork

Michael Jordan
basketball player ★ 1963—

At the dawn of the millennium, he topped many "greatest" lists. His number, 23, is instantly recognizable—thousands of kids across the country wear it. Ask most people who's the greatest athlete in the world and you'll get the same answer: Michael Jordan.

At the 1982 National Collegiate Athletic Association play-offs, Georgetown led the University of North Carolina (UNC), Jordan's team, by one point. With 17 seconds left in the game, Jordan fired a 17–foot jumper through the net. The UNC Tar Heels took the championship. Jordan headed for the Olympics. Cocaptain Jordan helped Team U.S.A. bring home the gold in 1984, a feat he repeated with the 1992 Olympic "Dream Team."

In 1984, Jordan was drafted by the Chicago Bulls. People came to see "Air" Jordan, the man immune to the laws of gravity. They weren't disappointed. In the 1986 play-offs, Jordan scored a record-breaking 63 points in *one game* against the Boston Celtics. He led the National Basketball Association (NBA) in scoring for 10 of his 11 full seasons. In 1986, Jordan racked up 3,041 points, joining **Wilt Chamberlain** as the only other basketball star to break 3,000 points in a season. Most Valuable Player Awards? Jordan earned five of them during regular seasons and was MVP six times in the finals. As for the Bulls, Jordan led the team to its first NBA championship in 1991. He followed up with five more during his Bulls career.

None of these statistics add up to the pure sensation that was Michael Jordan in play. "His Airness" could leap as high as 44 inches off the court. He'd hover over the basket a few dazzling seconds, then *swish*! Jordan became the most idolized, televised, talked about, written-up player in basketball history. He had multimillion-dollar endorsement contracts with, among others, Nike, which sold millions of Air Jordan sneakers. Fans were stunned when Jordan announced his retirement in 1993, a few sad months after his father was murdered.

Jordan played minor league baseball for two seasons. Then two simple words made him front-page news again: "I'm back." On March 19, 1995, Jordan once again donned a Chicago Bulls jersey, this time number 45, since the Bulls had already retired his famous 23. (Jordan was wearing it again in a few weeks.) Basketball fans went wild. Air Jordan gave them what they wanted—high-flying, record-breaking basketball—for two more seasons. He retired in 1999 again. But again, not for good.

On October 30, 2001, Michael Jordan, by now nearly 39, bounded out of the Washington Wizards locker room to face the New York Knicks. (The Knicks won, 93–91.) Jordan donated his $1 million first-year salary as a Wizards player to a relief fund for the World Trade Center disaster.

One of Michael Jordan's most famous shots is this one in the last 40 seconds of game six in the 1998 NBA finals against the Utah Jazz. The Utah Jazz were ahead of the Bulls by one point before Jordan scored. The Bulls won.

and intelligence win championships." — MICHAEL JORDAN

Chief Joseph
Nez Percé leader ★ c.1840–1904

In the 1860s, the Nez Percé of northeast Oregon were in the same situation as many other Native Americans. Pioneers and gold miners wanted their land and the government wanted them to move to a reservation. Chief Joseph bravely tried to resist both, but when he realized the battle would be lost, he made an even braver decision: to lead his people to freedom.

About 750 Nez Percé men, women, and children set out in the summer of 1877. They climbed rugged mountains and crossed rivers through Oregon, Washington, Idaho, and Montana. For months, Chief Joseph and his 200 or so warriors outfoxed and outfought the thousands of U.S. troops who pursued them. Finally, on October 5, 1877, the U.S. Army surrounded the hungry, exhausted tribe in the Bear Paw Mountains. The Nez Percé had traveled 1,400 long, hard miles. They were only a day's walk from Canada—and freedom.

The Nez Percé were exiled first to Kansas, then Oklahoma. Many died along the way. Chief Joseph made several trips to Washington, D.C., to plead with politicians to return his people to their homeland. Instead, they were removed to a reservation in Washington state, cut off from other Nez Percé.

Jackie Joyner-Kersee
Olympian ★ 1962—

Jackie Joyner-Kersee won a 1984 silver medal for the heptathlon, a grueling seven-event Olympic competition that includes the long jump, the high jump, the shot put, the javelin, the 200-meter dash, the 100-meter hurdles, and the 800-meter run. It was the start of a headline-making, record-breaking Olympic career. In 1986, Joyner-Kersee set a world record for the heptathlon, winning more points than anyone in history. Two years later, she won a 1988 Olympic gold medal for the heptathlon, breaking her own world record. She also became the first American woman to win a gold medal for the long jump, after soaring 24 feet and 3½ inches. She scored the heptathlon gold medal at the 1992 Olympics.

The woman many people call the "World's Greatest Female Athlete" is retired. She founded the Jackie Joyner-Kersee Youth Center Foundation and has raised more than $12 million to provide services and sports facilities for children in East St. Louis, Illinois, her hometown. She was voted Female Athlete of the Century by *Sports Illustrated for Women.*

*Jackie Joyner-Kersee wins the heptathlon finals at the 1992 Olympics in Barcelona, Spain. Her sister-in-law was **Florence Griffith-Joyner.***

Buster Keaton in The General.

Buster Keaton

actor ★ 1895–1966

Joseph Frank "Buster" Keaton grew up in the theater. His godfather was **Harry Houdini**. His parents were vaudeville actors. Buster, an amazing acrobat and comic, had top billing in the family act by the time he was five! But what really put his name up in lights were the movies.

Keaton left stage-acting for the big screen in 1917. Three years later, he formed his own film studio. Keaton wrote, directed, and starred in 12 feature-length and 19 short silent films between 1920 and 1928. He created his famous screen character, a bewildered hero swept up by the maddening, mechanical, modern world. Keaton's trademark was his "stone" face. His facial movements were very controlled: a raised eyebrow here, a frown there, a sideways glance. But he became even more famous for his acrobatics. Keaton did all of his own stunts, from the death-defying to the slapstick. He had a great sense of comic timing and was a master of visual gags and deadpan humor. His film masterpieces included: *The Three Ages* (1923), *Sherlock, Jr.* (1924), and *The Navigator* (1924). These three films were Keaton's biggest box-office successes. Critics consider Keaton's *The General* (1927) to be among the best movies ever made. It was one of the first films to be preserved by the Library of Congress.

Helen Keller

social activist ★ 1880–1968

A childhood disease left Helen Keller deaf, blind, and mute. She lived in a dark, silent world, unable to communicate with anyone. Until Anne Sullivan came along in 1887.

Sullivan had trained at the Perkins Institute for the Blind in Boston. Anne taught Helen to read Braille, to use the manual alphabet, and to feel sign language. The two lived and worked together for 50 years, until Sullivan's death.

Helen Keller was an extremely determined young woman. She learned to speak by feeling and imitating mouth movements. Keller graduated from prestigious Radcliffe College in 1904. She was a staunch feminist and a pacifist. She also joined the Socialist Party of America in 1909 and became friends with the party's leader, **Eugene V. Debs**.

A world traveler and a patron of the arts, Keller lived a rich, full, independent life. She helped organize 30 state commissions for the blind and lectured in support of the American Foundation for the Blind. She also donated $2 million to the foundation. Keller became one of the first people to write articles about blindness for major magazines. Her autobiography, *The Story of My Life* (1902), was an international best-seller. In 1963, Keller was awarded the Presidential Medal of Freedom.

John F. Kennedy
35th president ★ 1917—1963

John Fitzgerald Kennedy (JFK) was president for only 1,037 days (1961–1963), but he inspired the nation.

Kennedy was a decorated World War II hero, a Massachusetts Congressman, and the Pulitzer prize-winning author of the book *Profiles in Courage* (1956) when he decided to run for president in 1960. Kennedy came from a wealthy Irish-Catholic family. At the time, many people wouldn't vote for Catholics, for fear they would put church above state. But JFK had never lost an election in his life. Not only that, the newest political tool, the television camera, loved the young, handsome, and enthusiastic 43-year-old candidate. In the first-ever televised presidential debates, Kennedy outshone his opponent, **Richard Nixon**. Still, the election was close. Nearly 70 million people voted. JFK beat Nixon by only 120,000 of those votes.

JFK boldly declared his presidency a "New Frontier" and promised to "get America moving again." Already a millionaire, he donated his presidential salary to charities.

President Kennedy ushered in the "Camelot" era, a time of optimism and energy. Kennedy created initiatives like the Peace Corps, which sent young Americans abroad to help developing nations. He urged Congress to fund the space program. But the Kennedy years were also marked by fears of communism and civil rights conflicts.

In 1961, a CIA-backed attempt to bring down Fidel Castro's Communist government in Cuba failed. President Kennedy was blamed. In 1962, the Soviet Union built nuclear missiles in Cuba. They were pointed at the United States. President Kennedy sent in the Navy to surround and blockade Cuba. For 13 scary days, the world's two superpowers were on the brink of war. Finally, the Soviets agreed to withdraw the missiles. The U.S. agreed not to invade.

> **"Ask not what your country can do for you—ask what you can do for your country."** —JOHN F. KENNEDY

That same year, East German Communists erected the Berlin Wall, which separated East Berlin and West Berlin. JFK promised retaliation for any Communist threat against democratic West Berlin. Meanwhile, JFK worried about the growing Communist guerrilla movement in Vietnam. At the time, the U.S. had fewer than 1000 U.S. military advisors in Vietnam; by 1963, Kennedy had upped that to 16,000.

President Kennedy and his attorney general, brother Robert F. Kennedy, faced tough political choices when it came to dealing with the violence that erupted at civil rights sit-ins, marches, and "Freedom Rider" bus trips in the South. Pressure from civil rights leaders and his own personal beliefs eventually convinced Kennedy to end discrimination in federally sponsored housing, to stop school segregation, and to encourage equal opportunity. Unfortunately JFK didn't live to see his ideas take shape.

Allen Ginsberg (1926–1997) (r.) was influential in getting Jack Kerouac (l.) published. Ginsberg was the most famous Beat poet. His groundbreaking work Howl *(1955) is one of the great modern American poems.*

Jack Kerouac
author ★ 1922—1969

In a 1948 interview, Jack Kerouac coined the term *Beat* to describe a generation not interested in stuffy social rules and old-fashioned art. Beats were interested in creativity not conformity.

Kerouac grew up in Lowell, a declining mill town in Massachusetts. He briefly attended Columbia University on a football scholarship. There he met the other two original Beats, writer William Burroughs and poet Allen Ginsberg. He also met Neal Cassady, a cowboy from Denver.

Kerouac teamed up with Cassady on some wild cross-county road trips. Jack immortalized their adventures in *On the Road* (1957). He wrote this novel in the spirited style he called "spontaneous prose." *On the Road* was a high-speed read, full of energy, street slang, and colorful characters. It was a wild literary trip through postwar America. Kerouac typed out his story in a three-week frenzy. The manuscript was a single 120-foot-long roll of paper. (In 2001, it was auctioned off for a record $2.2 million.)

It took Kerouac seven years to find someone willing to publish his novel. *On the Road* has now sold more than 3.5 million copies just in the U.S. Kerouac published several more works, including *The Dharma Bums* and *The Subterraneans* (both 1958) and *Desolation Angels* (1965).

Jack Kilby
engineer ★ 1923—

Jack Kilby's tiny invention had a huge impact on the world. It made the Information Age possible. You can't click on a TV or PC, chat on a cell phone, or use most electronic devices without the silicon microchip.

Kilby, an electrical engineer, was working at Texas Instruments in Dallas in 1958. The TI lab was empty because it was summer, so Kilby went to work on his own miniature component. That's when he got "The Monolithic Idea": do space-saving horizontal wiring, manufacture all the pieces together from the same material, and put them inside a tiny integrated circuit (IC) chip. It worked.

On October 10, 2000, Jack Kilby was awarded the Nobel Prize for physics, for his invention that changed the world.

In February 1959, Kilby applied for a patent for his IC. In June, Robert Noyce, a scientist working at Fairchild Semiconductor Corporation, filed for an IC patent, too. He'd designed a microchip without wires, which was easier to manufacture. Both men are now commonly considered coinventors of the IC microchip.

Jack Kilby also coinvented the pocket calculator (1965) and holds patents on 60 other electronic products.

to live, mad to talk, desirous of everything at the same time."

When B. B. King and Lucille get together, they start playing the blues. "Lucille" is King's trademark name for his guitars.

B. B. King
blues musician ★ 1925—

His real first name is Riley. The "B. B." stands for Blues Boy. His last name figures into his title, "King of the Blues."

B. B. King has reigned in the blues world for nearly six decades. King got his start in 1948 in Memphis, Tennessee, a hot spot in the blues scene. The young bluesman played on the radio and in local clubs, barn dances, and roadhouses. In 1951, his song "Three O'clock Blues" hit the charts and King hit the road, performing all across the U.S. But it was his single "The Thrill Is Gone" (1969) that really put B. B. King on the country's musical map. His distinctive style—heartbreaking bent notes, staccato single notes, and passionate, earthy vocals—has kept him there.

King has won 11 Grammy Awards, including one in 2001 for *Riding with the King*, his multiplatinum collaboration with Eric Clapton. He still sings the blues . . . about 250 times a year in concerts all over the world.

Billie Jean King
tennis player ★ 1943—

Billie Jean King likes to win. At 18, she was half of the youngest pair to take the women's doubles title at the famous Wimbledon, England, tennis tournament. By 1967, King had won six major titles. In 1971, she became the first woman to earn more than $100,000 in one season, when she won 17 singles and 21 doubles tournaments. Billie Jean scored a total of 20 Wimbledon titles in her career, winning her 20th match in 1979 with doubles partner **Martina Navratilova**.

King was an outspoken leader in women's tennis on and off the courts. She trounced male chauvinist Bobby Riggs in the famous 1973 "Battle of the Sexes" match. She founded the Women's Tennis Association in 1973 to promote professional women's tennis and fight for prize money equal to men's tournament awards. King's last major appearance on the court was in 1983 when, at age 39, she reached the singles semifinals at Wimbledon. She later became the first woman commissioner in professional sports at the World Team Tennis League.

"Injustice anywhere is a threat

Martin Luther King, Jr.
civil rights leader ★ 1929—1968

In 1954, Martin Luther King, Jr., a young Baptist minister, took a pastor's job in Montgomery, Alabama. His preaching soon spread beyond his pulpit.

King grew up in Atlanta, Georgia. He was an exceptional student who enrolled in Atlanta's Morehouse College at 15. After college, he studied at Crozer Theological Seminary in Chester, Pennsylvania. There, King read the works of Mahatma Gandhi, leader of India's independence movement. He embraced Gandhi's ideas about change through nonviolence.

In 1955, King got a chance to test this philosophy. After the arrest of **Rosa Parks**, he helped lead the successful Montgomery bus boycott. King became a national hero. He was only 27 years old.

Martin Luther King delivers his famous "I Have a Dream" speech at the 1963 March on Washington. In 1986, King's birthday was declared a national holiday.

King emerged as the powerful leader of the civil rights movement. He was an outstanding speaker: Threats, mobs, bombings, beatings, and jail didn't silence him.

In 1957, King and the Reverend Ralph Abernathy formed the Southern Christian Leadership Conference (SCLC). SCLC conducted voter registration drives across the South. King and the SCLC mounted a major campaign against segregation in Birmingham, Alabama, in 1963. King led sit-ins and protest marches. Birmingham's racist police chief, Bull Connor, responded with fire hoses, attack dogs, beatings, and jail. King was thrown in solitary confinement. He answered critics' charges about his actions with his stirring and now-famous "Letter from Birmingham Jail."

Birmingham was a major victory. City and business officials agreed to integrate many public places. But the effect of King and the SCLC's campaign reached beyond Birmingham. Press coverage of the violence that had been unleashed on peaceful protestors shocked the nation. The civil rights movement drew more support. On August 18, 1963, more than 250,000 people joined an historic march on Washington, D.C. They cheered and wept as Martin Luther King delivered what became his most memorable speech, "I Have a Dream."

King was awarded the Nobel Peace Prize in 1964. The struggle continued. In 1965, King led a voter registration drive in Alabama. It turned into a freedom march from Selma to Montgomery, the state's capital. The peaceful marchers were beaten and tear-gassed by state police.

In 1968, King traveled to Memphis, Tennessee, to support striking black sanitation workers. In a speech there on April 3, he declared, "I've looked over and seen the promised land. I may not get there with you." The next day King was dead, assassinated by James Earl Ray. King's work lives on.

Stephen King
author ★ 1947—

Killer cats. Killer cars. Killer kids. Stephen King has made a fortune out of frightening characters! The crowned "King of Horror" has sold more than 100 million copies of his books. In 1999, he earned $65 million, making him the world's second-highest-paid author.

During the 1970s, King worked as a schoolteacher in Maine. At night, he worked in a laundry. His first best-seller, *Carrie* (1974), changed all that. He could afford to write full-time.

King is not only one of the most popular modern authors, he's one of the busiest. Since 1975, he's published more than 48 books (some of them under the pen name Richard Bachman). Many of his creepy, suspenseful novels, like *Carrie*, *The Shining* (1977), *Cujo* (1981), *Pet Semetary* (1981), *Misery* (1987), and *The Girl Who Loved Tom Gordon* (1999), were later turned into creepy, suspenseful movies.

*Stephen King occasionally plays guitar in a band, the Rockbottom Remainders, along with **Amy Tan** and **Matt Groening**.*

In the summer of 1999, King was severely injured when he was hit by a van while jogging near his home in Maine. (He later bought the van so he could smash it with a sledgehammer.) After his accident, Stephen King wrote the well-received work *On Writing* (2001), which is part autobiography, part how-to book, and part essay on his craft.

In 2002, Maxine Hong Kingston moved from writing fiction to poetry with her book To Be the Poet.

Maxine Hong Kingston
author ★ 1940—

When she was young, Maxine Hong Kingston wanted to read books that had Chinese characters who were not just stereotypes. There were none in her local library. Kingston grew up and wrote the kinds of stories she had looked for as a child.

Maxine Hong Kingston's *Woman Warrior, Memoirs of a Girlhood Among Ghosts* won the 1976 National Book Critics Award for nonfiction. Kingston uses female narrators to tell the story of her family's immigration from China; her childhood in Stockton, California; the family laundry business; and the rich heritage of Chinese culture, language, and myths that were part of her upbringing. She also explores the difficulties women face in Chinese and American societies. *Woman Warrior* was named one of the top 10 books of the decade by *Time* magazine.

Kingston's second book, *China Men* (1980), won the American Book Award and has all male characters. It is an intimate look at the history of the Chinese laborers who built the railroads and worked the mines in the American West during the 19th century.

Tripmaster Monkey: His Fake Book created a sensation when it was published in 1989. Some critics favorably compared Kingston's main character to Mark Twain's Huckleberry Finn.

"There can't be a crisis next week.

Henry Kissinger
secretary of state ★ 1923—

No one would argue that Henry Kissinger isn't one of America's most original thinkers about global politics. But the arguments about his ideas have never stopped.

Kissinger served as President **Richard Nixon**'s national security advisor from 1969 to 1973. In 1973, Kissinger, who was born in Germany, became the first naturalized U.S. citizen appointed secretary of state. He served in this cabinet role under Nixon and President Gerald Ford.

Nixon and Kissinger worked closely, often secretly, on foreign policy. They brokered new relations and treaties with China and the Soviet Union in the 1970s. Kissinger won the 1973 Nobel Peace Prize for negotiating the withdrawal of American troops from Vietnam. In 1974, he frequently traveled between meetings in Washington and the Middle East. This "shuttle diplomacy" helped resolve explosive issues involving Israel, Egypt, and Syria.

In his years as national security advisor and secretary of state, Kissinger was also involved in secret operations. During the Vietnam War, he played a key decision-making role in the illegal bombings of Cambodia and Laos, which resulted in many civilian deaths. Kissinger was also connected with CIA operations to overthrow Chile's elected president, Salvador Allende.

Sandy Koufax
baseball player ★ 1935—

Sandy Koufax's sports career started with a college basketball scholarship. He also played on the University of Cincinnati's baseball team. Major League Baseball came calling after scouts reported on his pitching. Koufax, a Jewish-American boy from Brooklyn, New York, signed with his hometown Dodgers. For several years he couldn't control his wild pitching. Finally, after taking some friendly professional advice from the Dodgers' catcher, Koufax came into his own on the mound. "The Man with the Golden Arm" dominated pitching from 1962 through 1966. His rocketing fastballs and impossible curveballs helped the Dodgers (now in Los Angeles) shut out the New York Yankees in the 1963 World Series and trump the Minnesota Twins in the 1965 World Series. During those five seasons, Koufax held a 111-34 win/loss record. He pitched four no-hitters, including a 1965 perfect game: no hits, no runs, no batters reaching first base. He was named Most Valuable Player of 1963 and unanimously chosen for three **Cy Young** Awards (1963, 1965, 1966), which honor great pitching. He retired in 1966 because of arthritis. Six years later he became the youngest baseball player ever inducted into the Baseball Hall of Fame.

Sandy Koufax set a National League record in 1965 when he struck out 382 batters.

My schedule is already full." —HENRY KISSINGER

Ray Kroc
fast-food entrepreneur ★ 1902–1984

What do paper cups, milk-shake mixers, and McDonald's all have in common? Ray Kroc.

Kroc was a paper-cup salesman in 1922. One of his big customers was Earl Prince. Prince had invented the Multimixer, a speedy five-spindle mixer. Kroc became the exclusive salesman for the Multimixer for 17 years.

In 1954, he visited a pair of his Multimixer customers, Mac and Dick McDonald. The McDonald brothers had a little restaurant in San Bernardino, California. The menu was simple: shakes, burgers, fries. It was cheap: 15¢ burgers. It was fast: The food rolled out in assembly-line fashion. Kroc convinced the brothers to let him start duplicating their restaurant. The first franchised McDonald's opened in Des Plaines, Illinois, the following year. (The site is now a McDonald's museum.) Within six years, hungry customers were chowing down across the country at 130 McDonald's restaurants.

Ray Kroc enjoying a burger. There are now 20,000 McDonald's around the world.

Kroc eventually bought out the brothers. He grew the McDonald's business and made the fast-food eateries famous for their quality, speed, and cleanliness. By 1963, Kroc could brag that one billion McDonald's burgers had been sold—and he did, on neon signs right under every restaurant's famous golden arches.

Michelle Kwan
Olympian ★ 1980–

When competitive figure skater Michelle Kwan takes the ice, she always wears a good-luck charm she got from her Chinese grandmother. But she doesn't depend just on luck. Years of hard work and long hours of practice have made Kwan one of the nation's brightest and talented young women on ice. Between 1992 and 2000, Kwan took home 51 gold medals, 17 silver medals, and 4 bronze medals in international skating competitions. Three of those golds were for World Professional Championships, four were for U.S. championships, and one of the silvers was the 1998 Olympic medal.

Kwan starting skating when she was five years old. She was the Junior World Champion at 13. At the 1998 U.S. National Championship, Kwan became the first female skater at the event ever to be awarded a perfect score—make that seven perfect scores for technical ability and eight perfect scores for artistry.

In 2002, Kwan finished first at the U.S. National Championship, and third at the Winter Olympics in Salt Lake City, Utah.

Michelle Kwan, who had hoped for a gold, took home a bronze medal at the 2002 Winter Olympics.

"The camera is an instrument that teaches

Migrant Mother *(1936) is one of Dorothea Lange's most famous photos. The woman pictured is 32-year-old Florence Thompson, a Cherokee from Oklahoma.*

Dorothea Lange
photographer ★ c.1895—1965

The Great Depression set the country reeling. Dorothea Lange caught the fear, failure, and despair of many Americans on film.

Lange was a portrait photographer in San Francisco. She couldn't overlook the people standing on breadlines for food handouts. She couldn't ignore the misery of people who'd come to California looking for work. Lange turned her camera on them. She and a university economist put together a report on the effects of the Depression. The report included Lange's photos. The federal government responded by building the first two migrant camps in California. These camps had toilets, showers, and stoves.

In 1935, Lange went to work for what became the Farm Security Administration (FSA). She documented the effect of the Depression on rural people and showed how the FSA was helping them. During the summers of 1936 to 1938, Lange spent time with farm people in Oklahoma and other Dust Bowl areas. Her pictures helped inspire support for government relief programs.

During World War II, Lange photographed Japanese-American internment camps on the West Coast of the U.S. In the 1950s, she produced photos of everyday family life.

Lewis Latimer
inventor ★ 1848—1928

Lewis Latimer is famous for his contributions to two of the world's most important inventions: the telephone and electric lighting.

Latimer, a draftsman in a Boston patent office, secured his own patent for a bathroom for train cars in 1874. Two years later, he feverishly drew the patent sketches for **Alexander Graham Bell**'s telephone. They were submitted with Bell's patent application just hours ahead of a competitor.

Latimer improved the way carbon filaments were mounted in incadescent lights. This made the Latimer lamp, patented in 1881, last longer. The following year he invented a superior carbon filament.

Latimer became a widely recognized authority on electric lighting. He oversaw the first lighting plants installed in New York, Philadelphia, and Montreal. In 1890, **Thomas Edison** hired him to head his legal department. Latimer drew the company's intricate patent sketches and defended those patents in court against piracy (unauthorized use). He also found time to continue inventing. Latimer secured patents for a room cooling/disinfecting device used in hospitals (1886); a locking rack for hats, coats, and umbrellas (1896); and a special bookshelf (1905).

people how to see without a camera." — DOROTHEA LANGE

Esteé Lauder
cosmetics entrepreneur ★ 1908—

Everything about Esteé Lauder—her products, packaging, advertising, and most of all, *herself*—suggested beauty and elegance.

Lauder started off mixing her own beauty products in her New York kitchen in the 1940s. She sold them herself, along with skin creams her chemist uncle concocted, in local beauty salons. Lauder knew two things would make her cosmetics business a success: perfect products and a personal touch. She had plenty of both. Lauder charmed and badgered department store buyers into selling her cosmetics line. To attract customers, she always gave them a free gift. This is now a standard marketing technique in the cosmetics industry.

By the 1960s, Esteé Lauder, Inc., was an international company with a full line of women's and men's beauty products. By 1993, Lauder was on the *Forbes* 400 list of people whose wealth was valued at $300 million or more. As of 2001, the company Esteé Lauder founded controlled 45% of the cosmetics market.

Jacob Lawrence
painter ★ 1917—2000

In 1938, sculptor Augusta Savage helped a fellow African-American artist, Jacob Lawrence, get a job with the federal Works Progress Administration (WPA). Lawrence, who lived in Harlem, New York, earned about $24 a week and had to turn over two paintings to the WPA every week. He began work in what became his signature style: series of paintings that tell a story. Some of his earliest subjects were **Harriet Tubman**, **John Brown**, and **Frederick Douglass**.

Lawrence's figures represent people in a very stylized way, much like African sculptures. He painted bold, stark shapes in strikingly vivid color combinations. He used patterns and angles to create unusual effects. His work has a flat, almost abstract, quality to it but is powerfully emotional.

When Lawrence was 23, he received a fellowship that allowed him to work on the piece that first brought him fame and fortune: *The Migration of the Negro* (1940–1941). The 60 dramatic panels of *Migration* explore the poverty, hope, and pain experienced by the thousands of African Americans who left the rural South for the urban North between 1910 and 1940. Lawrence became an art world sensation. He went on to paint acclaimed series such as *Life in Harlem* (1943) and *Struggle: From the History of the American People* (1955).

"One great cause of failure is

Mother Ann Lee
Shaker leader ★ 1736—1784

These Shaker sisters are shown around 1830, when Shakerism was near its peak.

Ann Lee, a former English millworker, belonged to the United Society of Believers in Christ's Second Appearing. The Believers were also called Shakers because of the shaking and dancing that went on at their meetings. Lee rose to the top of the congregation, who called her "Mother." She preached that God was both male and female, that men and women were equal, and that sexual relations were unnecessary. Lee also believed she was the spirit of Jesus Christ.

In 1776, Mother Ann had a vision about America. She and eight followers fled England for the colonies and started a Shaker community in Watervliet, New York. It was difficult to attract followers at first, but Lee was very charismatic and there was a great awakening of religious feeling sweeping the area. The Shakers' simple lifestyle and ideals of gender and racial equality also appealed to many people. By the time Mother Lee died, 11 Shaker communities had started. There, men and women lived in separate houses. They raised their own food and invented tools like the clothespin and the circular saw. The Shakers became famous for their simple, handcrafted homes and furniture.

Bruce Lee
actor ★ 1940—1973

Bruce Lee, the "Fastest Fist in the East," single-handedly—actually with both hands *and* flying feet—made kung fu popular in the United States.

Born in San Francisco, California, Lee was raised in Hong Kong. He returned to the U.S. in 1958. Through intensive martial arts study and practice, Bruce Lee turned his body into a virtual fighting machine. He was so muscular he could do push-ups on one finger. In 1964, his lightning moves brought the champs to their knees and fans to their feet at the Long Beach International Karate Championship in California. It was the first major demonstration of kung fu in the U.S.

Lee was immediately signed to play the sidekick Kato on television's *The Green Hornet* (1966). When further media roles didn't follow, he went to Hong Kong to make action films. They made Lee a very popular—and wealthy—star. His films were released in the U.S. as *Fist of Fury* (1972) and *The Chinese Connection* (1973). They were box-office hits. Hollywood took notice and gave Lee money to make an American film. But a month before *Enter the Dragon* was released in 1973, Bruce Lee suddenly died of a brain swelling. *Return of the Dragon*, made earlier, was released after his death.

Lee did all of his own amazing acrobatic stunts in his movies.

lack of concentration." — BRUCE LEE

Robert E. Lee
Confederate general ★ 1807–1870

President **Abraham Lincoln** offered him command of the entire federal army. But Robert E. Lee followed his beloved Southern state, Virginia, into the Confederacy.

Lee became head of the Army of Northern Virginia in 1862. Throughout the Civil War, he was handicapped by shortages of soldiers and supplies, but he was a brilliant military thinker and an inspirational leader. Lee repelled Union forces during the 1862 Peninsular Campaign. After a victory at the second battle of Bull Run (Manassas) he marched his army north, invading Maryland. The battle of Antietam was a costly draw for General Lee, but he continued his bold strikes. He defeated the Union army at the battles of Fredericksburg and Chancellorsville, Virginia (1863). Then General Lee and his men headed for Gettysburg, Pennsylvania. The bloody battle raged for three days (July 1–3, 1863). When it was over, 28,000 Confederates, more than one third of Lee's army, were killed, captured, or wounded. The survivors were forced into retreat.

After a 10-month siege, Lee lost control of Petersburg, Virginia, the supply link to Richmond. The capital of the Confederacy fell on April 3, 1865. Lee's army was shoeless, ragged, exhausted, and starving. On April 9, General Robert E. Lee surrendered at Appomattox Court House and went home. He later served as the head of Washington College in Lexington, Virginia. It's now called Washington and Lee.

Spike Lee
film director ★ 1957–

Spike Lee uses hip humor and cool filmmaking skills to tackle some hot topics in his films. He's explored urban racial tension (*Do the Right Thing,* 1989), interracial couples (*Jungle Fever,* 1991), and urban violence (*Summer of Sam,* 1999).

Lee's first widely distributed film was *She's Gotta Have It* (1986). Shooting time was 12 days on one location. The budget was $175,000. Box office gross? $7 million.

Success made it possible for Lee to get Hollywood backing for his next features. One of his most ambitious films was *Malcolm X.* Lee's epic biography of the slain African-American leader opened in 1992 and was a box-office success. Lee also received critical acclaim for his documentary *4 Little Girls* (1997).

He's directed music videos for artists like **Stevie Wonder** and **Miles Davis**. His Nike commercials are legendary, especially the ones featuring Lee and **Michael Jordan**. Spike Lee's work has helped open up the media world for other African Americans.

Spike Lee writes, directs, and often edits and stars in his own movies. Many of them are set in Brooklyn, New York, where he grew up.

Carl Lewis won 65 long-jump national and international competitions in a row, from 1981 to 1991.

Carl Lewis
Olympian ★ 1961—

Carl Lewis won nine gold Olympic medals and one silver. He was undefeated in the long jump for 10 consecutive years. He set world records for the 100-meter sprint. Lewis, like his hero, **Jesse Owens**, was one of the great all-time track-and-field stars.

Lewis qualified for the 1984 Olympics in Los Angeles. He came home with four gold medals. He sped across the finish line at 28 miles per hour to win the 100-meter race. Lewis's long jump beat the competition by a foot. In the 200-meter sprint, he set an Olympic record at the time (19.80 seconds). He ran anchor (fourth runner) and helped his team win the 4x400-meter relay. Lewis also won gold medals at the 1988 Seoul Olympics (long jump and 100-meter sprint). He did it again at the 1992 Barcelona Olympics with a gold medal as part of the relay team. He soared a record-breaking 28 feet, 5½ inches to become the first person to win the Olympic long jump three times.

At 35, Carl Lewis was still a champ. His mighty long-jump leap at the 1996 Atlanta Olympics earned him his ninth gold medal.

John L. Lewis
labor leader ★ 1880—1969

This giant of the labor rights movement stomped through union halls and government and business offices. He left friends and enemies in his dust.

John L. Lewis, a former mine worker, was president of the United Mine Workers of America (UMWA) union from 1920 through 1960 and of the Congress of Industrial Organizations (CIO) from 1936 through 1940. It was a controversial reign.

Lewis rebuilt the flagging UMWA in the 1930s. His forceful leadership brought higher salaries and improved working conditions for skilled workers. Then Lewis expanded his union plans. At a 1935 American Federation of Labor (AFL) convention, Lewis proposed organizing unskilled laborers. The AFL disagreed. Lewis

pulled out (and *punched* out an opponent as he left!). The UMWA became part of the CIO, the new group of unions Lewis formed. Lewis also sent out UMWA people to help start other unions, such as the United Steelworkers of America and the United Auto Workers.

Meriwether Lewis and William Clark
explorers ★ 1774–1809 (Lewis); 1770–1838 (Clark)

President **Thomas Jefferson** had just spent $15 million on the Louisiana Purchase, France's former lands between the Mississippi River and the Rocky Mountains. Now he needed to see what he'd bought for the nation.

The president's secretary, Meriwether Lewis, and Lewis's friend, William Clark, agreed to organize a Corps of Discovery. They put together their expedition between December 1803 and May 1804. Lewis organized the supplies. He brought "gifts for the Indians," everything from beads, calico shirts, and fishhooks, to silver peace medals. He packed scientific books and instruments, ammunition, medicine, and food. He also bought 13 red leather-bound journals for recording the trip. Clark trained the crew, which included his slave, York, an interpreter, and 41 river men and soldiers.

On May 14, 1804, Clark and the Corps of Discovery set sail up the Missouri River from Camp Wood in Illinois. Lewis joined them with more supplies upriver a few days later.

The explorers traveled through 7,689 miles of wilderness. They followed the Missouri River north through the Dakotas and west through Montana. Then they crossed the Rocky Mountains and followed the Snake and Columbia rivers west to the Pacific Ocean. The round-trip journey took two years, four months, and nine days. It was adventurous—and dangerous.

In the Great Plains, game was plentiful but winter temperatures could drop to -45° F. In the mountains, the starving crew ate tree-bark soup. Lewis and Clark's route took them along uncharted rivers with treacherous, roiling rapids. They traveled through snow and hail "the size of pigeons' eggs." There were snakebites, fleabites, and frostbite, and even an attack by a grizzly bear.

William Clark's sketch of a trout, seen on the expedition.

> "... we suffered everything Cold, Hunger & Fatigue could impart, or the Keenest Anxiety for the fate of [the] Expedition in which our whole Souls were embarked."
>
> **— MERIWETHER LEWIS**

Guided by **Sacajawea**, Lewis and Clark traveled through lands peopled by many different groups of Native Americans. Most of them helped the explorers, providing food, shelter, and geographical information.

Throughout their trip, Lewis and Clark both kept incredibly detailed journals about the nearly 50 tribes they met and about the 178 plants and 122 animals they had never seen (or *eaten*) before. They collected many specimens and once sent back a "barking squirrel" (prairie dog) to the president.

Lewis and Clark ended their journey in St. Louis on September 23, 1806. Lewis was appointed governor of the Louisiana Territory in 1807. He died two years later. Clark became brigadier general of the Louisiana militia and then governor of the Missouri Territory and superintendent of Indian affairs in the West.

Maya Lin
artist, architect ★ 1959—

In 1981, a committee of architects, sculptors, and designers chose one design out of 1,421 entries submitted for a Vietnam veterans memorial. The winning design was a V-shaped sculpture of polished black granite, inscribed with all 58,175 names of the armed services men and women killed or missing in action in Vietnam. The winning designer was Maya Lin, a 21-year-old graduate student at Yale.

Lin's Vietnam Veterans Memorial was dedicated in 1982. Her design was startling and controversial. Some people called it a "big, black scar" and thought it was insulting. Many more people found the experience of walking around "The Wall" and feeling the names on its smooth walls powerfully moving. It is one of the most visited memorials in the country.

Maya Lin made her first model of the Vietnam Veterans Memorial in her college dining room. She used mashed potatoes!

Lin's works are very specific to their sites. She integrates natural forms and fluid lines. She uses materials such as water, wood, and rocks to create architectural sculpture that is meant to be touched—and touching. Lin's Civil Rights Memorial (1989) in Montgomery, Alabama, is a sheet of water running over a simple granite table. It is inscribed with names of fallen civil rights leaders and a biblical phrase: "We are not satisfied and we shall not be satisfied until justice rolls down like waters and righteousness like a mighty stream." Her sculpture Women's Table (1993) at Yale University uses a spiral of 0s and numerals to signify the number of women enrolled in Yale over time.

Maya Lin describes herself as an artist rather than an architect. To avoid being labeled and limited, she gave up making monuments in 1989. She has designed homes, landscapes, and art installations, such as Wave Field (1993) at the University of Michigan. Lin studied flight, fluid dynamics, and water waves to create the 10,000-square-foot work of sculpted grass. Her piece 10 Degrees North at the Rockefeller Foundation in New York City uses a world map with unique projections and icons to remind people that "we're looking at the world from our point of view." Lin also did innovative designs for the **Langston Hughes** Library in Clinton, Tennessee; the Reading a Garden installation at the Cleveland Library (Ohio); and the Museum of African Art in New York City. In 2002, Lin's winter garden opened in American Express's office in Minneapolis, Minnesota. It has a warped floor meant to suggest the curve of the earth and a wall of flowing water that freezes in the winter.

Lin runs her own design studio in New York. She has won numerous awards, including the Presidential Design Award.

Abraham Lincoln
16th president ★ 1809—1865

This is the last studio photograph taken of Abraham Lincoln. It was made on February 5, 1865.

Plain-faced and plainspoken, but complex, compassionate, and smart, "Honest Abe" is often called America's greatest president.

Abraham Lincoln was born in a log cabin in Kentucky. He grew up on the frontier, with about a year's worth of formal education picked up here and there. Lincoln was mainly self-schooled, but ambitious. In between reading his beloved Shakespeare, the Bible, or *Robinson Crusoe*, young Abe worked as a fence rail-splitter, a ferryman, a store clerk, a surveyor, and a postmaster. He also borrowed some books and taught himself to be a lawyer.

Tall and craggy, Lincoln had a folksy way about him that people loved. They also loved his jokes, puns, and funny stories. But Lincoln was a serious thinker and a persuasive writer and speaker. In 1858, the Illinois Republican party convinced him to run for senator against **Stephen A. Douglas**. The famous Lincoln-Douglas campaign debates on slavery and statehood brought Lincoln national attention. He lost the senate seat but won the Republican bid for the presidency two years later.

Before Lincoln even took office, 11 Southern states had seceded and formed the Confederate States of America. A month after his inauguration in March 1861, the Confederates attacked Fort Sumter in South Carolina. That which Lincoln loathed and feared most had begun—civil war!

The Civil War dominated Abraham Lincoln's presidency (1861–1865). He often walked through the streets of Washington late at night, alone and deeply troubled by the horror of the Civil War. People died in unprecedented numbers. Abraham Lincoln's most famously powerful and moving speech, the Gettysburg Address (1863), was delivered on the Pennsylvania battlefield where nearly 28,000 Confederate and 23,000 Union soldiers died in just three days of fighting.

But Abraham Lincoln also believed that the *United* States had to be preserved. The president himself thought slavery was wrong, but he didn't think the U.S. Constitution gave him or the federal government the power to ban it. So Lincoln found political solutions. He issued the Emancipation Proclamation (1862), which freed all slaves in rebellious areas as of January 1, 1863. The proclamation said nothing about the status of slaves in the Union or border states.

After firing a series of unsuccessful generals, President Lincoln made General **Ulysses S. Grant** commander of the Union forces in 1864. The war came to a bloody close a year later.

Abraham Lincoln didn't live to help rebuild the nation he had struggled to save. On April 14, 1865, President and Mrs. Lincoln went to Ford's Theater. John Wilkes Booth, a Confederate fanatic, burst into the presidential box and shot Lincoln in the head.

Lincoln's body lay in state in 14 cities. Thousands of mourners paid their respects. The president was then buried in Springfield, Illinois.

Charles Lindbergh
aviator ★ 1902–1974

On May 21, 1927, a startled fisherman looked up as a plane buzzed his boat. The pilot shouted down "Which way is Ireland?" It was Charles Lindbergh, in the 27th hour of his historic solo flight over the Atlantic Ocean.

In the early 1920s, Lindbergh worked as a stunt-flying barnstormer and as an airmail pilot. In 1927, he went after a $25,000 prize offered for the first transatlantic flight.

On May 20, 1927, Lindbergh took off from Roosevelt Field, New York. To keep the plane's weight down, he didn't even take a radio or a parachute. Lindbergh spent the next 33½ hours

Charles Lindbergh, the "Lone Eagle," in front of his single-engine, 28-foot plane, Spirit of St. Louis, *in 1927.*

in the crammed cockpit of the *Spirit of St. Louis*. He ate only sandwiches and often had to fight sleepiness. He flew 3,600 miles, sometimes through fog and ice. When he landed outside Paris, France, a crowd of 100,000 stormed the landing strip. Lindbergh was an instant celebrity.

Back in New York, Lindbergh was treated to the largest ticker-tape parade in American history. He became *Time* magazine's first Man of the Year. Lindbergh then flew the *Spirit of St. Louis* all over the country. Thirty million people turned out to see him on his three-month tour. Lindbergh's commitment and fame helped expand the aviation industry.

Jack London
author ★ 1876–1916

By the time he was 22, Jack London had already been a sailor, a hobo, a college student, and a gold prospector. Then he chose his toughest job—author.

London started on a colorful life after a poor childhood in Oakland, California. He enlisted on a boat sailing for Japan in 1892. Five years later, he headed for Alaska and the Klondike gold rush. London took the long way home—he rafted 2,000 miles down the Yukon River.

Back in San Francisco, London went to work in a factory. He decided to get out of this dreary job through writing. London set himself a goal: 1,000 words per day. With the life he'd led, he had plenty of raw material for his adventure stories. London struggled for a few years trying to sell his work. Then in 1900, his short-story collection, *The Son of the Wolf*, inspired by his Klondike trip, struck gold.

Best-seller followed best-seller: *The Call of the Wild* (1903), *The Sea-Wolf* (1904), *White Fang* (1906). London wrote more than 50 books, including novels, short-story collections, and political essays. He became the highest-paid writer of his time—and one of the most popular.

"I would rather be a superb meteor...than a

Nancy Lopez

golfer ★ 1957—

Nancy Lopez was practically born a golf champ. As a child, she put in long hours of practice. By the time she was 12, she was winning competitions. Lopez became a professional golfer in 1978. She immediately broke several records and became the first woman to win five Ladies Professional Golf Association tournaments in a row. She also earned nearly $200,000, more than any other male or female rookie pro golfer at the time.

Lopez maintained this winning streak throughout the 1980s. She was the champion in 40 tournaments and became a multimillionaire. In 1987, she was elected to the Ladies Professional Golf Association Hall of Fame.

In 1997, Lopez celebrated winning her 48th career title. She also crossed the $5 million career earnings line. Still a competitive golfer, Lopez is considered one of the most influential women in the sport.

Nancy Lopez shows her strong form.

Joe Louis was famous for his powerful left hook and two-fisted punches. That's what knocked out Max Schmeling.

Joe Louis

boxer ★ 1914—1981

Joe Louis's gloves flew like lightning, but connected like wet cement. That's why he was the longest-reigning heavyweight champion of the world.

The "Brown Bomber" grew up in Detroit. When he started boxing, he won 50 out of 54 amateur bouts. All but seven were knockouts. Louis was just as successful when he turned pro—27 wins, 23 of them knockouts. In 1935, Louis became the first African American to be named Associated Press Athlete of the Year. Two years later, he fought his way to the world's heavyweight crown.

Louis was heavyweight champ from 1937 to 1949. One of his most famous bouts took place in New York in 1938. Adolf Hitler was in power in Germany. He praised German boxer Max Schmeling as an example of the dominance of the white race, one of the hateful ideas of Nazism. Louis was already beloved by the African-American community at a time when segregation and racism were widespread in the U.S. The "Brown Bomber" stepped into the ring as more than a world-class boxer. He was the hero and hope of millions of black people. For many Americans of all colors, he represented the power of democracy over tyranny. Louis flattened Schmeling in two minutes, four seconds. KO!

sleepy and permanent planet." —JACK LONDON

Nat Love
cowboy ★ 1854—1921

The title of his popular 1907 autobiography says it all: *The Life and Adventures of Nat Love, Better Known in the Cattle Country as "Deadwood Dick," Written by Himself: A True History of Slavery Days, Life on the Great Cattle Ranges and on the Plains of the "Wild and Woolly" West, Based on Facts, and Personal Experiences of the Author.* Love was born a slave in Tennessee in 1854. Like many former slaves, he migrated west after the Civil War. In the late 1860s, nearly 5,000 men, or one out of seven cowboys, were African-American. Love could ride, rope, and shoot with the best of them. He was famous for breaking in wild broncos and got his nickname, "Deadwood Dick," from his champion performance at a Dakota rodeo when he was only 22. By 1889, Love had tired of the long cattle drives, the gambling and gunfights, and the hard life of a cowboy. He dismounted and got on the "Iron Horse" instead, working as a Pullman porter on the railroad.

Nat Love roped, saddled, and mounted a wild mustang in nine minutes, shot 14 bulls-eyes, and won $200 to become champion at the Deadwood, Dakota, rodeo.

Juliette Gordon Low
Girl Scouts of the U.S.A. founder ★ 1860—1927

At first, the uniforms were dark blouses, long skirts, and black wool stockings, not the familiar green scouting outfits. Now, there are more than 3.7 million Girl Scouts in the United States, but the original troop was just several girls. The Girl Scouts in America have come a long way!

Girl Scout founder Juliette Gordon Low moved from the United States to Great Britain after marrying. There, she met Sir Robert Baden-Powell in 1911. Baden-Powell was the founder of the Boy Scouts and a similar group called the Girl Guides, which his sister, Agnes, helped run. The Baden-Powells encouraged Low to start Girl Guide troops, too. She did, organizing several troops in England and Scotland.

In 1905, Low's husband died. She returned to her native Savannah, Georgia, in 1912 and brought the Girl Guide movement with her. Low's group quickly became a popular national organization. By 1913, the group had changed its name to Girl Scouts. Low served as first president of the Girl Scouts. She continued to promote this active new option for girls and raised funds for the organization.

Juliette Gordon Low (standing, center) and Girl Scouts in the mid-1920s.

George Lucas
film director, producer ⋆ 1944—

In 1973, George Lucas wrote and produced a low-budget movie called *American Graffiti*. It was a nostalgic story about California teenagers, drive-ins, and drag races. The movie grossed $50 million and got five Oscar nominations.

The boy who loved Flash Gordon and Buck Rogers comics was now a millionaire. He had the vision and power to create a whole new sci-fi world. Lucas wrote a movie myth for the modern age, a classic story of good versus evil, set in a distant galaxy. He added cool, high-tech special effects and blow-out sound effects. When *Star Wars* was released in 1977, it blasted through all box-office records and won seven Academy Awards. Lucas's sensational space saga continued with four more films. The latest is *Star Wars: Episode II, Attack of the Clones* (2002).

George Lucas (l.) helped launch an era of film blockbusters with his Star Wars phenomenon.

In the 1980s, George Lucas teamed up with **Steven Spielberg** and produced the swashbuckling, Oscar-winning Indiana Jones movies. Lucas also founded a special effects company, Industrial Light & Magic, which put the wizardry in the *Harry Potter* movies (2001, 2002, 2003) and the "live" dinosaurs in the *Jurassic Park* movies (1993, 1997, 2001).

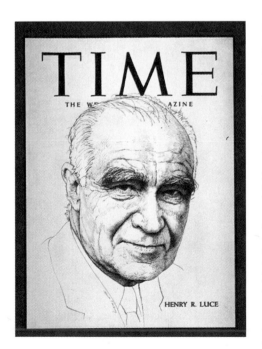

Henry Luce
publisher ⋆ 1898—1967

Henry Luce knew that people were going to be very busy in the new era he called "The American Century." So he cofounded a magazine for the 20th-century American: *Time*.

In 1922, Luce and his partner, Briton Hadden, quit their reporters' jobs, raised $86,000, and went into the magazine business. Hadden oversaw the editorial. Luce handled the finances.

The first issue of *Time* came out on March 3, 1923. The magazine's news articles were organized into handy departments. The feature writing was concise but lively. When Hadden died in 1929, Luce took over as editor, and he started building a media empire.

In 1930, Luce came up with a business magazine called *Fortune*. Six years later, he created the stunning, exciting photojournalism magazine *Life*. Luce also had his finger on the nation's pulse when he launched *Sports Illustrated* in 1954.

Henry Luce served as editor-in-chief of Time, Inc., until 1964. The media group he founded, AOL/Time Warner, is now one of the world's largest.

"If men were angels, no government

General MacArthur in 1942.

Douglas MacArthur
general ★ 1880–1964

Douglas MacArthur was brilliant—he graduated with the third highest grade point in the history of West Point. He was flamboyant—he wore a long scarf and carried a riding crop into battle in World War I (and received seven Silver Stars for bravery). And he was egotistical—he fought with his commanding officer . . . the president!

From 1935 to 1942, MacArthur was military commander of the Philippines, which was then a commonwealth of the U.S. When the Japanese invaded the Philippines in 1941, MacArthur's forces were overwhelmed. The general was ordered to evacuate. He vowed to return.

MacArthur was named supreme commander of the Allied forces in the Southwest Pacific during World War II. His successful "island hopping" offensive targeted specific Pacific islands for recapture. By 1944, the Philippines were recaptured. A year later, atom bombs had ended World War II. On September 2, 1945, the Japanese formally surrendered to MacArthur aboard a U.S. battleship in Tokyo Bay. Allied forces then occupied Japan, where MacArthur served as military commander until 1950.

That same year, war broke out between North and South Korea. South Korea was backed by U.S. forces under General MacArthur. U.S. forces later battled with China, North Korea's ally. While President **Harry Truman** was trying to work out a cease-fire, General MacArthur issued an unauthorized military threat to the Chinese. President Truman issued an authorized message to MacArthur: He was fired.

Dolley Madison
first lady ★ 1768–1849

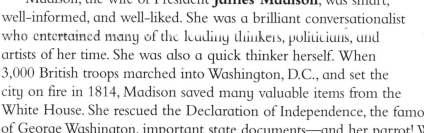

As first lady, the vivacious "Queen Dolley" Madison set new standards in fashion, entertainment, and food. She made turban headdresses all the rage. She liked American dishes served at her famous official dinners and receptions. She even convinced Congress to spend money on fixing up the decrepit White House.

Madison, the wife of President **James Madison**, was smart, well-informed, and well-liked. She was a brilliant conversationalist who entertained many of the leading thinkers, politicians, and artists of her time. She was also a quick thinker herself. When 3,000 British troops marched into Washington, D.C., and set the city on fire in 1814, Madison saved many valuable items from the White House. She rescued the Declaration of Independence, the famous Gilbert Stuart painting of George Washington, important state documents—and her parrot! When the British finally left, Dolley lobbied to rebuild America's capital.

would be necessary." — JAMES MADISON

James Madison
fourth president ★ 1751–1836

The "Father of the Constitution" was actually a slight, boyish-looking man who weighed only 100 pounds. But at the Constitutional Convention of 1787, James Madison loomed large.

The convention lasted 86 days. Madison, a deep political thinker, argued his points on 71 of those days. He was the only person to take notes on how the Constitution was created. Madison also thought it did not go far enough in protecting citizens' rights. As a member of the House of Representatives, he led the fight to pass what is now the Bill of Rights (1791).

Madison served as **Thomas Jefferson**'s secretary of state and was then elected to two terms as president himself (1809–1817). They were not easy terms. "War Hawks" in Madison's Republican party convinced the president to declare war on England for attacking American ships. In the ensuing War of 1812, the British captured Washington, D.C., but Baltimore, Maryland, repelled British attack.

"Mr. Madison's War" was finally over on January 8, 1815, when the British were trounced in New Orleans by General **Andrew Jackson**.

Charles Wilson Peale (1741–1827) painted this miniature of James Madison.

Madonna
singer, actress ★ 1958—

She amazes her audiences and outrages her critics. She's shrewd about business. She's savvy about her image, whether that's dance-club queen, **Marilyn Monroe** vamp, spiritual new mother, or pumped-up rocker. She's a brash performer who puts on a good show. This Queen of Pop intends to reign for a long time.

Madonna Louise Veronica Ciccone grew up in Detroit, Michigan. She first appeared on the pop music scene in 1983. Her hit songs such as "Holiday," "Material Girl," "Ray of Light," and "What It Feels Like for a Girl" have brought her international fame. Her on-stage antics have made her infamous.

Grammy-winning Madonna has 24 hit singles that went gold. She is tied with the Beatles for second place behind **Elvis Presley** for most gold singles in U.S. history.

Madonna has also starred in several movies, including *Desperately Seeking Susan* (1985), *Dick Tracy* (1990), *A League of Their Own* (1992), and *Evita* (1996).

"You can't separate peace from freedom because

Malcolm X
Muslim leader ★ 1925–1965

Malcolm Little went into jail an angry young man. He came out Malcolm X, a self-educated, radicalized Muslim.

While he was serving a sentence for burglary, Little learned about the Nation of Islam, a Black Muslim group. Released in 1952, he studied with **Elijah Muhammad**, the leader of the Nation of Islam. Malcolm Little became Malcolm X. (The *X* symbolized the fact that many African Americans' real names had been lost generations ago during slavery.)

Malcolm X rose through the ranks of the Muslim ministry. His message was radical: Black people had to upgrade their lives "by any means necessary." He promoted black separatism, black businesses, and clean living. Membership in the Nation of Islam rose from 400 to 10,000 by 1960 because of him.

In 1964, Malcolm X split with Elijah Muhammad over the identity and direction of the Nation of Islam. He traveled to Mecca, Saudi Arabia, where he met Muslims of all races. The pilgrimage changed Malcolm's life. When he came back, he planned to work with black civil rights groups and even with some white people.

Malcolm X didn't get to implement his new ideas. On February 21, 1965, he was gunned down in the Audubon Ballroom in New York City's Harlem. Three members of the Nation of Islam were convicted of the murder.

Wilma Mankiller
Cherokee chief ★ 1945—

Wilma Mankiller, a Cherokee, became the first woman Native American chief in 1985.

Mankiller grew up poor in Mankiller Flats, Oklahoma. In 1957, the Mankillers moved to San Francisco, California. There Wilma was inspired by the American Native Indian Movement (AIM) of the 1960s.

After college, Mankiller returned to Oklahoma. She got an entry-level job with the Cherokee Nation. She worked her way up and was promoted to chief in 1985 to finish out her boss's term. Mankiller was elected in her own right in 1987 and reelected in 1991 and 1995.

During Chief Mankiller's years in office, tribal membership increased to 140,000 people and revenues skyrocketed. She was a powerful lobbyist for health, education, and job training programs. She worked hard to revive cultural pride through programs such as the Institute for Cherokee Literacy, where young tribal members learned to read and write the Cherokee language.

no one can be at peace unless he has his freedom."

— MALCOLM X

Horace Mann
educator ★ 1796—1859

As a college student, Horace Mann was an outstanding orator and debater. He would need those skills to convince the nation of the need for "free, universal, and public education." Mann was elected to the Massachusetts legislature in 1827. He won important reforms in the care of the mentally ill. He worked to repeal the laws that threw debtors in prison. He studied Massachusetts schools and found that the teachers were ill-educated, the students were harshly dealt with, and the schoolhouses were falling apart.

When Massachusetts set up the country's first State Board of Education in 1837, Mann gave up a successful law career to become the board's secretary. His ideas about better-paid teachers and longer school years often faced stiff opposition because people did not want to pay for public education. But Mann was eventually able to build more public schools, including 50 high schools. He opened "normal schools" for teacher training and raised teachers' salaries. In 1848, he was elected to the U.S. Congress. Mann took his education plans to the national level.

Mickey Mantle
baseball player ★ 1931—1995

"The Mick" had two things going for him that would eventually make him a baseball superstar—speed and strength.

As a child, Mickey Mantle practiced switch-hitting, batting left and right. He was a high-school ballplayer in Commerce, Oklahoma, when a Yankees scout signed him up in 1949.

Mantle spent two seasons with the Yankees' minor league team. He played right field, then center field for the Yankees, and was a disappointment at first. But by 1952, "The Mick" began to get in the swing. His batting average rose to .311. He smacked out 23 home runs, including a record-breaker. Four years later, he won the Triple Crown for highest batting average, most home runs, and most RBIs (runs batted in).

Roger Maris (l.) with Mickey Mantle (r.) in 1961.

The Yankees and "The Mick" were a winning combination. Mantle scored three Most Valuable Player Awards (1956, 1957, 1962) and appeared in 20 All-Star games. While he was on their team, the Yankees won 12 pennant races and seven World Series. In 1961, Mantle and fellow Yankee Roger Maris were slugging it out to see who could beat **Babe Ruth**'s single-season home-run record. Mantle's season was cut short due to an infection, so Maris won with 61 home runs to Mantle's 54. This record wasn't broken until 1998 (by **Mark McGwire**).

Wynton Marsalis

jazz musician ★ 1961—

Forty acclaimed classical or jazz albums. Nine Grammys. One great trumpet player: Wynton Marsalis.

Marsalis was born in New Orleans, Louisiana, the birthplace of jazz. A genius of a trumpet player, he studied classical music at the prestigious Juilliard School in New York. He also played with Art Blakey and Herbie Hancock's jazz groups.

An expert on jazz history, Marsalis believes modern jazz should honor its roots. His recordings, such as "Black Codes from the Underground" (1985), reflect this idea. So does one of his most important works to date, "Blood on the Fields" (1995), a stirring composition for voices and orchestra that sets a love story amid the harsh world of slavery.

In 1996, *Time* magazine named Marsalis one of the 25 most influential people in America. Marsalis has composed original jazz music for concerts, film, television, and dance, including pieces for **Alvin Ailey** and Twyla Tharp. He's the artistic director of Jazz at Lincoln Center, a department he helped create. He's also a leader in music education and has won a Peabody Award for his television series, *Marsalis on Music*.

Wynton Marsalis's "Blood on the Fields" won the Pulitzer prize for music in 1997. It was the first jazz composition ever awarded the honor.

George C. Marshall

secretary of state, general ★ 1880—1959

General George C. Marshall was a career military man and a clear, strategic thinker with incredible organization skills. In 1939, President **Franklin Roosevelt** appointed him Army chief of staff. World War II had started in Europe. Marshall urged Congress to help the U.S. prepare for war. He lobbied for drafting soldiers, for a bigger military budget, and for increased military manufacturing. Once the United States was drawn into World War II, General Marshall oversaw planning, policy, and military relations with European Allied commanders. President **Harry Truman** called him the man who "won the war."

In 1947, Truman chose George Marshall as his secretary of state. Postwar Europe was in ruins; millions of people were starving. Secretary Marshall spearheaded the European Recovery Plan, which everybody called the Marshall Plan. In four years, the U.S. underwrote $13 billion worth of food, funds, goods, and machinery to rebuild Europe. The plan worked. By 1951, European farm and manufacturing productivity was above prewar levels. There was political stability. It was the greatest humanitarian aid project ever launched. It won George C. Marshall the Nobel Peace Prize in 1953.

"Equal means getting the same thing,

John Marshall
secretary of state, U.S. Supreme Court justice ★ 1755—1835

John Marshall went from being secretary of state to being chief justice of the Supreme Court . . . overnight!

Marshall was one of President **John Adams**'s "midnight appointments." On his way out of office, Adams put many judges in place. A Federalist, Adams wanted to make sure that his party's ideas about a strong central government would survive incoming Democratic-Republican President **Thomas Jefferson**'s term. Marshall's decision on the case *Marbury vs. Madison* in 1803 firmly established the idea of judicial review. This meant that the Supreme Court could void an act of Congress if that act went against the U.S. Constitution. Marshall's explanation of judicial review also showed that the executive, legislative, and judicial branches were equal partners in a government of "checks and balances."

Justice Marshall served 34 years on the bench.

The motto carved on the Supreme Court is "Equal Justice Under Law." Thurgood Marshall (center) helped make this motto ring true for all Americans.

Thurgood Marshall
U.S. Supreme Court justice ★ 1908—1993

On October 2, 1967, "Mr. Civil Rights" became "Your Honor." Thurgood Marshall was sworn in as the first African-American Supreme Court justice.

From 1939 to 1961, Marshall headed the Legal Defense and Educational Fund of the National Association for the Advancement of Colored People (NAACP). He spearheaded the NAACP's legal battle to integrate universities, schools, housing, transportation, and other public facilities. He organized legal strategies to fight unjust laws that barred African Americans from voting, serving on juries, and belonging to political parties.

As an NAACP lawyer, Marshall argued 32 cases before the U.S. Supreme Court. He won 27 of them. The most famous was *Brown v. Board of Education of Topeka* (1954). Marshall successfully argued that "separate, but equal" education policies were unconstitutional. The nine Supreme Court justices agreed with him *unanimously*! The decision was a civil rights milestone.

In 1961, President **John F. Kennedy** nominated Thurgood Marshall for a federal judgeship. President **Lyndon B. Johnson** nominated Marshall for solicitor general in 1965. He was the first black person in the job. Two years later, Johnson nominated Marshall for the Supreme Court. Justice Marshall sat on the bench for 24 years. His rulings showed a respect for individual rights and a commitment to social and political equality.

at the same time, in the same place." — THURGOOD MARSHALL

The Marx Brothers in Duck Soup. From l. to r.: Chico (Leonard Marx); Zeppo (Herbert Marx); Groucho (Julius Henry Marx); and Harpo (Adolph Marx).

Marx Brothers
comedy actors ★ 1886–1961 (Chico);
1888–1964 (Harpo); 1890–1977 (Groucho)

Chico, Groucho, Harpo—their stage names alone were funny. Add the sight gags, the zinging quips, and the hilarious puns, and you've got the Marx Brothers, America's funniest family act.

The Marx Brothers got their start in vaudeville, and then moved to Broadway musicals. But their real claim to fame are the 12 Hollywood movies they made together, classics such as *The Cocoanut,* (1929), *Animal Crackers* (1930), *Monkey Business* (1931), and *A Night at the Opera* (1935). Each movie had the Marx Brothers trademarks: Rollicking chaos, zany humor, and mocking social commentary tied together by crazy plots and crazier ad libs. Each of the brothers had his own trademark, too. Groucho was the cigar-chomping, fast-talking "professor" with the outlandish mustache. Chico wore a pointed peasant hat and spoke in broken English and made-up Italian. Harpo never spoke at all. He wore a curly wig and a big, baggy coat stuffed with all kinds of props. At the sight of a pretty blond, he'd whip out an old-fashioned car horn, start honking, and give chase. Sometimes a fourth brother, Zeppo (1901–1979), acted the straight man in the middle of the hilarious chaos.

Cotton Mather
minister, writer ★ 1663–1728

Cotton Mather was an unusual man for his times. Like most people in Puritan New England, he believed in witches. Unlike most people, he also believed in advanced medical ideas, like smallpox inoculations.

Enlightenment—scientific *and* spiritual—was Mather's lifelong pursuit. He was a celebrated minister at the Second Church of Boston (Old North Church), one of the largest congregations in America at the time. He wrote nearly 500 works on subjects ranging from theology, history, and biography to medicine and science. In one work, Mather gave detailed instructions for identifying a witch. He was often blamed for the hysteria of the Salem witch trials in 1692, but in fact, he criticized how the trials were conducted.

Mather wrote about witchcraft in Salem and other persecutions in *Wonders of the Invisible World* (1693). His most famous work was *Magnalia Christi Americana* (*The Annals of Christ in America,* 1702). Like much of his work, this book promoted Puritanism.

and that's no great loss, either."

Louis B. Mayer helped found the Academy of Motion Picture Arts and Sciences in 1927. This group gives out the Oscars.

Louis B. Mayer
film entrepreneur ★ 1885–1957

From 1937 to 1945, movie tycoon Louis B. Mayer was the highest-paid boss in America.

Mayer, who was originally from Russia, got his start when he renovated a run-down movie house in Haverill, Massachusetts, in 1907. He quickly turned his business into a chain of theaters. Business boomed when Mayer became the only distributor in the Northeast for the first movie blockbuster, **D.W. Griffith**'s *The Birth of a Nation* (1915). In 1918, the movie mogul went to Hollywood.

Within 10 years, Louis was running MGM (Metro-**Goldwyn**-Mayer). He brought along his brilliant production head, Irving Thalberg. MGM dominated box offices during the 1930s and 1940s. Mayer was a genius at figuring out what the public liked and selling it to them. Under Mayer, MGM turned out spectacles like *Ben Hur* (1925), dramas like *Grand Hotel* (1932), comedies like *Dinner at Eight* (1933), and musicals like *The Wizard of Oz* (1939). The studio's stars included **Clark Gable**, **Elizabeth Taylor**, **Katharine Hepburn**, Spencer Tracy, **Judy Garland**, and the **Marx Brothers**. He ruled MGM with an iron fist and iron-clad contracts.

Willie Mays
baseball player ★ 1931—

Willie Mays hit 660 career home runs, a record topped only by **Hank Aaron** and **Babe Ruth**.

Mays started playing ball as a teenager in the Negro Leagues. After **Jackie Robinson** broke the color barrier in 1947, Mays signed with the New York Giants. He played for them from 1951 to 1972.

Mays was an outstanding hitter and an unbelievable fielder. One of his most famous catches happened during the 1954 World Series. With the score tied in the eighth inning, Cleveland Indian Vic Wertz exploded a line drive over Mays's head, deep into centerfield. Mays took off . . . straight ahead and fast! Only once in his sprint did he look back to check on the ball. When it finally fell earthward, nearly 480 feet from home plate, Mays was there. He caught the ball, and without stopping, twirled on one foot and hurled it back into the infield. The crowd went wild.

This kind of playing, coupled with Mays's power hitting, earned him two Most Valuable Player awards (1954, 1965). His career batting average was .302, even though his ballplaying was interrupted by a two-year stint in the Army during the Korean War.

Joseph McCarthy
senator ★ 1908—1957

The Korean War, the revolution in China, and the Soviets testing an atom bomb made many Americans nervous about communism in the 1950s. Senator Joseph McCarthy preyed on those fears.

From 1950 to 1954, this Republican senator conducted a "witch hunt" for Communists. McCarthy declared that he had a list of 205 Communists working in the State Department. When pressed by his fellow senators, McCarthy couldn't produce the list. But that didn't stop "McCarthyism" from running rampant for four years.

Senator McCarthy wielded extraordinary power as chairman of the Permanent Subcommittee on Investigations of Governmental Operations. He accused all kinds of people of being Communists. His claims were based on suspicions, rumors, lies, or personal vendettas. He ruined countless careers

Joseph McCarthy (r.) consults with his lawyer, Roy Cohn (l.), during the 1954 Army hearings.

and reputations and never firmly proved that even one person he questioned was a Communist.

In 1954, **Edward R. Murrow** broadcast a damning show of McCarthy clips. Around the same time, McCarthy accused the U.S. Army of harboring Communists. The Army fought back with its own inquiry into some of the Senator's wheeling and dealing. In December 1954, the Senate voted to condemn McCarthy for his behavior and remove him as chair of a Senate committee.

Barbara McClintock
geneticist ★ 1902—1992

In 1941, the Carnegie Institution of Washington made Dr. Barbara McClintock an ideal job offer: a laboratory, a home, a salary . . . and a cornfield.

McClintock had been conducting studies on the individual chromosomes of maize, or wild corn, since her first year of graduate school at Cornell University in 1924.

In 1944, Dr. McClintock studied what she called "transposition." Most scientists at the time believed

Dr. Barbara McClintock accepts the prestigious Lasker Award for medical research in 1981.

genes were stable or fixed. McClintock suspected this was not true, based on her observations of color mutations in some corn kernels in her fields. When McClintock delivered a paper on her radical theory to 100 scientists in 1951, there was complete silence.

Though no one took her "jumping genes" theories seriously, McClintock continued her research. In the 1970s, research into DNA, the basic element of genes, suggested that some of McClintock's theories might be correct. She was showered with attention and awards, including the Nobel Prize for medicine.

"When you know you're right, you don't

Cyrus McCormick
inventor ★ 1809—1884

In the early 19th century, even the fastest reaper could only work through one acre of wheat in a day. Wheat rots if it's not cut in time, so farmers could only plant small amounts of it. Cyrus McCormick changed all that.

In 1831, he invented a reaping machine. It had several V-shaped openings on a fixed bar, and knives that moved back and forth to cut the grain. For the next several years, McCormick improved on his reaper (and faced constant competition from rival inventor Obed Hussey). By 1843, he was selling his machines for $3,000 each.

McCormick moved to Chicago, Illinois, right in the middle of the Great Plains. His business thrived. Not only did he have a great product, but he was also an innovative marketer. McCormick sold his reaper to farmers on the installment plan, in which they paid some part of the price each month. Otherwise, the farmers never would have had the money to buy a reaper in the first place. McCormick promised a money-back guarantee on his machines. He also got testimonials from satisfied customers and printed them as newspaper advertisements.

Elijah McCoy
inventor ★ 1843—1929

U.S. Patent No. 129,843 was "the real McCoy"—Elijah McCoy's patent for a lubricating cup, that is.

McCoy, the son of escaped slaves, grew up in Ontario, Canada. When it came to mechanical things, young McCoy was incredibly gifted. He was educated in Edinburgh, Scotland, and became an engineer. Unfortunately, when he then came to the U.S., no one was interested in an African-American engineer.

McCoy hired on with the Michigan Central Railroad as a fireman/oilman. He shoveled two tons of coal an hour into the blazing boiler that provided steam for the engine. The train's moving parts also had to be oiled often. That meant stopping the train. McCoy figured there must be a more efficient way. He spent nights designing a lubricating cup that would release oil automatically. In 1872, he patented it.

Other manufacturers tried to imitate Elijah McCoy's lubricating cup, but none worked as well. Customers always asked for "the real McCoy."

Because of prejudice, train companies were slow to get on board with McCoy's invention. But eventually they did—and so did shipping companies, and later, mining and factory operations. McCoy went on to improve the lubricating cup and invent other useful items, like the portable ironing board and the lawn sprinkler. He held 57 patents on his work. In 1920, he formed The Elijah McCoy Manufacturing Company. They produced the graphite lubricator McCoy had designed for the new superheater trains.

care what others think." —BARBARA MCCLINTOCK

Mark McGwire
baseball player ★ 1963—

Roger Maris's single-season home-run record stood for 37 years—until "Big Mac" stepped up to the plate on September 8, 1998, and blasted out his 62nd home run. Ironically, it was his shortest home run of the year.

Mark McGwire was recruited by the Oakland Athletics in 1986. McGwire was named 1987 Rookie of the Year. He made the All-Star team regularly. McGwire and fellow slugger Jose Canseco, who were nicknamed the "Bash Brothers," helped bring Oakland into the World Series three times in a row, and win the championship in 1989.

Oakland traded McGwire to St. Louis in 1997. The following year saw first baseman McGwire locked in a heated home-run race with Chicago Cubs player Sammy Sosa. Both men kept slugging away; the sports media and fans were frenzied. McGwire hit 70 home runs that year, for a record-breaking single season total. (In 2001, San Francisco Giant Barry Bonds broke McGwire's record with 73 single-season homers.) McGwire's powerful, upper-cut swing had earned him the fifth-place spot for all-time career home runs when he retired after the 2001 season. McGwire had 583 career home runs to his name.

Margaret Mead
anthropologist ★ 1901—1978

Margaret Mead was fascinated by anthropology. Her best-selling books drew other people into that fascination, too.

Mead studied anthropology, or how people live and behave, at Barnard College in New York. She then traveled alone to Samoa and other Pacific islands in 1925, when she was 23. Mead studied cultural behavior and values. She wrote her findings in *Coming of Age in Samoa* (1928), which became a best-seller. Mead followed with *Growing Up in New Guinea* in 1930 and *Sex and Temperament in Three Primitive Societies* in 1935.

Although much of Mead's work focused on "primitive" people, she also wrote about American culture and examined male and female behavior across cultures. She was a curator at New York's American Museum of Natural History from 1926 to 1969. In 1961, she headed President **John F. Kennedy**'s Commission on the Status of Women. Mead's interest in Pacific island life continued throughout her life.

thing on your body." — MARK MCGWIRE

George Meany
labor leader ★ 1894–1980

In 1955, the American Federation of Labor (AFL), founded by **Samuel Gompers**, and the Congress of Industrial Organizations (CIO), founded by **John L. Lewis**, merged. George Meany became the first AFL–CIO president.

Meany came to the job with an impressive experience. Born in New York City, Meany was the son of a plumber. He became a plumber himself, a union plumber. Meany joined the United Association of Plumbers and Steam Fitters. He rose through labor ranks and became president of the New York State Federation of Labor in 1934. There he honed his skills at making a labor organization a powerful political force. This would prove to be Meany's legacy.

As secretary-treasurer of the AFL (1939) and president of the AFL–CIO (1955–1980), Meany wasn't afraid to use labor's political muscle, both inside and outside of his organizations. He survived problems with some of the AFL–CIO's member organizations, such as Jimmy Hoffa and the Teamsters Union, and Walter Reuther's United Auto Workers. Meany effectively worked for higher wages, better working conditions, and broader insurance coverage for union workers. Under his leadership, AFL–CIO support became a major factor in presidential elections. A show of support from Meany and the AFL–CIO could bring a politician thousands of votes from the union's membership.

Herman Melville
author ★ 1819–1891

In 1841 Herman Melville was a deckhand on the whaler *Acushnet*. Life on board was deadly boring if no whales were sighted—and could be deadly if they were! Melville jumped ship after 18 long, harsh months at sea. He lived with the people of Marquesa, an island paradise in the South Pacific. Eventually, Melville worked his way home by enlisting as a sailor on a U.S. Navy warship. He'd been gone three years.

Onshore, Herman Melville's sailing and whaling experiences flowed onto the page. He wrote two colorful adventure novels based on his stay among the cannibals on Marquesa and on Tahiti. Critics and the public loved *Typee* (1846) and *Omoo* (1847). They were less kind to his next work, a book now considered one of America's greatest masterpieces, *Moby Dick, or The Whale* (1851). The story of Captain Ahab's obsession with killing the great white whale who chewed off his leg sold poorly. Melville's reputation as an author sank. Melville died poor and unknown. His other famous work, *Billy Budd* (1924), was published 33 years after his death.

"My candle burns at both ends; It will not last the night;

Edna St. Vincent Millay
poet ★ 1892—1950

Free-spirited and independent, Edna St. Vincent Millay represented the "new woman" of the 1920s. She was also the most famous poet of her time. Millay read her poetry to packed halls. In 1923, she became the first woman to win the Pulitzer prize in poetry. Her books sold thousands of copies, even during the Depression.

Critics raved about Millay's first poem, "Renascence" (1912), when it was published in a literary competition. In 1917, Edna graduated from college and moved to New York. *Renascence and Other Poems*, her first book, also appeared.

Millay's fascinating circle included other writers, actors, artists, and political revolutionaries. The beautiful, captivating poet lived a wild life. Her poem "First Fig" helped define the Roaring Twenties. Her second poetry collection, *A Few Figs from Thistles"* (1920), broadened her audience. *Ballad of the Harpweaver* (1923) brought her the Pulitzer. Millay's widely praised sonnets, like those collected in *Fatal Interview* (1931), blended her unique modern voice, deep soul, and classical style.

Arthur Miller
playwright ★ 1915—

When the curtain fell on the first performance of *Death of a Salesman* in 1949, the audience was completely silent. They were awed by Arthur Miller's masterpiece.

Miller, the son of Jewish immigrants, grew up during the Depression and World War II. He saw how pursuing the American dream—success, status, money—could twist a person. He explored ideas about responsibility, family relations, and morality in his plays. He also used his own experiences as inspiration. *Death of a Salesman* drew on memories of his father's business losses and Miller's own work in the garment business. The play won several awards, including the Pulitzer prize. *The Crucible* (1953) is based on the Salem witch trials of the 1600s, but on another level the play is a criticism of Senator **Joseph McCarthy**'s hearings on communism, which Miller opposed. *A View from the Bridge* (1955) and *After the Fall* (1964) have their roots in Miller's short-lived marriage to **Marilyn Monroe**.

Arthur Miller is the author of many other plays, the movie script for *The Misfits* (1961), an autobiography, and several nonfiction books. His most recent play is *Resurrection Blues* (2002).

But, ah, my foes, and, oh, my friends—It gives a lovely light!"

— EDNA ST. VINCENT MILLAY

Shannon Miller
Olympian ★ 1977—

Whether performing on beam, bar, or floor, gymnast Shannon Miller is famous for her artistry and athleticism. She is the most decorated American gymnast in history.

Miller and the six other members of the U.S. Olympic gymnastics team made history in 1996. The "Magnificent Seven" became the first Americans to take home Olympic gold medals in team gymnastics. Shannon Miller didn't stop there. She scored 9.862 for her routine on the balance beam. Because of that amazing performance, Miller became the first American female gymnast to win an individual gold medal.

Miller was a veteran of the 1992 Olympics. There, she won two silver medals (beam; all-around) and three bronze (uneven parallel bars; floor exercise; team). Between 1993 and 1994, Miller swept the World Championships. She won a total of five gold medals, including two consecutive all-around titles, an American record.

After the incredible victory of the "Magnificent Seven," Miller retired in 1996. An injured knee prevented her from making a comeback at the 2000 Olympics. But what laurels to rest on—seven Olympic medals and nine World Championship medals!

Maria Mitchell
astronomer ★ 1818—1889

Maria Mitchell (l.) with her telescope and Vassar students, 1870.

On October 1, 1847, Maria Mitchell was "sky sweeping," searching the night sky with a telescope. She discovered a new comet. The king of Denmark gave her a gold medal for her comet discovery.

Mitchell worked by day as a librarian on Nantucket, an island off Massachusetts. There she could also get books to study mathematics and navigation. But her true work and joy began at night, up on the roof, looking at the stars through her father's telescope.

In 1848, based on her discovery of the comet now named "Miss Mitchell's Comet," Mitchell became the first woman elected to the American Academy of Arts and Sciences. Her work also captured the attention of women leaders of the time, and in 1858, a group of them gave her a new, very precise telescope on behalf of "the women of America."

Mitchell was appointed professor of astronomy and director of the observatory at Vassar Female College in 1865. She focused most of her studies on the sun, Saturn, and Jupiter. In 1873, Mitchell founded the Association for the Advancement of Women (AAW), to encourage other women to reach for the stars.

N. Scott Momaday
author • 1934—

The 1969 Pulitzer Prize for fiction went to a first novel by an unknown author. He's not unknown anymore.

N. Scott Momaday is one of the nation's most respected and successful contemporary Native American writers. He's written novels, poetry, literary criticism, folktale collections, and essays on Native American culture and on the environment. His Pulitzer Prize-winning novel is *A House Made of Dawn*. It's a powerful story about a Native American World War II veteran who returns home and finds himself in his own private war between modern society and his ancient traditions.

Momaday's own life spans two worlds. He was born in Oklahoma and grew up on the Apache, Pueblo, and Navajo reservations of the Southwest. He studied American and English literature at prestigious Stanford University in California, where he earned his Ph.D. in 1963.

Momaday has been a professor of English literature at several universities. He's also a dedicated scholar of Native American oral traditions, which have greatly influenced his own fiction writing and poetry. The author is an honored member of the ancient Kiowa Gourd Dance Society and holds more than 12 honorary degrees.

James Monroe
fifth president ★ 1758—1831

The White House, which had been burned by the British in the War of 1812, was under repair. So newly elected president James Monroe (1817–1825) set off on a 15-week tour of the nation. The people loved him; the press declared his presidency the "Era of Good Feeling."

Still, President Monroe, a member of the Democratic-Republican party, had his hands full. One of the biggest issues he faced was slavery. During Monroe's presidency, several western territories asked to be admitted to the Union. If they were admitted, they would then send representatives to Congress. So the balance of power in Congress depended upon whether these western territories were admitted as slave states or "free soil" states, which banned slavery. The Missouri Compromise of 1820 was the federal government's attempt to satisfy the North and the South on the slavery issue. President Monroe opposed the compromise. He said it interfered with individual states' rights. But since he feared civil war more, Monroe didn't veto the bill.

The fifth president's most enduring legacy was the Monroe Doctrine, which he delivered to Congress in 1823. In it, Monroe plainly and boldly warned European nations that they could no longer colonize or interfere with the affairs of North or South America. The Monroe Doctrine, though not a law, set an important standard for U.S. foreign policy.

"The best form of government is that which is most likely to prevent the greatest sum of evil." —JAMES MONROE

Marilyn Monroe
actress ★ 1926–1962

Marilyn Monroe's beginnings were far from glamorous. Born in Los Angeles, California, she bounced around from foster homes to orphanages. She married at 16 and went to work in an aircraft company. There, an army photographer asked her to model for an article on women workers. Monroe kept on modeling for a few years, got divorced along the way, then tried Hollywood. Her small role in *The Asphalt Jungle* (1950) got people's attention. That year she also made a striking appearance in *All About Eve*, starring **Bette Davis**. Twentieth-Century Fox signed her and promoted Monroe as a "dumb blond bombshell" in movies like *Gentlemen Prefer Blondes* (1953). Monroe's movies earned more than $200 million.

Many people thought of Monroe as only a sexy film goddess, but she was also a great comedy actor. Critics loved her in funny movies like *The Seven-Year Itch* (1955) and *Some Like It Hot* (1959).

Monroe's private life was complicated. She married and divorced **Joe DiMaggio** and **Arthur Miller**. While Monroe was one of the world's most recognizable women, she was deeply unhappy. She died of an overdose of sleeping pills before finishing the autobiography she had been writing.

Joe Montana
football player ★ 1956–

"Joe Cool" Montana was one of the hottest quarterbacks ever in the National Football League (NFL).

The San Francisco 49ers drafted Montana in 1979 and he played his first full season for them in 1981. His claim to fame became the impossible comeback. In 30 games, the 49ers trailed in the fourth quarter. Each time, Montana saved the day with a last-minute play, most famously "The Catch" of 1981. In the 1981 NFC championship game, the Dallas Cowboys were ahead, 27–21. With 58 seconds remaining, Montana rolled far right and threw a six-yard pass that no one thought would work. It did. Montana had sent his team to its first Super Bowl.

Montana wore the 49ers jersey for 11 seasons. The San Francisco team took home the trophy in Super Bowl XVI, XIX, XXIII, and XXIV (1982; 1985; 1989; 1990). In three of those Super Bowls, Montana was voted Most Valuable Player (MVP). He also won the NFL MVP award twice.

In 1993, Montana started playing with the Kansas City Chiefs. Two years later, Montana retired. But no one can retire Cool Joe's career: 40,551 yards, 3,409 completions, 273 touchdowns.

None of Joe Montana's passes in a Super Bowl was ever intercepted.

Rita Moreno
performer ★ 1931—

Moreno as Anita in West Side Story.

Puerto Rican star Rita Moreno became the first and only female performer to win all four of the top entertainment awards: the Oscar, the Emmy, the Tony, and the Grammy.

As a young actress, Moreno was often typecast or given roles as a sexy, fiery Latina. Her big break came in the 1962 film version of **Leonard Bernstein**'s *West Side Story*. Moreno played Anita, a tough, strong-minded character in this Romeo-and-Juliet love story set in the gang world of 1950s New York City. Although the movie's now-dated portrayal of Hispanics was stereotypical, its message promoted tolerance. Moreno won an Oscar for Best Supporting Actress. She was able to use her newfound fame to gain more power over her career.

Moreno starred in 30 films and several top Broadway plays, including *The Ritz*, for which she won a 1973 Tony Award. Through her work on *Sesame Street* and on a sound track for the *Electric Company* television show, Moreno provided children with a positive, inspiring Hispanic role model. And she earned an Emmy and a Grammy in the bargain. Rita Moreno proved to Hollywood and Broadway that women of color shouldn't only be cast in "ethnic" roles.

J. P. Morgan
financier ★ 1837–1913

He was so rich that he bailed out the government *twice*!

John Pierpont Morgan opened a banking firm in 1871. It became one of New York's top financial companies. In 1885, Morgan started buying, building, and reorganizing railroads. During the 1893 financial depression, he scooped up more railroad companies when their prices fell. Morgan soon owned one-sixth of America's railways. This made him a very rich man.

During the financial panic of 1895, Morgan stepped in. He lent the U.S. government $62 million by buying bonds to raise the money. Of course Morgan profited on those bonds. Six years later, he bought **Andrew Carnegie**'s steel company. Morgan merged it with some of his other businesses. He formed U.S. Steel, America's first billion-dollar corporation, in 1901. In 1907, Morgan used his wealth to help save New York City from a financial crash during a stock market panic.

Morgan was a great art collector. His outstanding collection is now at the Metropolitan Museum of Art and the J. P. Morgan Library in New York City.

"Writing is discovery; it's talking

Toni Morrison

author ★ 1931—

Toni Morrison has always looked within herself, her family, and her community to gather material for her novels and essays. Her deep soul-searching has produced some of the most powerful books about the African-American experience ever written. Those books are read by millions of people.

Morrison's real name is Chloe Anthony Wofford. (Toni is a nickname; Morrison is a married name.) She was born in Lorrain, Ohio, where she grew up surrounded by poverty during the Great Depression. As a child, she heard

In 1993, Toni Morrison became the first African-American woman to win the Nobel Prize for literature.

about the racial violence her grandparents had faced as sharecroppers in the South. She also heard the stories and folktales about her heritage. This gave her a strong sense of the injustices African Americans had endured and the spirit through which they survived. All of these were important influences on Morrison as a writer.

She enrolled at Howard University in Washington, D.C., in 1949 to study English literature and got her master's degree at Cornell University in 1955. After teaching for a time, and marrying and divorcing, Morrison moved to New York City and became an editor at Random House in 1965. There Morrison focused on getting more books by African Americans into print. Meanwhile, she worked on her own writing and published her first novel, *The Bluest Eye* (1970). Critics hailed this moving story of three young girls searching for their African-American identities in a world that values blond hair and blue eyes.

During this time, Morrison also produced *The Black Book,* an African-American history. She was inspired by the photographs and other artifacts she saw while working on this book. As a result, Morrison wove an historic look at racism in the U.S. into her next book, *Song of Solomon* (1977), which was a best-seller. It won the 1977 National Book Critics' Circle Award. More important, the book was such a financial success that Morrison could devote herself to writing full-time. When Morrison's next book, *Tar Baby,* came out in 1981, it made *The New York Times* best-seller list, and Toni made the cover of *Newsweek.* She was the first African-American woman featured on the front of the magazine.

While researching *The Black Book*, Morrison found an 1851 newspaper clipping about an escaped slave who killed her daughter rather than see her captured and returned to slavery. Morrison turned this true story into one of her most powerful works, *Beloved* (1987). *Beloved* won the 1988 Pulitzer prize and is part of a trilogy about African-American history. In 1993 Morrison won the 1993 Nobel Prize for literature for her outstanding skill and sensitivity as a writer. More than 500,000 copies of her other books sold in the three months after she was named a Nobel winner. Morrison continues to write and to teach at Princeton University.

deep within myself." — TONI MORRISON

Samuel Morse

inventor ★ 1791—1872

Samuel Morse painted this portrait of himself in 1812. He also founded the National Academy of Design.

Samuel Morse was a well-established artist, but new discoveries about electricity sparked his interest in invention.

In 1835, Morse developed a telegraph. He built it himself using an artist's canvas stretcher, parts of an old clock, and a battery. His telegraph worked by electrical impulses traveling along wires. By 1838, he had created "Morse code," a system of dots and dashes that stood for letters of the alphabet. The telegraph's electrical impulses transmitted this code.

Morse found partners, but little public interest in his telegraph and code. Luckily in 1843, he persuaded Congress to give him $30,000 to demonstrate the capabilities of his invention. On May 24, 1844, Morse telegraphed from the Capitol Building in Washington, D.C. Forty miles away, in Baltimore, Maryland, at the other end of the telegraph wires, his historic message came through clearly: "What hath God wrought?"

Telegraph wires soon linked all parts of the nation. By 1858, they linked North America and Europe. Morse code became an international form of communication.

Lucretia Coffin Mott

abolitionist, suffragist ★ 1793—1880

Lucretia Mott, a Quaker minister, practiced what she preached. She was opposed to slavery, so she never bought cotton cloth, cane sugar, or any other product of slave labor. Her home was a stop on the Underground Railroad. She was barred from the first American Anti-Slavery Society convention in 1833 because she was a woman, so she founded the Philadelphia Female Anti-Slavery Society. When Mott and the other American women delegates were denied seats at the 1840 World Anti-Slavery Convention in London, she joined her new friend, **Elizabeth Cady Stanton** in the fight for equality. Mott and Stanton helped organize the historic Seneca Falls Woman's Rights Convention in 1848.

Some people praised Lucretia Mott's public speeches, but others jeered and even physically threatened her.

Lucretia Mott traveled across the country lecturing on abolition, equal rights, social reform, temperance, and world peace. This did not always make her own life peaceful. An anti-abolitionist mob once raided a meeting of her Philadelphia antislavery society and set the building on fire. The violent mob then headed toward the Motts' house, but fortunately was stopped.

Mott was named president of the American Equal Rights Association, a group devoted to African-American and women's suffrage, in 1866. She continued to be publicly and privately active until her death at the age of 87.

"Nature always has something

Elijah Muhammad
religious leader ★ 1897–1975

Elijah Poole was a Detroit factory worker when he took over a new local African-American religious movement in 1934. Poole changed his name to Muhammad. He turned the Nation of Islam into a powerful national organization.

Elijah Muhammad was called the "Messenger of Allah." His message to African Americans was self-knowledge, self-discipline, self-esteem, and unity. Muhammad preached that black people should become economically independent. They should refrain from using drugs, alcohol, and violence. They should learn more about their heritage. They should unite as black people—and separate from white people. Muhammad's ideas about black separatism were controversial, but the Nation of Islam attracted a strong following, especially among African Americans who struggled in poverty.

During the 1950s and 1960s, the Nation of Islam thrived under Elijah Muhammad. It eventually included Muslim-run schools, farms, stores, restaurants, a newspaper, and a bank, among other businesses. Muhammad ran the Nation of Islam from his Chicago temple. Membership soared. A prison convert, **Malcolm X**, became Muhammad's right-hand man. In 1965, the two split over the future direction of the Nation of Islam. Muhammad remained in charge, but was accused of corruption and of being involved in Malcolm X's assassination.

John Muir
environmentalist ★ 1838–1914

When he wasn't wandering through America's wilderness, the "Father of Conservation" was working hard to protect it.

Born in Scotland and raised in Wisconsin, John Muir was a keen observer of nature and mechanically gifted. (He invented a timer that tipped him out of bed in the morning.)

After an injury that nearly blinded him, Muir devoted himself to nature studies. He set off on a 1,000-mile trek from Indianapolis to the Gulf Coast. In Florida, he shipped out to Cuba. Muir kept careful notes of his trip. Next, he set his sights on California.

Muir fell in love with the snowy peaks of California's Sierra Nevada Mountains and the sensational beauty of its Yosemite Valley. He discovered living glaciers in the Sierras in 1871 and wrote about them. In his lifetime, he wrote 300 articles and 10 books about his nature studies and travels.

By the 1880s, farmers, ranchers, and miners all wanted a piece of the wilderness lands. Muir succeeded in having Yosemite declared a national park in 1890. Two years later, he helped found the Sierra Club to promote environmental awareness and establish a system of national parks.

rare to show us." —JOHN MUIR

Edward R. Murrow
journalist ★ 1908–1965

The London Blitz. The Berlin bombings. The liberation of Nazi death camps. Edward R. Murrow brought the horrors and heroism of World War II home to Americans—through the airwaves.

Murrow was CBS's European director in 1937. When war broke out, he broadcast his radio news shows live. Millions of people tuned in to Murrow's news-breaking, fearless reports.

Murrow's CBS weekly radio show, *Hear It Now* (1950–1951) soon became *See It Now* (1951–1958) when television arrived. Murrow had a good eye for a story, a willingness to dig deep and investigate, and the courage and honesty to present his findings. One of the show's most famous episodes exposed the outrageous behavior of Senator **Joseph McCarthy** during his infamous Congressional hearings on communism.

From 1953 to 1959, Murrow also hosted another weekly program, *Person to Person*. Television audiences loved getting an inside scoop on glamorous celebrities at home. In 1961, Murrow left CBS. President **John F. Kennedy** appointed him head of the U.S. Information Agency. Murrow was awarded the Presidential Medal of Freedom in 1964.

Ralph Nader
activist, politician ★ 1934–

Ralph Nader's first book, *Unsafe at Any Speed* (1965), put him in the fast lane to fame.

Nader, an attorney, spearheaded the consumer rights movement. He believes consumers have the right to know everything about things they plan to buy, and to be protected from harmful products and manufacturing. His groundbreaking, best-selling 1965 book exposed the auto industry for producing unsafe cars. Within a year, Congress had held hearings and passed industry safety regulations. It was the first of many

Nader campaigns that resulted in safer foods, cleaner air and water, and fairer insurance costs.

In the late 1960s and the 1970s, Nader founded several nonprofit groups to make sure that consumers' interests were taken seriously by business and the government. Nader's pioneering efforts helped establish U.S. government agencies: the Consumer Product Safety Administration; the Occupational Safety and Health Administration; and the Environmental Protection Agency. Nader led the battle to get the Freedom of Information Act passed, which gave citizens the right to ask for copies of government files, records, and reports.

Nader ran for president on the liberal Green Party ticket in 1992 and 1996. There wasn't much fanfare. Things were different in 2000. More people were willing to listen to Nader's message about how corporations were running—and ruining—the nation.

"We have a choice in this country. Either the people are going to be

Joe Namath
football player ★ 1943—

When Joe Namath signed with the New York Jets in 1965, he brought power, precision, and *style*. The Jets brought Namath a $400,000-plus three-year contract and a fancy car. Namath became the highest-paid rookie in pro football at the time.

As Jets quarterback (1965-1976), Namath became the first player to pass more than 4,000 yards in a season (1967). He saved the day in the 1968 American Football League (AFL) championship game against the Oakland Raiders. With the Jets trailing by three points, and only minutes left in the game, Namath shot off his third touchdown pass of the game. The Jets won the championship. They were going to Super Bowl III (1969).

After his performance in Super Bowl III, Joe Namath was voted AFL Most Valuable Player. He also acted in several films and television shows.

Namath was a flashy guy off the gridiron. He wore fancy clothes and long hair. He liked dancing, clubs, and the New York high life.

When Namath predicted that the Jets would trounce the favored Baltimore Colts at Super Bowl III, people thought he was idly boasting.

They were so wrong. In a now legendary game, Namath hurled 28 passes, 17 of them complete, covering 206 yards. The final score? 16–7 . . . Jets! They were the first AFL team to win the Super Bowl.

Joe Namath retired in 1977 after one season with the Los Angeles Rams. He was inducted into the Pro Football Hall of Fame in 1985.

Martina Navratilova
tennis player ★ 1956—

When Martina Navratilova left the singles tennis circuit in 1994, she had the best record of wins by any man or woman in the history of tennis.

The Czechoslovakian-born champ defected in 1975 and settled in the U.S. She won the first of a record-breaking nine Wimbledon singles victories in 1978 and played on a winning doubles team with **Billie Jean King** in 1979. Navratilova's hard work led to 15 Grand Slam singles titles and 25 Grand Slam doubles titles.

In her 20-year career, Navratilova played more than 1,600 tennis matches, earned more than $19 million, and was often named top athlete by various sports organizations. She is also a national spokesperson for the gay and lesbian rights movement. She was inducted into the International Tennis Hall of Fame in 2000.

sovereign or big business is going to be sovereign." —RALPH NADER

Louise Nevelson

sculptor ★ c.1899–1988

Louise Nevelson is one of the great contemporary sculptors, though she worked for several decades before her pieces achieved this status.

A Russian-Jewish immigrant, Nevelson began studying full time at the Art Students League in New York in 1928. By 1933, Nevelson's abstract sculptures made of wood, stone, metal, and other materials were being exhibited. Her first one-woman show was in 1940.

Over the next 10 years, Nevelson created the large sculptures, such as *Moon Garden Reflections, Sky Cathedral* (1958), and *Dawn's Wedding Chapel II* (1959) that made her famous. Many of her sculptures are wooden and boxlike. They include layers of different "found" objects, anything from wheels to bowling pins to chair legs. Nevelson painted these sculptures one color—black, white, or gold.

By the 1960s, Nevelson's work was shown in major museums. In the 1970s, she started creating large sculpture environments, where the outdoor setting and her sculptures worked together.

Jack Nicklaus

golfer ★ 1940–

From 1962 to 1986, whenever Jack Nicklaus took out his clubs, the golf world prepared another trophy. Nicklaus was a flawless putter and a power driver. He won 18 major pro golf events, more than any other player.

After an outstanding amateur career, Nicklaus turned pro in 1961. It didn't take long for Nicklaus to start winning—and earning—big! He was famous for his determination and for his absolute concentration on his stroke. That helped Nicklaus win six Masters tournaments, five Professional Golf Association (PGA) championships, five PGA Player of the Year awards, four U.S. Opens, and three British Opens. Nicklaus took on, and often beat, the reigning king of the greens, **Arnold Palmer**, in one of pro golf's great rivalries.

Jack Nicklaus was nicknamed the "Golden Bear" because he was big, blond, and fierce when it came to golfing.

Nicklaus made headlines at the beginning of his career and toward the end. In 1962, he became the youngest person to win the U.S. Open. Twenty-four years later, Nicklaus won his sixth Masters and became the oldest player ever to do so.

"I am not a crook." — RICHARD NIXON

Richard Nixon
37th president ★ 1913–1994

Richard Nixon's presidency (1969–1974) was as complicated as his personality. Nixon, a former senator from California, had long been a zealous anti-Communist. Yet, as president, his biggest foreign policy successes were with Communist countries.

Nixon was the first president to visit Communist China. He met with Chairman Mao Tse-tung in 1972 to establish diplomatic relations. That same year, Nixon also visited Moscow in the Soviet Union and signed an arms-control treaty with the

Richard Nixon refused to admit his guilt in the Watergate break-in. He flashed his signature "victory" sign on leaving the White House.

Soviets. Nixon was internationally recognized for his "détente" policy, which encouraged cooperation rather than confrontation between the U.S. and these two superpowers.

Nixon's Vietnam War policies were less popular. There were widespread, sometimes violent, antiwar protests in the U.S. Despite the public uproar in 1972, President Nixon ordered the infamous, heavy "Christmas bombing" to force the North Vietnamese back to the peace table in Paris, France. By January 1973, the war was over, but President Nixon had other troubles at home.

In 1972, there had been a break-in at the headquarters of the Democratic National Committee in the Watergate complex in Washington, D.C. The burglars arrested were linked to the Committee to Reelect the President (CREEP). They had been looking for information that the Republicans could use against the Democrats. An investigation by *Washington Post* reporters Bob Woodward and Carl Bernstein led all the way to the Oval Office.

President Nixon denied having anything to do with stories that surfaced about money-laundering, political dirty tricks, and a Republican "enemies list." He also denied covering up the Watergate break-in. In February 1973, a Congressional committee started investigating whether anything illegal or unethical happened during the 1972 presidential campaign. Word leaked out that Nixon had recorded all his conversations in the Oval Office. The committee subpoenaed the tapes. Nixon refused to hand them over. On July 24, 1974, the U.S. Supreme Court unanimously ordered him to turn over all the tapes. The tapes were very incriminating. The House Judiciary Committee voted for three articles of impeachment.

On August 8, 1974, President Richard Nixon resigned on nationwide television rather than face impeachment. One month later, Vice President Gerald Ford took office. He pardoned Nixon, so the former president would not face any criminal charges.

Isamu Noguchi
artist ★ 1904–1988

Exploring his American and Japanese heritages was a struggle and an inspiration for Isamu Noguchi. The attempt had a profound effect on the innovative sculptures and landscapes and the theater, furniture, and architectural designs that made him famous.

Noguchi abandoned medical school for art in the 1920s. He studied in New York, Paris, Japan, and China. At first, he earned a living by sculpting traditional busts. But Noguchi was more interested in working with abstract and organic shapes.

Several visits to traditional Japanese gardens gave Noguchi the idea to create entire sculpted landscapes. In 1952, Noguchi created *Ikiru* (To Live), two memorial bridges in Hiroshima, Japan, where

Isamu Noguchi stands next to Brilliance, one of his 250 works in the Isamu Noguchi Garden Museum in New York City.

the first atomic bomb had been dropped. Four years later, he designed the beautiful sculpture garden at the UNESCO offices in Paris, France. Noguchi went on to design site-specific sculptures, gardens, fountains, parks, and playgrounds in 17 American cities and several other cities worldwide. His set designs were used in dance productions by **Martha Graham**, **George Balanchine**, and **Merce Cunningham**. Noguchi also felt sculpture should be part of everyday life. In the 1940s, he designed his now-famous *Akari*—bamboo-and-paper lamps—and his blob-shaped coffee tables. Both had a big impact on modern design.

Annie Oakley
sharpshooter ★ 1860–1926

Even as a child, Phoebe Ann Moses helped support her family by shooting and selling game. She earned enough to pay off the mortgage on the family farm outside Cincinnati, Ohio. In 1876, the teenager entered a shooting match with a champion marksman, Frank Butler. She won the match—and a husband. She and Frank were soon married.

Phoebe changed her name to Annie Oakley and appeared in vaudeville shows. Oakley became world-famous when she and Frank joined **Buffalo Bill Cody**'s Wild West Show in 1885. She toured with them throughout the U. S. and Europe for more than 15 years. Annie Oakley's skill with a gun was legendary. She could shoot a dime from between her husband's thumb and fingers and shoot the flames off candles while standing on a galloping horse. She continued performing even after being injured in a railroad accident in 1901. Annie Oakley's was captured on film by **Thomas Edison** in 1894. **Irving Berlin** later wrote a famous musical called *Annie Get Your Gun* about the woman many called "Lady Sure Shot."

"Don't be afraid to reach for the stars."

— ELLEN OCHOA

Ellen Ochoa
astronaut ★ 1958—

Not many people get a chance to play the flute while floating weightless in a space shuttle. Ellen Ochoa did when she went up on the space shuttle *Discovery* in 1993.

Ochoa is a record-breaking astronaut—she was the first Hispanic woman in space. She's an outstanding scientist with degrees in physics and electrical engineering. She's an inventor who shares three patents on highly specialized optical systems. One of them is an important tool in space robotics.

In 1991, Ochoa was one of 23 people out of 2,000 applicants chosen for astronaut training. Ochoa then joined the National Aeronautics and Space Administration (NASA) as a research engineer. She continued her work in optical systems at NASA's Ames Research Center.

The 1993 *Discovery* flight was Ochoa's first mission in space. It lasted nine days. On board the orbiting shuttle, Ochoa retrieved satellites with robotic arms. She also studied the sun's energy and how solar activity affects Earth's atmosphere.

The following year, Ochoa went up in space again on the shuttle *Atlantis*. Back on Earth, she then served as NASA's chief of the Astronaut Office and helped develop the international space station. Ochoa was back in space on board the *Discovery* in 1999 when it became the first shuttle to dock at the space station. Again, she worked with the robotics arms. This time she was moving equipment—*four tons of it*—from the *Discovery* to the space station.

Astronaut Ellen Ochoa in the cargo bay of the space shuttle Discovery. *She coordinated the hardware equipment that would be transferred to the space station.*

Ellen Ochoa has logged more than 719 flight hours. She has received seven NASA achievement awards, the Hispanic Heritage Leadership Award, and the Hispanic Engineer Albert Baez Award for Outstanding Technical Contribution to Humanity. In 1999, Ochoa was appointed by President **Bill Clinton** to his Commission on the Celebration of Women in American History.

Sandra Day O'Connor
U.S. Supreme Court justice ★ 1930—

The first thing that changed when Sandra Day O'Connor took her seat on the Supreme Court bench in 1981 was that court members would henceforth be called "Justice," instead of "Mr. Justice."

O'Connor graduated third in her class in 1952 from Stanford Law School. The only job offer she got was legal secretary. She went into government legal work instead. By 1965, O'Connor was assistant attorney general for Arizona.

During the next 16 years, O'Connor accomplished many things. She was elected to the Arizona state senate and later served as a county judge. She was appointed by the governor to the higher Arizona state court of appeals. By 1979, O'Conner thought she was at the height of her career. Then President **Ronald Reagan** nominated her for the U.S. Supreme Court.

On September 25, 1981, the Senate voted 99–0 in favor of Sandra Day O'Connor becoming the first woman appointee in the 191-year history of the Supreme Court. Justice O'Connor frequently votes with her more conservative colleagues. But she is also an independent thinker who often casts the court's tie-breaking vote.

Justice O'Connor participated in the landmark Supreme Court ruling during the 2000 presidential election. She voted with the 5–4 majority to stop ballot counting in Florida. The Supreme Court's decision effectively put **George W. Bush** in office.

Georgia O'Keeffe
painter ★ 1887—1986

Georgia O'Keeffe once wrote that her first memory from childhood was of "light all around." This sensitivity grew deeper with age.

O'Keeffe attended the Art Institute of Chicago and the Art Students League in New York City in 1904. In 1916, a friend showed O'Keeffe's work to famous photographer Alfred Stieglitz. He exhibited O'Keeffe's work at his well-known 291 Gallery in New York. O'Keeffe and Stieglitz married in 1924.

O'Keeffe's first paintings were pure abstractions of shape and light. Her work slowly evolved into images of recognizable objects, viewed from unusual angles or distances. She did a famous series of large, sensual flower paintings. O'Keeffe fell in love with the Southwest countryside in 1929 and returned every summer to paint for the next 17 years. After her husband's death in 1946, O'Keeffe settled in New Mexico permanently. The starkness of the desert landscape

Georgia O'Keeffe, photographed by her husband, Alfred Stieglitz (1864–1946), in 1929.

held a special attraction for her. Her paintings of skulls and bones, crosses, adobes, and desert scenes are among her most famous works.

"I will make even busy New Yorkers take time

Jacqueline Kennedy Onassis
first lady, editor ★ 1929–1994

Jacqueline Kennedy served as first lady for 1,037 days. She made every day count.

Kennedy had worked hard to get her husband, **John F. Kennedy**, elected president. She had campaigned, held fund-raisers, and written a weekly column, "Campaign Wife," in the months leading up to the election.

As first lady, Jackie Kennedy set new standards of style. She influenced women's fashions. Kennedy convinced the U.S. Congress to declare the White House a national museum. She restored the Executive Mansion, paying great attention to historical detail and authenticity. In 1962, nearly 56 million people tuned in to watch the first lady

President John F. Kennedy called Jackie Kennedy his "number one ambassador of good will."

give the first televised tour of the White House.

After witnessing her husband's assassination in 1963, Kennedy retired into private life with her children. In 1968, she married Aristotle Onassis, a Greek millionaire, but was widowed again when Onassis died in 1975. Jackie Kennedy Onassis moved to New York City and became a book editor. She is remembered as one of the nation's most popular first ladies.

Eugene O'Neill
playwright ★ 1888–1953

Eugene O'Neill turned to playwriting when he was hospitalized for tuberculosis in 1912. By that time, he'd already been a gold prospector, a newspaper reporter, and a sailor who visited South America, England, and Argentina. The colorful people he met along the way and O'Neill's own family provided plenty of characters for his dramas.

In 1916, O'Neill and some other artists formed the Provincetown Players, an experimental theater group. They staged O'Neill's one-act plays in Provincetown, Massachusetts, and in New York City's Greenwich Village. Four years later, O'Neill's play *Beyond the Horizon* went to Broadway—and won the Pulitzer prize.

During the 1920s, O'Neill experimented with writing and staging. He produced some of his finest work: *The Emperor Jones* (1920), *Anna Christie* (1921), *Desire Under the Elms* (1924), and *Strange Interlude* (1928). He also picked up three more Pulitzers and

Eugene O'Neill is often called the first great "truly American" playwright. He wrote more than 60 plays.

the 1936 Nobel Prize for literature. He later wrote masterpieces of chilling realism, such as *The Iceman Cometh* (produced 1946), *Long Day's Journey into Night* (produced 1956), and *A Moon for the Misbegotten* (produced 1957).

to see what I see of flowers. **—GEORGIA O'KEEFFE**

When Robert Oppenheimer watched the first nuclear explosion, he thought of a line from the Bhagavad Gita, a sacred Hindu text: "Now I am become Death, the Destroyer of Worlds."

J. Robert Oppenheimer
physicist ★ 1904—1967

July 16, 1945, 5:29 A.M. A terrific fireball bursts over Alamogordo, New Mexico. A deafening roar follows. Blinding light burns brighter than 20 suns. A mushroom cloud rises 41,000 feet high. Robert Oppenheimer clings to a post to keep from falling over. He's just exploded the world's first atom bomb.

In 1942, Oppenheimer, a brilliant physicist and political progressive, agreed to head the Manhattan Project, a secret government-funded plan to build an atom bomb. Time was of the essence. World War II was raging and the U.S. feared that the Nazis might develop nuclear technology first. Oppenheimer set up a laboratory in remote Los Alamos, New Mexico. He oversaw the 1,500 scientists, engineers, and other personnel working on the top secret project. They developed the atom bombs that destroyed the cities of Hiroshima and Nagasaki, Japan, on August 6 and 9, 1945.

Like many people, Oppenheimer realized the dangers of a nuclear arms race. As director of the Institute for Advanced Study at Princeton University (he succeeded **Albert Einstein**) and as a member of the Atomic Energy Committee, he supported arms control agreements and using atomic power for energy, not weapons.

Osceola
Seminole leader ★ c.1800—1838

The "Tiger of the Everglades" was not going to be caged on a reservation. When the U.S. government ordered all Native American tribes to move west in 1832 and 1833, Osceola, a leader of the Seminoles refused to leave Florida. He rallied his people, and the African Americans living among them, and fought the Second Seminole War (1835–1837). Osceola and his warriors repeatedly attacked U.S. troops and then disappeared into Florida's swampy Everglades. The government spent nearly $20 million trying to flush them out.

What the Army couldn't win by fighting, they won by lying. Osceola, under the flag of truce, came to meet with Army officials at Fort Moultrie, South Carolina, in 1837. The general there promptly threw Osceola in prison, where he died three months later. The Seminoles continued to fight until 1842, when most—but not all—of them surrendered and were forced to move to Oklahoma.

Elisha Graves Otis
inventor ★ 1811—1861

Elisha Otis had so much faith in his elevator safety brake that he tested it himself—from *inside* a moving elevator.

Otis was a clever mechanic who worked at a New York bed factory. He saw how difficult and dangerous it was to move workers, equipment, and goods on the simple freight elevators of the time. Those elevators used counterweights and ropes. Ropes sometimes broke. Otis went to work on a safer option.

At the 1854 Crystal Palace Exposition in New York City, Otis had himself hoisted up in an open-shaft elevator. When he was way up above the gaping crowd, he ordered the lifting rope cut. The elevator didn't plummet. Otis had outfitted the shaft with large, ratcheted metal teeth. When the rope was cut, the elevator car was caught and held in these teeth. The first

Three years after Elisha Otis dramatically demonstrated his "safety elevator," the first passenger elevator was installed in a New York department store.

"safety elevator" had passed the test. Otis's invention would make the world's modern skylines possible.

Jesse Owens
Olympian ★ 1913—1980

In 1935, at the Big Ten track-and-field championships in Michigan, Jesse Owens broke or equaled six world records—including the broad jump with one single leap. The very next year, the "Ebony Antelope's" victories would be even more world-shaking.

Owens, the grandson of a slave, was on the 1936 U.S. Olympic team. That year, the games were held in Berlin, Germany, where Adolf Hitler and the Nazis ruled. They planned to use the Olympics as a showcase for their beliefs about white supremacy. Owens ruined their plans. He tore up the track, winning gold medals in the 100-meter and 200-meter sprints. He soared through the air, taking another gold for the broad jump. His lead-off helped the U.S. relay team win the 400-meter race, bringing Owens his fourth gold medal.

Three of Jesse Owens's 1936 Olympic golds set new records. Ten years after his death, Owens was awarded the Congressional Gold Medal.

Back home in Cleveland, Ohio, good times lasted only as long as the ticker-tape parades. Owens had to work a variety of jobs to support his family. He often was paid to race anything from horses to cars. It was demeaning work. Owens also couldn't escape racial prejudice, despite his international fame. But his sportsmanship paid off. In the 1950s, Jesse Owens became a highly paid inspirational speaker, giving talks about sports and personal values.

Satchel Paige
baseball player ★ c.1906–1982

As a child in Mobile, Alabama, Leroy Robert Paige earned money (and his nickname) by hauling satchels from the city's train station. As an adult, Satchel Paige earned the admiration of millions by hurling fastballs and curveballs.

From 1925 to 1947, Paige pitched in the Negro Leagues, the only venues then open to African-American ballplayers. He earned $30,000 to $35,000 a season, way more than most Major League players. He also formed his own traveling team, Satchel Paige's All-Stars. This team "barnstormed" around the country, playing exhibition games.

Some estimates say Paige played nearly 2,000 games, and pitched somewhere between 50 and 100 no-hitters. He had an amazing array of fastballs, including his famous "hesitation pitch." Mid-pitch, Paige's left leg hesitated, delaying the follow-through of his arm. Batters never knew when the ball was coming!

During the 1940s, Paige played for the Kansas City Monarchs. He helped them win the 1942 Black World Series.

After **Jackie Robinson** broke the color barrier, Paige was finally signed by a major league team, the Cleveland Indians. In 1948, at 42, he became the first black pitcher in the American League.

On his barnstorming tours, Satchel Paige billed himself as the "World's Greatest Pitcher, Guaranteed to Strike Out the First Nine Men."

Thomas Paine
philosopher ★ 1737–1809

Tom Paine, a failed corset-maker, left England for the American colonies in 1774. The revolution was simmering. Paine helped it reach a boiling point by writing *Common Sense* (1776). In his famous pamphlet, he explained why a war for independence was necessary. He outlined bold new ideas about a democratic government and a society based on equality. *Common Sense,* was credited with converting American colonists to the revolutionary cause.

Paine joined the Continental army. During the war's most difficult period, he wrote *The American Crisis* (1776) on top of a drumhead. It opened with the famous line, "These are the times that try men's souls." General **George Washington** used it to rally his weary troops before their famous surprise attack on Trenton, New Jersey.

After the war, Paine returned to Europe. He published another fiery but best-selling pamphlet, *The Rights of Man* (1791). It defended the French Revolution, called for social reform, condemned the class system, and argued for freedom of religion and the press.

Paine returned to America in 1802. He had become a notorious figure because of his attack on Christianity in *The Age of Reason* (1794). Ignored and outcast, Paine died in poverty.

"Tyranny, like hell, is not

Arnold Palmer
golfer ★ 1929—

Before the 1950s, the only place you'd see a good golf game was at a ritzy country club. Then Arnold Palmer—and television—came along.

Palmer, the 1954 U.S. Amateur golfing champion, turned professional in 1955. Three years later, he won his first Masters title, just one stroke ahead of his competition. In fact, Palmer became famous for his close calls and the daring strokes he took to catch up (or sometimes *lose* a lead!). His exciting playing style and energetic personal style made Palmer a fan favorite. At any tournament, crowds of cheering, clapping supporters who called themselves Arnie's Army followed the golf pro. So did the television cameras. Palmer played a great role in making golf media-friendly and popular.

In peak form from 1958 to 1964, Palmer won four Masters, two British Opens, and a U.S. Open. He became the first pro-golf millionaire. Twice he was named Player of the Year by the Professional Golf Association (PGA). In 1962, Palmer lost the U.S. Open to a new, upcoming player, **Jack Nicklaus**.

Palmer established the U.S. Senior PGA Tour for older golfers in 1980—and then promptly won its championship.

Standing 27 feet away from the 17th hole, Arnold Palmer birdied in the 1960 Masters tournament. That means he used one stroke fewer than average to get the ball in.

Charlie Parker
jazz musician ★ 1920—1955

Charlie "Bird" Parker was one of jazz's great geniuses and one of its great tragedies.

Parker played alto sax in hot, jazzy, gangster-ridden Kansas City, Missouri, in the 1930s. At times, he was laughed off the stage for his self-taught, offbeat way of playing jazz.

In the early 1940s, Parker played in New York City, the center of the jazz world. At first, he played in swing bands, which is how he met **Dizzy Gillespie**. Parker experimented with innovative new jazz techniques, rhythms, and chords. He became the master of bebop and one of the world's most influential jazz players. He also fell heavily under the influence of drugs and alcohol. In 1946, he had a nervous breakdown.

Parker was blowing his sax again within a year and had formed a quintet that included **Miles Davis**. During the 1950s, he toured clubs in Europe and the U. S. But Parker was never too far from drugs and alcohol. In 1955, he died of pneumonia. The great sax player was only 35 years old.

easily conquered." —THOMAS PAINE

"The only tired I was,

Ely S. Parker's Seneca birth name,
Ha-sa-no-an-da, meant "Leading Name."

Ely S. Parker
commissioner of Indian affairs ★ 1828—1895

Ely S. Parker was born on the Seneca Tonawanda reservation in western New York. He was educated in white schools, where he was an exceptional student. At 18, Parker went to Washington, D.C., with Seneca leaders to negotiate land treaties with Congress. They were unsuccessful. (However, in 1857 Parker negotiated a treaty that let the Seneca buy back most of their Tonawanda reservation.)

Law school followed, but Parker was not considered "American," so he wasn't allowed to practice. He became an engineer instead and worked on the Erie Canal. In 1857, his work took him to Illinois where he was befriended by a local shopkeeper: **Ulysses S. Grant**.

Parker became Grant's aide during the Civil War and quickly rose through the military ranks. When Grant became president, he appointed Parker commissioner of the Bureau of Indian Affairs in 1869. He was the first Native American to hold the post. Parker tried to clean up the corrupt bureau, protect both government and tribal interests, and deliver on treaty promises of food, clothing, and other supplies to the tribes.

Gordon Parks in 1997, with his photo American Gothic.

Gordon Parks
photographer ★ 1912—

While working as a waiter on a train, Gordon Parks found a magazine with powerful photos of migrant workers. Parks was so moved he bought a camera himself. On layovers, he haunted Chicago's tenements and teeming South Side streets. Parks shot photos of the poor people he saw there. By 1941, he landed a job at the federal Farm Security Administration. He was the first African American to do so.

Hired by **Henry Luce**'s *Life* in 1948, Parks became the magazine's first black staff photographer. He worked there until 1972. Parks focused his lens on everybody from celebrities to civil rights leaders. Parks saw his camera as a tool in the struggle for social and political justice. His famous photo essays followed everyday people as they grappled with segregation in 1950s Alabama or poverty in Harlem. He documented the life and death of **Malcolm X** and the rise of the Black Panthers.

Parks has written more than 12 books, including memoirs, novels, poetry, and photography books. He also directed the hit Hollywood movie *Shaft* (1971).

172

was tired of giving in." — ROSA PARKS

Rosa Parks
civil rights activist ★ 1913—

Rosa Parks stood up for her rights by sitting down.

On December 1, 1955, the 42-year-old seamstress refused to give up her seat on a Montgomery, Alabama, bus to a white passenger. Her arrest sparked a massive boycott.

Parks had joined the National Association for the Advancement of Colored People (NAACP) in 1943 and served as its secretary. After her arrest, Parks and the NAACP urged African Americans not to ride segregated city buses. A young Montgomery pastor, **Dr. Martin Luther King, Jr.**, helped lead the boycott. For 381 days, thousands of African Americans walked, rode bicycles, or car-pooled across Montgomery. The bus company lost money. Parks and her husband lost their jobs because of their activism. But the whole country heard about the boycott, which helped fire up the civil rights movement nationally.

Rosa Parks being fingerprinted after her arrest in 1955. She was fined $14. Parks is known today as the "Mother of the Civil Rights Movement."

In 1956, Parks's case went to the U.S. Supreme Court, which ruled that segregation in public places was unconstitutional. A year later, Parks and her family moved to Detroit, Michigan, where they felt safer. Parks worked for Michigan congressman John Conyers for 25 years. Rosa Parks has received many awards, including the Congressional Gold Medal of Honor (1999).

George S. Patton, Jr.
general ★ 1885—1945

Legendary World War II general George S. Patton, Jr. sported a gold helmet and pearl-handled revolvers. "Old Blood-and-Guts" Patton was a complex man but a fearless commander.

Patton conducted brilliant campaigns in North Africa and Sicily from 1942 to 1943. He led the Second Corps in Africa and the Seventh Army in Italy to important Allied victories. Then Patton tarnished his reputation by yelling at two shell-shocked soldiers in a hospital. After being forced to apologize for his bad behavior, Patton took command of the Third Army. Under the fiery, flamboyant general, the Third Army's tanks and troops blazed across France and helped liberate Paris in 1944. His army moved faster than any other in history. In less than a year, Patton had reclaimed 6,484 miles of German territory. At the crucial Battle of the Bulge in the Ardennes section of Belgium, Patton's Third Army broke through German lines to rescue trapped U.S. troops. This was one of Patton's boldest, most grueling military moves.

George Patton died after a car accident in 1945.

"Once you put your hand to the plough you don't

Alice Paul wrote the first equal rights amendment, called it the Lucretia Mott Amendment, and got it introduced to Congress in 1923.

Alice Paul
suffragist ★ 1885—1977

Alice Paul was willing to risk jail and worse to get what she wanted: the right to vote.

Paul, a prominent member of the National American Woman Suffrage Association (NAWSA), helped organize a massive parade on March 3, 1913, the day before President **Woodrow Wilson**'s inauguration. Five thousand suffragists marched down Pennsylvania Avenue in Washington, D.C. Alice Paul led the parade.

Paul formed the radical National Woman's Party (NWP) in 1917. She thought more action was necessary to win the right to vote for women. The NWP targeted Congressional Democrats and held them responsible for not getting the women's suffrage amendment passed. They staged protests and were repeatedly jailed for their militancy.

The NWP kept the pressure on President Wilson. In January 1917, they picketed the White House daily and more than 265 suffragists were arrested, including Paul. To discredit her, Alice Paul was jailed in solitary confinement in the psychiatric ward of a prison. Three years later, Paul's radical efforts paid off. The 19th Amendment was ratified in 1920. Alice Paul and millions of women across the country could finally cast their ballots.

Linus Pauling
chemist ★ 1901—1994

Linus Pauling taught at the California Institute of Technology for 36 years.

Proteins. Peace. Scientist Linus Pauling was heavily invested in both. That's how he became the only person ever to win two unshared Nobel Prizes.

In the 1930s, Pauling became interested in protein chemistry. He studied amino acids, (the building blocks of protein), hemoglobin, and antibodies. Still, he puzzled over an essential question: What was the structure of protein molecules?

In 1948, Pauling suffered from kidney disease. While recovering, he sketched polypeptides, the chain of bonds and amino acids that build proteins. He folded his sketches back and forth. He formed a helix (a 3-D spiral) and he found an answer. His "alpha helix" was the basic shape of protein. (This had a big impact on the DNA studies of **James Watson** and Francis Crick.)

After World War II, Pauling lobbied for a nuclear test ban treaty. His U.S. passport was revoked for his political activity. Pauling was unable to leave the country until he was awarded the 1954 Nobel Prize for chemistry.

From the 1950s on, Pauling studied the scientific connections between nutrition and health. In 1963, he was awarded the Nobel Peace Prize, and in 1975, the National Medal of Science.

Walter Payton
football player ★ 1954—1999

His nickname, "Sweetness," came from his personality. It doesn't even hint at the power and intensity Walter Payton brought to his football playing.

Payton was the Chicago Bears' star running back from 1975 to 1987. In fact, he was the star running back of the entire National Football League (NFL). He holds the NFL record for rushing—16,726 yards! In one 1977 game against the Minnesota Vikings, Payton ran an amazing 275 yards. Six years later, he beat **Jim Brown**'s rushing record of 12,312 yards. Overall, Payton had 10 seasons in which he gained more than 1,000 yards.

As running back, Payton could be a freight train or an artful dodger. His speed and skill won him two Most Valuable Player awards (1977, 1985). With Payton in their uniform, the Bears bested the San Francisco Giants and the Los Angeles Rams in the 1984 play-offs. Then they roared to a 46–10 win against the New England Patriots in Super Bowl XX. Two seasons later, Payton retired. In honor of his great teamwork, the Bears hung up Number 34, too.

Payton died of cancer when he was only 45.

Robert E. Peary
explorer ★ 1856—1920

Robert E. Peary lost eight toes to frostbite. He was once so close to starvation that he ate his sled dogs. But he got what he wanted. He got to the North Pole.

Peary led seven Arctic expeditions between 1891 and 1909. **Matthew Henson** accompanied him on all of his Arctic trips. It took five difficult expeditions before Peary crossed the perilous Greenland Ice Cap and succeeded in locating the most northern shore of Greenland in 1900. He collected important scientific and surveying data on these trips. He even hauled back three colossal meteorites.

In winter 1909, Peary and his crew returned to the Arctic. They landed at Ellesmere Island, Canada. Twenty-three men, 133 dogs, and 19 sleds set out across the frozen Arctic Ocean on March 1. The temperature was subzero, the terrain treacherous. As they got farther along, Peary streamlined the team to ease the strain of travel. A smaller party of men, dogs, and sleds continued the trip north. The rest set up camp. On April 6, 1909, Peary, Henson, and members of the Inuit, Oatah, Seegloo, Ookeah, and Eginwah tribes planted an American flag at the North Pole.

Robert E. Peary had to disprove a rival explorer's claim that he had reached the North Pole first. Congress declared Peary the winner in 1911.

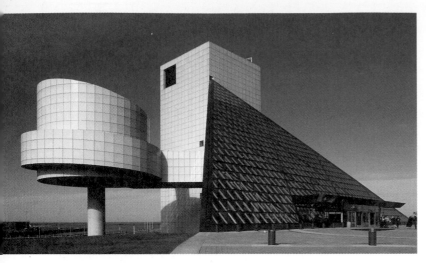
I. M. Pei designed the Rock and Roll Hall of Fame in Cleveland, Ohio. It was completed in 1995.

I. M. Pei
architect ★ 1917—

Ieoh Ming Pei has built a world-class reputation using geometric shapes in a whole new way.

Pei earned degrees in architecture from the Massachusetts Institute of Technology (MIT) and Harvard University's Graduate School of Design. In 1955, he formed his own architectural firm.

Pei designed the **John F. Kennedy** Library in Boston in 1964, which brought him national recognition and new jobs. In 1979, Pei designed a wing for the National Gallery of Art in Washington, D.C. Pei's East Building is a modern, geometric addition made of the same pink marble as the original building. It includes a waterfall and a giant tetrahedron skylight. The American Institute of Architects named it one of the Ten Best Buildings in the United States.

In 1983, Pei was asked to renovate the Louvre, the famous French museum built in the early 1200s. Many people didn't want it changed. It took 10 years for Pei and his firm to reconfigure the museum. When they were finished, the Louvre's ornate old building shone through Pei's new, sheer, 71-foot glass pyramid, which now serves as the museum's entrance.

Pei's innovative architectural plans have turned into award-winning buildings throughout the world.

William Penn
founder of Pennsylvania and Delaware ★ 1644—1718

William Penn was a wealthy Englishman who shocked his family and friends by becoming a Quaker. In the 17th century, Quakerism was punishable by fines, beatings, or imprisonment. Penn suffered all of that for his strong religious beliefs.

King Charles II of England owed Penn's father money. To repay the debt, in 1681 he gave William Penn a large tract of land in America, to be called Pennsylvania. Penn turned it into his Holy Experiment. People who moved to his colony could worship as they pleased. All trials would be held by jury. All children would be taught to read and write. There would be peaceful treaties with the Native Americans who already lived in Pennsylvania. They would be paid for land the colonists wanted.

Penn never really lived in his colony, but when he came over from England to visit, he designed the colony's beautiful capital, Philadelphia, the "City of Brotherly Love."

"There can be no friendship when

Frances Perkins
secretary of labor ★ 1880–1965

In 1933, President **Franklin D. Roosevelt** appointed Frances Perkins secretary of labor. She was the first woman ever to serve in a presidential cabinet. She championed laws that changed the position of the American worker forever.

When Perkins took office, the country was in the midst of the Great Depression. Fifteen million people were unemployed. Perkins reorganized the Department of Labor and made it more effective and efficient. During the 12 years (1933–1945) she served as labor secretary, she helped establish major New Deal programs. They included the Federal Emergency Relief Administration (1933), the first program for unemployment relief; and the National Recovery Administration, to establish fair business practices and union bargaining rights.

*After Roosevelt's death in 1945, Frances Perkins resigned. In 1946, President **Harry Truman** appointed her to the Civil Service Commission.*

Secretary Perkins believed that working people had the right to a fair wage, decent hours, and benefits if they lost their jobs and when they retired. Her most enduring legacies are the Social Security Act of 1935 and the Fair Labor Standards Act in 1938.

Commodore Matthew Perry used "gunboat diplomacy," or the threat of force, to establish relations between the U.S. and Japan.

Matthew Perry
naval officer ★ 1794–1858

In the 19th century, Japan was by choice an isolated nation, closed to most foreigners. In 1853, U.S. Commodore Matthew Perry sailed into Yedo (Tokyo) Bay, Japan, with four Navy ships. He carried a letter from President Millard Fillmore requesting that the Japanese open up their ports to American merchant ships. "Old Bruin" Perry didn't plan to take no for an answer.

Perry was a seasoned naval officer and skilled diplomat. He'd commanded the first American steam warship and fought in the Mexican-American War in 1847.

The shogun, or ruler of Japan, and many of the Japanese wanted Perry to leave. Perry insisted upon dealing with only high-level Japanese officials. He delivered the message himself and then sailed off, giving the Japanese a few months to think over the proposal.

In February 1854, Perry sailed back to Japan. This time he had 10 ships. He met with Japanese officials. On March 31, 1854, they signed the Treaty of Kanagawa, which opened up two Japanese ports to American boats.

there is no freedom." — WILLIAM PENN

"Make them laugh, make them cry, and back to

The French cheer the arrival of "Black Jack" Pershing in Boulogne, France, on June 13, 1917.

John Pershing
brigadier general ★ 1860—1948

John Pershing's military career spanned cavalry battles to world war. He was a tough disciplinarian, not always popular but feared and respected.

Pershing was nicknamed "Black Jack" because he had commanded African-American troops on the American frontier. In 1898, he did so again in the Spanish-American War. When **Teddy Roosevelt** led his famous Rough Riders in the charge on San Juan Hill, Cuba, Pershing was right there, too. He led the black soldiers of the 10th Cavalry.

During the Mexican Revolution, Pershing led 5,800 U.S. soldiers across the U.S.-Mexico border. In 1916, they pursued Mexican rebel leader Pancho Villa, who had attacked Columbus, New Mexico. A year later, Pershing was crossing European borders.

In 1917, the United States entered World War I. President **Woodrow Wilson** named Black Jack Pershing head of the American Expeditionary Force (AEF). It was a grand name, but in reality, America had no standing army and little military equipment. Pershing built, trained, and mobilized an army. On the European battlefront, he often argued tactics with his Allied peers. However, Pershing commanded the 200,000 American soldiers whose participation in the Meuse-Argonne offensive led to the end of the war in 1918.

King Philip
Wampanoag leader ★ c.1639—1676

The Wampanoag called their chief by his real name, Metacom. The English called him King Philip, because he sometimes wore European clothes. That name stuck to one of the bloodiest wars in American history.

Metacom's father, Massasoit, had helped the first white settlers at Plymouth, Massachusetts. By the time his son became chief, Wampanoag lands and rights were being encroached upon. Metacom gathered warriors from several tribes and struck back. His army was ready: They had guns *and* armor.

King Philip's War (1675–1676) raged through New England. More than 600 colonists died. So did nearly 3,000 Wampanoag. Metacom was surprised and killed by a raiding party.

Vengeful colonists stuck King Philip's head on a pole in their fort in Plymouth. It stayed there for 25 years.

178

Mary Pickford
actress, studio head ★ 1893—1979

Mary Pickford was Hollywood's first major female star. On-screen, she was a sweet, innocent heroine. Off-screen, she was a sharp businesswoman and a tough negotiator.

Pickford, born Gladys Smith in Canada, started out as a child stage actress. She hit Broadway by the time she was 14 and picked up the name Mary Pickford. Two years later she went to Hollywood. In 1909, the 16-year-old actress charmed **D. W. Griffith**, the famous Hollywood director, into casting her. By the time she was 23, Pickford had appeared in dozens of plays and movies.

Beautiful, blond, and talented, Pickford was an emotional, expressive actress. Audiences melted at her deep, soulful gazes and her rosebud lips. Pickford usually played a wholesome, lovable, childlike girl with the spirit of a heroine. Some of her classic, sweet silent-film characters include *Tess of the Storm Country* (1914), *Cinderella* (1915), *Rebecca of Sunnybrook Farm* (1917), and *Pollyanna* (1920). Her acting style influenced other silent-screen stars such as Lillian Gish.

Mary Pickford, "America's Sweetheart."

Pickford knew her impact at the box office and made the most of what it was worth. She fought for contracts that gave her more money and more control. By 1917, she was earning $350,000 per picture. In 1919, Pickford made an excellent business move. She, Griffith, and actors **Charlie Chaplin** and Douglas Fairbanks, Sr. organized their own movie studio, the United Artists Corporation. Through UAC, these famous artists controlled ownership and distribution of their films. A year later, Pickford and Fairbanks married. In 1927, the glamorous husband-and-wife team became the first movie stars to put their footprints in the cement sidewalk in front of Grauman's Chinese Theater. This "Walk of Fame" is now a Hollywood tradition.

Mary Pickford worked steadily through the 1920s and early 1930s, making nearly 200 silent films and four "talkies." In 1929, she cut her hair, changed her image, and vamped it up in her first talking picture, *Coquette*. She won an Academy Award for the film.

In 1933, Pickford retired from acting. Three years later, she became vice president of United Artists, which made her one of the most powerful women in Hollywood. She produced several films and wrote four books, including her autobiography. She joined other Hollywood stars and helped establish a retirement home and hospital for aged actors. In 1975, Pickford was presented with a special Academy Award for her outstanding contributions to the film industry.

Susan La Flesche Picotte
doctor ★ 1865–1915

Dr. Susan La Flesche Picotte was the first Native American woman to earn a medical degree. She graduated at the head of her class at Woman's Medical College in Philadelphia before she was even 24. She then returned to her birthplace, an Omaha reservation in Nebraska, to practice medicine.

Picotte became an unofficial leader of the Omaha. She opened up a medical practice in 1889 and treated both Native American and white patients. In her 25 years as a doctor, she is said to have treated all 1,300 members of her Omaha tribe at one time or another. Picotte was a tireless advocate for better health care for her people. She chaired the local board of health and fought for sanitation improvements. She also traveled to Washington, D.C., to lobby for a ban on liquor sales on the reservation. Liquor, introduced by white settlers, had caused many social and health problems among the Native American tribes. In 1913, Picotte established a modern hospital in Walthill, Nebraska, a reservation town.

Molly Pitcher
American Revolution soldier ★ 1754–1832

There are actually many Molly Pitchers. The name was a term used by soldiers during the American Revolution. When soldiers were thirsty in the middle of battle, women brought them water. The soldiers nicknamed them "molly pitchers."

Mary Ludwig Hays, a famous heroine of the American Revolution, is commonly called Molly Pitcher. Hays was a dairy maid in Carlisle, Pennsylvania. She followed her husband, John Hays, when he joined Pennsylvania's 7th Regiment. Like many colonial women, Hays traveled with the Continental army, doing laundry, cooking, and nursing, until the Battle of Monmouth.

The battle took place on June 28, 1778, in Monmouth, New Jersey. It was a sweltering day. Mary Hays brought water to the men on the hot, smoky battlefield. In the midst of the battle, her husband collapsed. An officer ordered Hays's cannon pulled back, because there was no one to fire it. Mary dropped her pitcher and started loading her husband's cannon. She fired that cannon throughout the bloody battle—even after enemy fire ripped through her petticoats. Some accounts say Mary was made a sergeant right on the battlefield by **George Washington** himself.

In 1822, 30 years after the Battle of Monmouth, the Pennsylvania legislature recognized Molly for "services during the American Revolution." They voted to give her a $40-a-year pension.

"I wish I could write as

Pocahontas
Powhatan historical figure ★ c.1595–1617

Matoaks als Rebecka daughter to the mighty Prince
Powhatan Emperour of Attanoughkomouck als Virginia
converted and baptized in the Christian faith and
Wife to the wor.ll M.r Tho. Rolff.

Pocahontas was hailed as an Indian princess when she was presented to the English court in 1616.

Many myths and legends have grown up around this Native American woman. Although information about her life is scarce, one thing seems to be true: Pocahontas, a Powhatan, was invaluable to the early settlers of Jamestown, Virginia.

Pocahontas was the daughter of **Powhatan**, chief of 30 tribes in the area. Her tribal name, Matoaka, meant "playful." She is credited with helping keep the peace between the Europeans and the Native Americans. Pocahontas often visited Jamestown, sometimes representing her powerful father, sometimes bringing food to the struggling colonists. (There is no accurate record that she saved the life of the colony's leader, Captain John Smith.)

In 1613, an English captain lured Pocahontas aboard his ship on the Potomac River. He held her hostage in order to force Powhatan to release some English prisoners. While a prisoner, Pocahontas learned English and converted to Christianity. In 1614, she married John Rolfe, the Jamestown planter who introduced tobacco to Virginia. The Rolfes traveled to England in 1616, where Pocahontas became ill and died.

Edgar Allan Poe
author ★ 1809–1849

His poems and short stories were filled with horror, doom, and ruin. So were many periods of his life.

Edgar Allan Poe was orphaned at three. He was disowned as a teenager by the wealthy family who had raised him. Poe enlisted in the army and later dropped out of West Point military academy. In the meantime, his poetry collection, *Al Aaraaf, Tamerlane and Minor Poems* (1829), was published.

Poe moved to Baltimore, Maryland, and worked as a magazine editor and literary critic at the *Southern Literary Messenger*. The magazine's circulation quintupled. But Poe drank and gambled, quarreled with his colleagues, and left his job. He married and moved to Philadelphia, Pennsylvania, then to New York City.

Poe was a brilliant critic and a popular storyteller. Readers loved the psychological horror of "The Tell-Tale Heart" and "The Pit and the Pendulum." In 1841, Poe wrote "The Murders in the Rue Morgue," the first modern detective story ever published.

Baltimore's football team, the Ravens, is named after Poe's famous poem "The Raven" (1845).

Poe's work made him a famous literary figure during the 1840s. But his wife's death, his debts, and alcohol made him melancholy. Poe died at 40 after a drinking binge.

mysterious as a cat." —EDGAR ALLAN POE

This 1950 photo captures Jackson Pollock's innovative painting technique.

Jackson Pollock
painter ★ 1912–1956

Jackson Pollock was a pioneer of Abstract Expressionism, a 1940s modern art movement. Pollock's art itself was all about movement: his and the paint's. Pollock didn't bother with easels, and sometimes he even dispensed with brushes. He spread his large canvas out on the floor. He flung, dripped, and poured paint onto the canvas. Sometimes he added texture with sand, nails, bottle caps, or cigarette butts. Some people called this art "Action Painting." (Some critics called Pollock "Jack the Dripper"!)

Pollock was born in Wyoming, raised in California, and came to New York City in 1926 to study art. There he met Lee Krasner, an artist who would both influence his work and later marry him.

American heiress Peggy Guggenheim commissioned Pollock's first large-scale work. *Mural* (1943) was 8 feet high and 20 feet long. Guggenheim became an important patron and helped Pollock and Krasner move to Long Island in 1945. They lived and worked there until Pollock's death in a car crash in 1956. That same year (and again in 1998) the Museum of Modern Art held a major retrospective exhibit of his work.

Cole Porter
composer ★ 1891–1964

Cole Porter, at the piano, in 1936

"Night and Day," "Anything Goes," "You're the Top," "I Get a Kick Out of You"—Cole Porter's songs were clever, witty, and sophisticated, just like their composer.

Porter came from a wealthy Indiana family. After college, he headed for New York City, where he wrote a few Broadway flops before penning the 1928 smash musical, *Paris*.

For the next 30 years, Porter composed and wrote 1,500 songs for stage and film musicals. His music was elegant, his lyrics often racy. His songs were performed by top stars of the day such as **Fred Astaire**, Ethel Merman, Bing Crosby, and **Frank Sinatra**. His music credits appeared on box-office hits like *Gay Divorcée* (1932), *Anything Goes* (1934), and *High Society* (1956). Even after a crippling horseback riding accident in 1937 left him in chronic pain, Cole Porter kept working. Many people consider the musical *Kiss Me, Kate* (1948), a show based on Shakespeare's *Taming of the Shrew*, to be his masterpiece.

Colin Powell
general, secretary of state ★ 1937—

Colin Powell, the first African-American secretary of state, didn't have an easy first year on the job: China captured a U.S. plane. Then the ongoing violence increased between Israel and Palestine. On September 11, 2001, the United States was attacked—the World Trade Center towers collapsed, and the Pentagon was in flames. The U.S. went to war in Afghanistan. The Middle East situation worsened. Powell used his military cool in all these crises.

Powell grew up in inner-city South Bronx, New York. He rose through the Army's ranks during his 35-year military career and became a four-star general. He served one tour of duty in Korea and two tours in Vietnam and was awarded several medals, including two Purple Hearts. Powell graduated from **George Washington** University and the National War College and held key commands overseas and at the Pentagon. He was deputy security advisor or national security advisor under Presidents **Reagan**, **Bush**, and **Clinton**. In 1989, the highly decorated general became the first African-American chairman of the Joint Chiefs of Staff. During his command, General Powell oversaw both the 1989 invasion of Panama and Operation Desert Storm (1991).

President **George W. Bush** appointed Powell secretary of state in 2001. Secretary Powell has earned a reputation for being moderate when it comes to foreign policy discussions.

Powhatan's brother once captured Captain John Smith and brought him before the great chief.

Powhatan
Powhatan leader ★ c.1550—1618

Wahunsonacock was Powhatan's real name. Powhatan was the name of his people, a Native American group that lived along coastal Virginia, and the Chesapeake Bay. Powhatan was also the name of a confederacy of 30 Eastern Woodland tribes, numbering about 15,000 people. Wahunsonacock headed that, too. The English colonists who came to Jamestown in 1607 found this all pretty confusing. So they called the chief himself Powhatan.

Powhatan was interested in trade with the colonists, particularly for guns. He told his people to help feed the starving Europeans and show them how to plant yams and corn. His daughter, **Pocahontas**, became a particular favorite among the colonists.

The colonists in return became more and more demanding. They wanted more food. They took more land. In 1610, Powhatan tried to get rid of the ragged settlers by cutting off their food supplies. Unfortunately, a fresh boat of Europeans arrived. They brought diseases that raced through the Powhatan confederacy. Wahunsonacock died in an epidemic in 1618.

183

Elvis Presley
rock 'n' roll singer ★ 1935—1977

Elvis Presley swiveled his hips, pouted his lips, let loose with a guitar riff—and set off a rock 'n' roll craze!

Elvis grew up in Mississippi and Tennessee where he heard gospel music in church and rhythm and blues from bars. He got his first guitar when he was 11 and started plucking country tunes.

Elvis paid $4.00 to cut his first record at Sun Studios in 1953. Within a year, Sun released Presley's version of "That's All Right." Within months, Elvis was famous. He topped the charts 18 times with songs like "Heartbreak Hotel," "Blue Suede Shoes," "Hound Dog," "Love Me Tender," and "All Shook Up." He starred and sang in 33 movies, including the classic *Jailhouse Rock* (1957). He cut 131 albums and singles that went gold or platinum. His first TV special (1968) was a sensation. Presley's concerts and Las Vegas shows were sell-outs. But Elvis was on a downward spiral. He holed up at his mansion, Graceland. He gorged on junk food and drugs. On August 16, 1977, Elvis Presley died of heart failure. All around the world people mourned "The King."

Elvis Presley's dancing was too racy for television in 1956. The producers of the Ed Sullivan Show filmed him from the waist up.

Leontyne Price
opera singer ★ 1927—

When she was a child, Leontyne Price's mother took her to hear **Marian Anderson** sing. Price already sang in church choirs in her hometown of Laurel, Mississippi. After hearing Anderson, she decided to make singing her life's work.

After graduating from college in 1948, Price got a scholarship to study at the Juilliard School of Music in New York City. In 1952, she debuted on Broadway as a singer in Virgil Thomson and **Gertrude Stein**'s opera, *Four Saints in Three Acts*. Price made her debut in classical opera seven years later with the San Francisco Opera. In 1961, she made opera headlines. After Price sang the last note of *Il Trovatore*, the audience at New York's prestigious Metropolitan Opera House applauded—for 42 minutes!

Leontyne Price was awarded the Presidential Medal of Freedom in 1964 and the National Medal of the Arts in 1985. She has also won more than 20 Grammys.

September 30, 2001. Leontyne Price came out of retirement to sing at a memorial concert for everyone affected by the 9/11 terrorist attacks.

popular, must have a dance." — TITO PUENTE

Tito Puente
musician ★ c.1923–2000

There's now a street in El Barrio, the Spanish Harlem section of New York City, called Tito Puente Way. It's a tribute to "El Rey," the "King of Latin Music," who grew up in the neighborhood.

Puente credited the neighborhood for exposing him to both jazz and Latin music. He incorporated both kinds of music into what he called "mambo instrumentals." After a stint in the U.S. Navy during World War II, Puente studied at the prestigious Juilliard School of Music. In 1948, he formed what would become the Tito Puente Orchestra. Puente and his big band played regularly at New York's Palladium club during the 1950s. He helped popularize mambo, cha-cha, merengue, and other Latin-influenced music.

Tito Puente produced more than 100 albums during his career, including the best-selling *Dance Mania* (1958), *Mambo Diablo* (1985), and *Mambo Birdland* (2000). He won five Grammy awards. Puente played hundreds of shows a year, often with other Latin stars like singer **Celia Cruz**. In 1963, his classic "Oye Como Va" was a huge crossover hit, and was later made even bigger by the group Santana.

A. Philip Randolph
civil rights activist ★ 1889–1979

Asa Philip Randolph organized his first labor protest when he was a waiter on a steamship. He led the fight to improve the substandard living conditions of the African-American crew.

Inspired by **W. E. B. DuBois**, Randolph soon looked for a larger platform for his message of equality and dignity in the workplace. He joined the Socialist party. In 1917, he started the *Messenger*, a radical magazine that addressed labor issues.

In 1925, Randolph organized the Brotherhood of Sleeping Car Porters. It took him 12 years to do it, but in 1937, the Pullman train company finally agreed to deal with the porters' union. It was the first labor contract negotiated between a corporation and an African-American organization.

Randolph was a tireless speaker, marcher, and organizer. He rallied blacks to join unions and fight for equal wages. In 1941, he brought enough pressure on President **Franklin Roosevelt** that the president signed an executive order making it illegal for defense contractors and federal agencies to discriminate because of race. Randolph also kept the heat on President **Harry Truman** until the armed forces were desegregated in 1948. Randolph organized the historic March on Washington on August 28, 1963, which drew 250,000 people. **Martin Luther King, Jr.,** gave his "I Have a Dream" speech there.

"Government is not the

Jeannette Rankin
U.S. representative ★ 1880–1973

When Jeannette Rankin took her seat in Congress in 1917, most women in the United States weren't even allowed to vote.

Rankin was elected to the U.S. House of Representatives by the people of Montana, one of the few places where women could vote. Congresswoman Rankin fought for passage of a federal women's suffrage amendment and also introduced several bills that supported the rights of women and children. A lifelong pacifist, Rankin voted against U.S. entry into World War I. Rankin's peace vote cost her the next election. She then spent several years working with **Jane Addams** and other women activists. In 1915, Rankin, Addams, and **Carrie Chapman Catt** helped found the Woman's Peace Party.

In 1940, Montana sent Rankin to the House of Representatives again. She voted her conscience again. In 1941, on the day after the bombing of Pearl Harbor, Rankin was the only Congressional member who voted against a declaration of war. She was not reelected.

For the rest of her life, Jeannette Rankin lobbied and lectured for women's rights and other social issues. In 1968, she headed a brigade of 5,000 women who joined a massive march on Washington to protest U.S. involvement in the Vietnam War. Rankin was then 87 years old.

Robert Rauschenberg
artist ★ 1925–

Animals. Vegetable dye. Car tires. Shoes. Avant-garde artist Robert Rauschenberg didn't limit himself to paint and canvas.

In a career that spans more than 50 years, Rauschenberg has produced paintings, lithographs, drawings, set designs and costumes, and art installations. He created the three-dimensional Combine, a term he coined. Combines are a combination of sculpture and painting. For example, Rauschenberg's *Bed* (1955) is a real pillow and quilt framed and covered with wide strokes and dribbling trails of paint. In *Monogram* (1955–1959), a stuffed goat with a paint-splashed

Robert Rauschenberg (l.) with dancer-choreographer **Merce Cunningham** in 2000.

muzzle wears a tire around its middle and stands on an abstractly painted platform.

Rauschenberg, who hails from Port Arthur, Texas, moved to New York City in 1949. His first solo exhibition was in 1958. From the 1960s on, Rauschenberg worked with silk screens, collages, and prints. Almost 30 years later, the Guggenheim Museum in New York City mounted a major retrospective exhibit of Rauschenberg's work in 1997, which included 400 pieces.

solution to our problems." — RONALD REAGAN

Ronald Reagan
40th president ★ 1911—

In 1980, this former movie actor, television host, and governor of California landed the starring role of his life: Ronald Reagan was elected president of the United States.

Reagan, a conservative Republican, served two terms (1981–1989). The oldest president ever elected, he was dubbed the Great Communicator because of the folksy ease with which he spoke to the public. People liked Reagan's upbeat, all-American, patriotic outlook. The president's economic policies were controversial, though "Reaganomics" reduced skyrocketing inflation and unemployment rates. But the national debt doubled and the budget deficit grew larger than those of all 39 previous presidencies combined.

After surviving an assassination attempt in 1981, Reagan was elected to a second term in 1984. The presidential election itself was the largest landslide in U.S. history. A high point of this term was when Reagan signed a nuclear missile control agreement in 1987 with the Soviet Union.

The Iran-Contra scandal also broke during Reagan's second term. President Reagan had secretly agreed to sell arms to Iran in exchange for release of American hostages. Members of his National Security Council illegally used the arms profits to fund a guerrilla war against the Nicaraguan government. Nonetheless, Ronald Reagan remained a popular president.

Red Cloud
Oglala Lakota Sioux leader ★ 1822—1909

Red Cloud (Makhpiya-Luta) did not trust the words of the "Great Father in Washington"—with good reason.

In the 1860s, the U.S. Army was building forts on Lakota territory. They wanted to open up the Bozeman Trail, which ran from Wyoming through Montana to Colorado, and let in settlers and prospectors. Red Cloud attacked. He and his warriors wiped out a troop of 80 soldiers near Fort Phil Kearny, Wyoming, in 1866. For the next two years, Red Cloud, along with **Sitting Bull** and **Crazy Horse**, kept up the assault. Finally, in 1868, the conflict, which is often called "Red Cloud's War," was resolved by the Fort Laramie Treaty. The Lakota would keep their lands in South Dakota, Montana, and Wyoming. But not for long.

Gold was discovered in South Dakota in 1874; the Lakota were ousted by 1877. Red Cloud and his people were removed to the Pine Ridge, South Dakota, reservation. There he fought a war of words to stir up public opinion against corrupt government agents and unfair laws against Native Americans.

"I have more than survived. I am living." — CHRISTOPHER REEVE

Christopher Reeve
actor, activist ★ 1952—

Audiences cheered Christopher Reeve when he played the heroic man of steel in the box-office hit *Superman* (1978) and its three sequels. Now he's playing an even more important and dramatic role. Reeve is an activist on behalf of research into spinal cord injuries.

Because of a horseback riding accident in 1995, Reeve is paralyzed from the neck down. His career was disrupted, but Reeve has not let it be destroyed. Just two years after his accident, he debuted as a director. His cable movie, *In the Gloaming*, was nominated for five Emmy Awards. A year later, Reeve starred in a remake of Alfred Hitchcock's thriller, *Rear Window*. He won a Screen Actors Guild Award for his performance.

Christopher Reeve got a thundering ovation when he appeared at the 1996 Academy Awards, not long after his paralyzing accident.

Reeve has made countless personal appearances, including testifying before Congress, in a bid to secure more funding for medical research and more rights for the disabled. He established the Christopher Reeve Paralysis Foundation in 1999 to further these goals. His best-selling book, *Still Me* (1998), is the moving autobiography of a real-life Superman.

Janet Reno
attorney general ★ 1938—

On March 12, 1993, Janet Reno became the first woman attorney general of the United States.

Reno came to the job with a reputation as a powerful advocate for children's rights and criminal justice reform. She earned that reputation during her 15 years as Florida's state prosecutor.

As the head of the U.S. Justice Department, Reno was both praised and panned. She got good marks for the investigations of the first terrorist attack on New York's World Trade Center (1993) and the Oklahoma City bombing (1995). Crime dropped and 100,000 federally funded police went to work during her tenure.

Attorney General Janet Reno oversaw the FBI, Drug Enforcement Agency, Bureau of Prisons, Immigration and Naturalized Services, U.S. marshals, and U.S. attorneys.

Reno took the heat for the FBI's deadly battle with a religious cult in Waco, Texas, in 1993. Congressional Republicans criticized her for not opening a special investigation into the possible mishandling of campaign funds by the Democrats. The Clinton White House was angered by Reno's role in allowing the investigation of the Whitewater financial scandal in 1993. Still, President **William Clinton** reappointed Reno attorney general in 1997. During her second term, Reno handled politically charged cases like the 1999 arrest of Dr. Wen Ho Lee, who was unjustly accused of leaking nuclear secrets; and the Elián Gonzalez custody/asylum case (2000).

Paul Revere

American Revolution leader ★ 1735–1818

Paul Revere, a Boston native, was an expert metalworker and engraver. He even designed false teeth. Revere, one of the original Sons of Liberty, was a leading patriot during the American Revolution. He delivered information to revolutionaries in other colonies. Reprints of his engraving of the Boston Massacre (1770) fueled patriotic fervor everywhere.

In 1863, Henry Wadsworth Longfellow celebrated the Boston silversmith in his poem, "The Midnight Ride of Paul Revere."

On April 18, 1775, British troops headed from Boston to Lexington and Concord, Massachusetts, to seize **Samuel Adams** and **John Hancock** and the patriots' arsenal of guns, gunpowder, and cannonballs. Revere planned to get there first to warn them of the coming attack. He set off on his famous "Midnight Ride" from Charlestown, Massachusetts. Revere charged through the night on horseback, sounding the alarm. Adams and Hancock escaped. Revere was captured near Lexington. The British took his horse, but he was released.

During the American Revolution, Revere was commander of the patriot forces that helped defend Boston Harbor. After the war, he expanded his prosperous business. He forged cannons and church bells and opened the first copper-sheet mill in the country. He also designed and engraved the new nation's first money.

Charles Richter

physics scientist ★ 1900–1985

A 2.0 earthquake would set a sign swinging. A 4.0 earthquake would shatter windows. A 6.0 earthquake would split the ground beneath your feet. A 7.0 earthquake would twist railroad tracks and release enough energy to heat New York City for a whole year. An 8.25 earthquake leveled San Francisco in 1906. Where do these numbers come from? The Richter scale.

Charles Richter was a physics scientist at the California Institute of Technology. During the 1930s, he started working at the Seismological Laboratory there. He studied seismic waves, the vibrating shock released by earthquakes or underground explosions. He recorded the seismic waves of more than 200 earthquakes a year in southern California. In 1935, Richter introduced a scientific scale for measuring the size and magnitude, or strength, of earthquakes. The Richter scale is not an actual instrument. It is made up of tables and charts used to analyze seismic readings.

Charles Richter was a professor at the California Institute of Technology until he retired in 1970. He was the author of several important books on seismology, the study of earthquakes.

Sally Ride
astronaut ★ 1951—

Astrophysicist Dr. Sally Ride was the first American woman in space and the youngest American astronaut ever to circle Earth. On June 18, 1983, she left Earth aboard the space shuttle *Challenger*. The mission lasted six days. On-board, Ride monitored science experiments while dealing with zero gravity. She also operated the robotic arm designed to retrieve and launch space satellites. When *Challenger* landed, Ride and the other four astronauts in the shuttle crew had traveled 2.5 million miles.

Dr. Ride went into space a second time in 1984. She was scheduled for a third space trip when the *Challenger* exploded on January 28, 1986. Ride was appointed to the commission that investigated and reported on the causes of the disaster.

Sally Ride was one of 35 people out of 8,900 applicants selected for NASA's astronaut program.

Her analysis suggested ways NASA's space exploration program should be redesigned. In 1987, Ride retired from NASA and went to work at Stanford University. She is now director of the California Space Institute and a physics professor at the University of California at San Diego.

Paul Robeson
actor, singer, civil rights leader ★ 1898—1976

Paul Robeson's powerful presence and remarkable voice made him a stage and film headliner. So did his role in the unfolding drama of the civil rights movement.

Robeson, the son of a slave, grew up in a time of racial segregation. Still, he managed to get a scholarship to Rutgers University, where he was class valedictorian in 1919. Robeson then earned a law degree from prestigious Columbia Law School. He also performed in a few amateur plays.

Because of prejudice, Robeson's law career faltered, but luckily he fell in with playwright **Eugene O'Neill** and the innovative theater group, the Provincetown Players. When Robeson played the lead part in O'Neill's *The Emperor Jones* (1925), he got rave reviews. But his role in the 1936 film version of the musical *Show Boat* made him a star. Robeson sang "Ole Man River" in one of the most powerful performances in American film history.

Robeson acted onstage and in movies. In 1943, he starred in Shakespeare's *Othello* onstage in New York in a then record-breaking 296 performances. His singing tours helped popularize slave spirituals and other African-American music.

In the 1930s, Robeson became active in social justice causes. Unjustly labeled "anti-American" by the media and government, his career suffered greatly because of his activism.

that it could not be breached on gridiron, court, diamond."

Jackie Robinson
baseball player ★ 1919—1972

Jack Roosevelt Robinson wore many uniforms in his lifetime. As a college student at the University of California, Los Angeles, he was a varsity athlete in basketball, football, track, and baseball. Robinson donned a Honolulu Bears jersey and played semipro football in 1941. He traded that in for soldier's khakis when he enlisted in the Army during World War II. But no matter what uniform he wore on the outside, inside Robinson was always the same: an outstanding athlete, a proud African American, and a man willing to fight for equality and respect.

In 1945, baseball fans took notice of Robinson, the rising new star in the Kansas City Monarchs uniform. The Monarchs were a Negro League baseball team. It was the only league open to African Americans. Branch Rickey, manager of the Brooklyn Dodgers, planned to change that.

Rickey signed Robinson in 1945. It was a major-league deal that changed the future of American sports. In 1947, Robinson put on a Dodgers' uniform, number 42, and became "Baseball's Great Experiment." For the first time in the 20th century, an African American was playing Major League Baseball.

In honor of Jackie Robinson's achievements, his famous uniform number 42 was retired in 1997.

Robinson endured death threats, ugly racial taunts, and objects thrown on the field—and those were just from the fans! In the dugout, some players shunned him. On the field, others spiked him or deliberately threw balls at him. He did not fight back. He knew many people were looking for any excuse to bar African Americans from baseball. Jackie Robinson didn't give them one.

The same year he broke the color barrier, Robinson was named Rookie of the Year. He blasted out 12 home runs, led the league in stolen bases (29), and ended the season with a .297 batting average. Two years later, he took the National League Most Valuable Player award. With his surefire fielding, power hitting, and sensational steals, Robinson helped the Dodgers capture six pennants in 10 years. He was a legendary runner who stole 197 bases during his career. Nineteen of them were home plate. In one famous play, Robinson, then 36 years old, stole home during a 1955 World Series game against the Yankees. His run helped the Dodgers finally win the championship title.

Jackie Robinson retired from baseball in 1957, but he continued to be a champion off the field. He became a businessman and an active, vocal leader in the growing civil rights movement.

John D. Rockefeller

industrialist ★ 1839—1937

*In 1913, John D. Rockefeller, Sr., (l.) was worth the equivalent of three times what **Bill Gates** is worth. He celebrated every September 26, the anniversary of the day he got his first job.*

In the 1860s, John D. Rockefeller, a successful Cleveland, Ohio, businessman, branched out into a new industry. It made him the richest person of all time.

Oil was a new, chaotic business not governed by many rules. Rockefeller was thrifty, efficient, disciplined, and systematic. He built an oil refinery in Cleveland in 1863. He cofounded the Standard Oil Company seven years later. Rockefeller wanted to control the oil business completely. That included raw materials, refining, marketing, and distribution. Rockefeller owned everything from oil fields to the timber used to make oil barrels. He bought out or drove out competing oil refineries. He wheeled and dealed with railroads to get the lowest shipping rates through shady agreements. By the end of the decade, his company, now called Standard Oil Trust, refined nearly 95% of U.S. oil. Rockefeller headed one of the country's most powerful monopolies. (Standard Oil's ruthless practices were later exposed by journalist Ida Tarbell in 1902 in her best-selling history of the company.)

In 1897, Rockefeller retired and became a philanthropist. He donated $530 million in his lifetime. His money helped found the University of Chicago and establish the Rockefeller Foundation and Rockefeller University, a medical research center in New York City.

Norman Rockwell

painter ★ 1894—1978

A postage stamp showing a 1929 Norman Rockwell illustration, "Doctor and Doll."

Norman Rockwell's paintings show an ideal America: happy, kind, devout, patriotic, and well-fed. Many Americans liked what they saw. Rockwell's art became enormously popular and was widely reproduced.

From the beginning, the New York–born artist wanted to be an illustrator. His goal was to paint a cover for the popular magazine *Saturday Evening Post*. Rockwell achieved his goal. His first *Post* cover appeared in 1916, and 316 more *Post* covers followed in a relationship that lasted until 1963. During that time, Rockwell also produced illustrations for ads and other magazines. In 1920, he did a painting for the annual Boy Scouts calendar. He continued doing this every year until his death.

Rockwell's work is famous for its warmhearted nostalgia and accurate historical detail. It also had an impact on the contemporary world. In 1942, Rockwell did a series of paintings celebrating the "four freedoms" President **Franklin D. Roosevelt** had talked about in a speech. During World War II, these paintings were exhibited around the country. They raised $132,992,539 for war bonds. In addition to his patriotic and homespun themes, Rockwell also painted American leaders. Some of his later works explored problems like racism and poverty.

192

"My folks didn't come over on the Mayflower,

Richard Rodgers and Oscar Hammerstein II

composer ★ 1902–1979 (Rodgers);
lyricist ★ 1895–1960 (Hammerstein)

"No girls, no gags, no chance," one critic predicted about Rodgers and Hammerstein's musical Oklahoma! *He was so wrong.* Oklahoma!, *choreographed by Agnes de Mille, was a smash hit and won a 1944 Pulitzer prize.*

"Oh, What a Beautiful Mornin'," "Do-Re-Mi," "Climb Every Mountain." Some of America's most famous, showstopping tunes have one thing in common: Rodgers and Hammerstein.

Composer Richard Rodgers and lyricist Oscar Hammerstein II had each achieved success and fame before forming their extraordinary partnership. Rodgers collaborated with lyricist Lorenz Hart from 1920 to 1943. Their work, including famous songs like "My Funny Valentine" and "The Lady Is a Tramp," was heard in Broadway shows and Hollywood movie musicals. Rodgers composed more than 1,000 songs in his lifetime. Hammerstein left law school to write musicals and operettas. One of his biggest hot-ticket musicals was *Show Boat* (1927), for which Jerome Kern wrote the music.

Rodgers and Hammerstein worked together for 16 years. Rodgers wrote the music and Hammerstein wrote the words for their nine hit musicals, including *Oklahoma!* (1943), *South Pacific* (1949), *Carousel* (1945), *The King and I* (1951), and *The Sound of Music* (1959). They revolutionized the American musical, which until then had been a loosely connected sequence of songs and dances. Rodgers and Hammerstein developed a more sophisticated type of musical, where the drama, staging, dance, music, and lyrics all worked together to tell a story.

Will Rogers

entertainer ★ 1879–1935

Will Rogers was born on a ranch in the Cherokee Nation (now part of Oklahoma). He learned to use a lasso to work on cattle drives. That rope came in handy in more ways than one.

Rogers became a trick twirler who could toss three lassos at once. He started touring in Wild West and vaudeville shows. Rogers tossed a little homespun humor into his act and took it to Broadway, as a star of the Ziegfield Follies (1916–1924). People loved him.

In the 1920s and 1930s, Rogers was the country's most popular folk hero. He starred in 71 Hollywood films. He became a well-known radio commentator and wrote a nationally syndicated newspaper column. Rogers usually opened with his trademark "All I know is what I read in the papers." Then he was off on a wry, witty commentary about presidents, politicians, and current events. Rogers had considerable clout with his audience. His support helped **Franklin Roosevelt** get elected president in 1932.

The nation's Cowboy Philosopher died in a plane crash en route to Alaska.

they were here to meet the boat." — WILL ROGERS

Eleanor Roosevelt

first lady, UN ambassador ★ 1884–1962

Eleanor Roosevelt logged in 38,000 miles of plane, train, bus, and car travel during her first year as first lady.

"It is not fair to ask of others what you are not willing to do yourself," first lady Eleanor Roosevelt once wrote. She was more than willing to do her share.

Roosevelt was from a wealthy, upper-class family in New York City, but threw herself into improving life for the poor. She worked at settlement houses and investigated sweatshops for the National Consumers League.

In 1905, Eleanor married her cousin **Franklin Delano Roosevelt** (FDR). The Roosevelts were an unusual pair. Eleanor was serious, shy, and considered homely. Franklin was outgoing and dashing. Their 40-year marriage was complicated, but the Roosevelts had a deep emotional bond and a shared commitment to social good. Eleanor convinced her husband to stay in politics after he was paralyzed by polio in 1921. In 1933, FDR was elected president. Eleanor came into her own.

Eleanor Roosevelt was a liberal reformer. Being first lady let her promote her ideas on a national scale. She was the first woman to hold a press conference at the White House. She held 350 of them, for women reporters only. Roosevelt broadcast her own radio program. In 1936, she started writing her own newspaper column, "My Day," which ran for 20 years.

Roosevelt lobbied for New Deal programs. She urged her husband to appoint the first woman cabinet member, **Frances Perkins**. She helped convince FDR to establish the Fair Employment Practices Committee in 1941 to fight racial prejudice in the war industries. Eleanor herself resigned from the Daughters of the American Revolution when they banned **Marian Anderson** from singing at Constitution Hall in 1939 because she was an African American.

The first lady represented FDR at national and international events. She also visited city slums and Dust Bowl shacks. She went down into the coal mines to talk to miners and out into the fields to talk to workers. She saw what the Great Depression had done to rural and urban communities. She reported everything she saw to her husband. Some people attacked Eleanor Roosevelt for having too many opinions and too much influence with the president. But to many Americans, she was a beacon of help and hope.

"You must do the thing you think you cannot do." — ELEANOR ROOSEVELT

After FDR's death in 1945, President **Harry Truman** made Eleanor Roosevelt a delegate to the United Nations (UN). She served as chairman of the Commission on Human Rights. In 1961, president **John F. Kennedy** made her chair of the Commission on the Status of Women. He also reappointed her to the UN. When Eleanor Roosevelt returned to the world body, the entire UN General Assembly gave her a standing ovation.

Franklin D. Roosevelt
32nd president ★ 1882–1945

Franklin Delano Roosevelt's 1932 presidential campaign song was "Happy Days Are Here Again." His confidence and good humor were just what the nation needed to lift it out of the Great Depression.

FDR was president from 1933 to 1945, an unprecedented four terms. When he was first elected, 5,000 banks had closed, 13 million people were out of work, and 25% of all farms had been foreclosed. Roosevelt promised all Americans a "New Deal." It was the first time a president insisted that helping the poor and managing the economy were the federal government's job.

During the first 100 days of his administration, Roosevelt rallied Congress and pushed through important measures. The newly formed Civilian Conservation Corps put three million young men to work building roads, dams, and other projects. The Agricultural Adjustment Act helped farmers hold on to their land. The National

Sixty million Americans tuned in to Roosevelt's "fireside chats," in which the president shared his ideas and plans via radio.

Recovery Administration improved wages and working conditions. The Public Works Administration put people to work on large-scale construction projects. The Tennessee Valley Authority, a flood control project, provided jobs, and it provided electricity to 400,000 farmers.

In 1935, FDR spearheaded the Works Progress Administration (WPA). WPA workers built bridges and public buildings. WPA artists painted public murals and recorded oral histories throughout the country. Roosevelt also supported history-making legislation. The Social Security Act (1935) provided income for retired people, unemployment insurance, and help for the disabled. Because of the Wagner Act (1935), workers' rights to belong to a union and collectively bargain, or negotiate as a group, were protected.

FDR's New Deal, like the warm, charming president himself, was enormously popular. His crippling polio and his presidential duties usually kept him at the White House. First lady

"The only thing we have to fear is fear itself." — FRANKLIN D. ROOSEVELT

Eleanor Roosevelt, whom FDR called his "eyes and ears," kept him well-informed about "ordinary" men and women. The nation began to recover. Then war broke out in Europe in 1939.

At first, the United States remained neutral—then came Pearl Harbor. On December 7, 1941, Japanese bombers attacked the U.S. naval and army bases. FDR told outraged Americans the day "will live in infamy." Then he asked Congress to declare war.

Roosevelt rallied the war effort at home and on the battlefield. In 1943, FDR met with Britain's prime minister Winston Churchill and Josef Stalin, the Soviet Union's premier. The "Big Three" planned strategies to end the war. But Roosevelt didn't live to see the full victory. On April 12, 1945, suffered a stroke and died. The nation wept.

"Speak softly and carry a big stick."

— TEDDY ROOSEVELT

Theodore Roosevelt
26th president ★ 1858–1919

President William McKinley's assassination in 1901 prompted one senator to complain that a cowboy was now president. He meant Teddy Roosevelt, who had, in fact, once been a cowboy. Roosevelt had also been the assistant secretary of the Navy, governor of New York, and vice president of the United States before serving two terms as president (1901–1909)—not to mention his famous charge up Cuba's San Juan Hill with his Rough Riders in 1898, during the Spanish-American War.

"TR" stepped into the presidency as if he were stepping into a boxing ring. He took on powerful industrialists who were forming trusts to fix high prices and low wages. He sent in federal troops to protect striking mine workers and brought all parties to the bargaining table. Teddy Roosevelt promised all Americans a "square deal."

Roosevelt was just as forceful in foreign affairs. He backed a rebellion in Colombia so he could buy land to build the Panama Canal. The Roosevelt Corollary to the **Monroe** Doctrine said the United States could intervene in Latin American affairs if necessary. Roosevelt became the first American to win the Nobel Peace Prize (1906) after he helped bring peace between warring Russia and Japan. He established five national parks, preserving nearly 200 million acres of land. An avid naturalist, Roosevelt once saved a bear cub in 1902. Shortly after, people started making "Teddy" bear stuffed toys.

Diana Ross
singer ★ 1944—

Diva comes from the Latin word for "goddess." Diana Ross is the American definition of the word.

Diana Ross and The Supremes (originally Florence Ballard and Mary Wilson) had 12 number-one hits between 1964 and 1967, a record no other female group has ever broken. Ross, Ballard, and Wilson grew up in a Detroit housing project. They started singing together while still in high school. In 1964, the Supremes' single, "Where Did Our Love Go," shot to number one.

Ross and The Supremes followed with hit after hit: "Baby Love" (1964), "Stop in the Name of Love" (1965), "You Keep Me Hanging On" (1966). But there was tension among the singers, and Ross had her sights set on even brighter stardom. In 1969, she went solo. Her solo albums have included hits, like "Upside Down," from the platinum album *Diana* (1980), and "Muscles" (1982), a chart-topping single written by **Michael Jackson**. Ross was also nominated for an Academy Award for playing **Billie Holiday** in the 1972 film *Lady Sings the Blues*.

Wilma Rudolph
Olympian ★ 1940—1994

Wilma Rudolph was the first American woman to win three gold medals at a single Olympics. It was an amazing feat for any athlete. For Rudolph it was close to a miracle.

As a child, Rudolph was stricken by polio and scarlet fever. Her left leg was paralyzed. It was an incredible struggle to just walk again. Wilma didn't stop until she was running.

Rudolph made the 1956 Olympic team while she was still in high school. She took home a bronze medal in the 400-meter relay. In 1960, she set a world record for the 200-meter dash. That same year, Rudolph went to the Olympics again. This time, she won three gold medals (100-meter sprint, the 200-meter dash, the 400-meter relay). Her hometown, Clarksville, Tennessee, wanted to throw her a

parade. At that time, public events in that state and other parts of the South were racially segregated. Wilma Rudolph was determined. Either the parade was integrated or she wasn't coming. She got what she wanted.

Rudolph set more track-and-field records before she retired in 1962. In 1993, she became the first woman to win the National Sports Award in recognition of her outstanding career achievements.

In 1964, Bill Russell (l.) scores his 10,000th point in an NBA game and hugs famed coach "Red" Auerbach (r.).

Bill Russell
basketball player, coach ★ 1934—

Bill Russell didn't just play basketball—he transformed it! He brought power and fury to the center position, aggressively blocking shots, snatching rebounds, and firing up fast breaks any way he could. Russell was playing a whole new ball game.

Basketball fans cheered Russell as he brought the University of San Francisco team out of obscurity and into a 55-game winning streak in 1955 and 1956. After graduating, Russell turned down offers from the National Basketball Association (NBA) and the Harlem Globetrotters. Instead, he played on the U.S. team in the 1956 Olympics—and took home the gold. Later that same year, Bill Russell signed with the Boston Celtics.

They would dominate the NBA for the next decade. Russell's unstoppable defense helped the Celtics score 11 NBA titles in 13 seasons (1957–1969). Russell himself won an unprecedented Rookie of the Year and Most Valuable Player (MVP) award in 1958. In all, he won five MVP awards (1958, 1961–1963, 1965) and was the first to win three of them in a row.

Russell played for and coached the Celtics from 1966 to 1969. He was the first African American to coach an NBA team.

"I hit big or I miss big. I like

Babe Ruth
baseball player ★ 1895—1948

One year (1930), George Herman "Babe" Ruth earned more than President Herbert Hoover. Two years (1920 and 1927), he hit more home runs by *himself* than any other entire baseball team did. For 21 years, fans jammed stadiums across the country to watch the Babe slug another one home.

America's favorite baseball player actually started out facing home plate. Ruth was a left-handed pitcher for the Boston Red Sox in 1914—a *star* pitcher. He won 20 games in a single season twice. He pitched 29⅔ scoreless innings in a row in World Series games. When he left the pitcher's mound for the batter's box, he often knocked out home runs. The Red Sox started using him more as a fielder and hitter.

The Yankees retired Babe Ruth's uniform number, 3. In 2000, Sports Illustrated named Ruth the best baseball player of the century.

In 1920, the owner of the Red Sox needed money to produce a Broadway show. So he sold Ruth's contract to the Yankees. New York would never be the same. (Neither would Boston!) With Ruth in Yankee pinstripes, the team won seven pennant races and four World Series between 1920 and 1933. Babe Ruth broke record after record, belting out 50 home runs a season (1926–1931), once topping that with 60 home runs in 1927 alone. He played in 10 World Series and hit 15 home runs in World Series play. In the 1932 World Series, Babe Ruth claims to have "called his shot." He pointed his bat to a spot in the centerfield and then smashed a home run out to it. By the time he retired in 1935, Ruth had a slugging average of .690 and a .342 career batting average. His career home-run record—714—held for nearly 40 years. Ruth transformed the game of baseball, bringing power hitting to the forefront of what was now "America's favorite pastime."

Babe Ruth was as famous off the field as on. In 1930 and 1931, Ruth earned $80,000, a fortune at a time when most of the country was sunk in the Great Depression. People eager for distraction gobbled up stories about the ballplayer and his glamorous high life. Ruth liked Cadillacs and fancy clothes. He threw wild parties and bought extravagant gifts for friends. He had an enormous appetite for anything he could eat or drink, from 18-egg omelets to alcohol. Babe Ruth loved publicity and liked being the first real national sports celebrity. He also did plenty of good works, especially for children in hospitals and orphanages.

When he died in 1948, Babe Ruth's body lay in state at Yankee Stadium. Hundreds of thousands streamed through the "House that Ruth Built" to honor the King of Clout, the Sultan of Swat—the Bambino.

to live as big as I can." — BABE RUTH

Nolan Ryan
baseball player ★ 1947—

Nolan Ryan, playing for the Texas Rangers, pitched his record-breaking seventh no-hitter game in 1991. He was 44 years old.

Nolan Ryan pitches his seventh no-hitter in a 1991 game against the Toronto Blue Jays.

In his 28-season major league career (1966–1993), Ryan wore the uniform of the New York Mets, the California Angels, the Houston Astros, and the Texas Rangers. His flaming fastballs helped turn the floundering Mets into the "miracle Mets," winners of the 1969 World Series. Ryan really came into his own while playing for the Angels. In 1975, he tied **Sandy Koufax**'s four no-hitter record. Four years later, he became a free agent and returned to his beloved home state, Texas. As pitcher for the Houston Astros, Ryan broke the strikeout record and held the top ERA (earned run average). He also became the first baseball player to earn a million-dollar salary. In 1989, he signed with the Texas Rangers. Though in his forties, Ryan was still an amazing pitcher. His balls shot from the mound at speeds faster than 90 miles per hour. He racked up three more no-hitters as a Rangers pitcher. With 5,714 career strikeouts, Nolan Ryan was baseball's number-one strikeout pitcher.

Sacajawea
explorer ★ c.1787—1812

Meriwether Lewis and **William Clark** hired fur trapper Toussaint Charbonneau as an interpreter for their 1805 expedition to the Pacific Northwest. Charbonneau brought his wife, Sacajawea, and two-month-old son. The Shoshone woman became an invaluable part of the team.

For the next year, the explorers traveled across the Rocky Mountains, through the Pacific Northwest, and back. It was an 8,000-mile trip. Sacajawea served as a translator and diplomat to negotiate peaceful passage through Native American lands. She showed everyone which wild foods were edible. She gathered firewood, cooked, and washed the laundry. She once saved valuable mapping instruments and records when an expedition boat overturned in a storm. Along the way, Sacajawea was reunited with her people, the Lemhi-Shoshone. Her brother had become their chief. She convinced him to provide horses and guide the explorers down the Clearwater and Columbia rivers. When the party neared the Pacific in 1806, Sacajawea made her only personal request of the trip. She wanted to see the "great waters" and "the monstrous fish." Lewis and Clark took her in their canoes. Sacajawea got her wish. She saw the ocean and a beached whale. After the expedition, Sacajawea returned to North Dakota. Her death was reported around 1812.

Jonas Salk

microbiologist ★ 1914–1995

Dr. Jonas Salk tried his polio vaccine on himself before it was tested on others.

In the 1940s, many scientists thought vaccines had to be made from live viruses. Jonas Salk had a radically different theory. He thought using "killed," or deactivated, viruses would work. As a graduate student at the University of Michigan, he tested his ideas. Salk was part of a government-funded project that developed the first killed-virus vaccine. It was used against the flu.

Salk got funding from the National Foundation for Infantile Paralysis (March of Dimes) in 1949 to work on a vaccine for polio, a virus that caused paralysis. Five years later, 650,000 children received Salk's controversial polio vaccine. At that time, another scientist, Dr. Albert Sabin, was promoting his own live-virus vaccine, taken in a sugar cube. The rivalry between the two doctors heated up when some children sickened after getting Salk's polio shot. Sabin said the program should be halted. Salk proved that it was a private lab making the vaccine that was at fault, not his scientific research.

Both men are now credited with helping to rid the world of polio.

Pete Sampras

tennis player ★ 1971–

His serves often clock in at 120 miles per hour With that kind of power, no wonder Pete Sampras was the number one tennis player in the world for six years straight (1993–1998).

In 1990, Sampras, a mere 19 years old, became the youngest person to win the U.S. Open. Ten years later, he had scored a record-breaking 14 Grand Slam titles (two Australian Opens, five U.S. Opens, and seven Wimbledon victories). Along the way, he collected $43 million in prize money.

Sampras is famous for his monster serves, strong backhand, and tough mental attitude about winning. In 2002, Sampras won his fifth U.S. Open and 14th Grand Slam title by defeating longtime rival Andre Agassi. At 31 years old, he became the oldest U.S. Open winner in more than 30 years. Sampras has won more major tournaments than any other tennis player.

Nearly five million television viewers watched Pete Sampras eliminate Andre Agassi from the U.S. Open in 2001.

"You always respect who you're playing."

— PETE SAMPRAS

Deborah Samson
American Revolution soldier ★ 1760–1827

The Official Heroine of the state of Massachusetts was chosen for her valor in the American Revolution—when she served as a *male* soldier!

Deborah Samson (her name is often misspelled as Sampson) bound her chest with a cotton strip, combed her hair back in a mannish style, and pulled on a pair of breeches. She enlisted in the Continental army as Private Robert Shurtleff in 1781 and fought in several battles against the British as a member of the 4th Massachusetts Regiment. When she was wounded near Tarrytown, New York, Samson pried a musket ball out of her thigh and sewed up the wound herself to keep her identity secret.

In 1802, Deborah Samson became one of the first American women on the lecture circuit. She appeared in her military uniform, did musket maneuvers, and told war stories.

"Private Shurtleff" rose to become a general's orderly. In Philadelphia in 1783, she became so deathly ill that undertakers came to take her away. Luckily, a doctor discovered Samson's heart was still beating. He also saw it was beating in a female body!

Army officials were shocked to learn the truth about Samson. Still, she *had* been a brave soldier. So on October 23, 1783, "Private Shurtleff" was honorably discharged at West Point military academy.

After the war, Deborah Samson married and had three children. In 1805, she was awarded a Congressional pension: the same $4.00 per month that male veterans got.

Barry Sanders
football player ★ 1968—

When Barry Sanders retired from the Detroit Lions in 1999 after 10 seasons, he had a record to roar about.

The running back first thrilled football audiences with his outstanding performances with Oklahoma State. Rushes? Sanders led the National College Athletic Association (NCAA) with 2,628 yards. Touchdowns? Another NCAA record, 39. Small wonder Sanders won the prestigious Heisman Trophy in 1988.

The following year, Sanders was drafted by the Lions. He was an unstoppable running back who started setting all kinds of records in the National Football League (NFL). Twice he was voted NFL Player of the Year (1991, 1997). In 1997, he rushed an incredible 2,053 yards, the second-highest mark in NFL history.

As a player, Sanders was known for hard work and a low profile. He was also known to say he was more interested in winning games than racking up statistics. Nevertheless, by the time he retired, Sanders had an impressive career record of 15,269 rushing yards. He was only 1,458 yards away from breaking **Walter Payton**'s rush record.

Margaret Sanger

reproductive rights activist ★ 1879–1966

Margaret Sanger was a nurse in New York in the 1910s. She devoted her life to providing information about birth control, a term she was the first to use.

Sanger traveled to Europe in 1913 to learn about contraceptives from doctors and government clinics. When she returned, she published her findings in a magazine, *The Woman Rebel*. She founded the National Birth Control League. When Sanger started her crusade, it was illegal to give out information about contraceptives. She was charged with sending obscene materials through the mail.

In 1916, Sanger opened the country's first birth control clinic in Brooklyn, New York. Hundreds of women lined up to learn about family planning. The clinic was soon shut down. Sanger was arrested and jailed for 30 days. Sanger continued to be arrested throughout the 1930s. But the public became more and more sympathetic to her message. Her efforts helped change the laws so that at least doctors could distribute contraceptives. In 1921, Sanger founded the American Birth Control League. The group is now called the Planned Parenthood Federation of America.

David Sarnoff

media executive ★ 1891–1971

David Sarnoff was a pioneer on a 20th-century frontier—communications.

In the early years of the century, Sarnoff was an operator at the Marconi Wireless Telegraph Company. His bosses promoted him, but didn't want to hear about the idea Sarnoff floated in 1916: a wireless "radio music box" that would bring music and entertainment into the home. Four years later, General Electric (GE) formed the Radio Corporation of America (RCA). GE started producing Sarnoff's Radiolas, and he became RCA's general manager.

In 1926, Sarnoff started an RCA subsidiary called the National Broadcasting Company (NBC). NBC linked different radio stations around the country to transmit national broadcasts of sports, music, and news. But Sarnoff had even bigger ideas. In 1929, he hired electronics pioneer Vladimir

David Sarnoff introduced television broadcasting to the United States at the 1939 World's Fair.

Zworykin to develop a marketable television. Sarnoff debuted RCA's television at the 1939 World's Fair and NBC started broadcasting television, the medium that would change the world. By 1950, 10 million American homes had televisions. Sarnoff continued as RCA's visionary leader until 1970.

"Competition brings out the best in

Charles M. Schulz
cartoonist ★ 1922–2000

Charles M. Schulz made 355 million people in 75 different countries laugh. That's a lot of translations of "Good grief!"

Schulz, who studied art through a correspondence course, created *Peanuts*, the most widely read comic strip in the world. *Peanuts* first appeared in syndication in 1950. It was a big hit. Who could resist big-headed, hapless Charlie Brown? Or loudmouthed Lucy? Or Snoopy, the coolest pet ever? Not many people. By 1965, the *Peanuts* gang appeared on television in *A Charlie Brown Christmas*. The show, the first of 50 television specials, has aired every holiday since. Shulz's lovable kids (and dog!) have appeared in films, a musical, and in best-selling book collections.

Charles Schulz won television's Emmy and Peabody awards and the prestigious Reubens Award from the National Cartoonists Society.

Schulz personally drew his *Peanuts* comic strip for 50 years. He infused it with a big dose of humor and an equally big dose of heart. In January 2000, he retired his daily strip because he was too ill to continue with it. He died the night before his last, "farewell" Sunday strip appeared. After Schulz's death, nearly 100 syndicated artists paid tribute to this cartoon master. On May 27, 2000, the characters in all their different comic strips were talking about the same thing: Charles Schulz's immortal *Peanuts*.

Dred Scott
freedom fighter ★ c.1799–1858

This slave's lawsuit for freedom shook up the whole nation.

Dr. John Emerson, a U.S. army surgeon, paid $500 for Dred Scott in St. Louis, Missouri. He then took his slave with him when he was transferred to the Wisconsin Territory, which banned slavery. Around 1837, Scott married Harriet Robinson. The two lived with the doctor, and later his widow, in both slave and free states.

In 1846, Scott, supported by abolitionists, sued for his freedom in a Missouri court. Scott was living in Missouri, a slave state. In his lawsuit, he argued that because he had lived in a place where slavery had been outlawed by the Missouri Compromise of 1820, he should be a free man. The Missouri Court agreed. The case went all the way to the U.S. Supreme Court. In an infamous ruling in 1857, the Supreme

Dred Scott was bought and freed by friends around 1857. He died a year later.

Court said that Dred Scott, as a slave, was property, not a citizen, and had no right to sue.

Abolitionists like **Frederick Douglass** were outraged by the Dred Scott decision. Southerners were delighted. The country moved another step closer to civil war.

products, and the worst in men." — DAVID SARNOFF

Sequoyah
Cherokee leader ★ 1770–1843

This great but illiterate scholar created a whole written language for his people. Sequoyah saw that there was power in the written word. He wanted his tribe to have some of that power. But the Cherokee had only a spoken language.

Sequoyah started by drawing pictographs, or picture symbols, for all the Cherokee words. That system was too unwieldy. So he spent 12 years creating symbols for the sounds of the Cherokee language. His alphabet included 86 characters.

The tribal council embraced his work. Sequoyah began teaching his fellow Cherokee how to read and write. By 1828, a weekly newspaper, the *Cherokee Phoenix*, was using Sequoyah's alphabet. The Cherokee language is still in use today.

Sequoyah called books and other written material "talking leaves." The giant Sequoia redwoods are named after him.

Dr. Seuss coined the word nerd in If I Ran the Zoo (1950). Here he is shown with Cat in the Hat.

Dr. Seuss
author ★ 1904–1991

Theodor Seuss Geisel always liked to draw cartoons. He scribbled them on the attic walls of his childhood home in Springfield, Massachusetts. He penned them for his college newspaper at Dartmouth College in New Hampshire and later for humor magazines. He was paid well to draw them when he worked in advertising. But he's most famous for the cartoons in his beloved children's books.

Geisel assumed the pen name Dr. Seuss in college. His first children's book, *And to Think I Saw It on Mulberry Street* (1937), was a best-seller. Other popular favorites followed. They all featured Seuss's zany pictures, quirky characters, and rollicking rhymes.

In 1957, Dr. Seuss wrote a book starring his own favorite character. *How the Grinch Stole Christmas* became a holiday favorite with millions of kids, too. But it was *The Cat in the Hat* (1957) that really made history. A magazine writer who thought the "Dick and Jane" books used to teach reading were boring suggested in his article that Dr. Seuss could write better beginning readers. Seuss took 223 easy-to-read words and did just that. Seuss topped himself with *Green Eggs and Ham* (1960), winning a bet that he could make a book using only 50 easy words.

Dr. Seuss wrote more than 47 books, which have been translated into more than 18 languages. His work has also been made into animated cartoons, films, and a musical. He was awarded the Pulitzer prize in 1984.

"Adults are obsolete children." —DR. SEUSS

William Seward

secretary of state ★ 1801—1872

In 1867, William Seward, secretary of state under President **Abraham Lincoln**, made a deal with the Russians. The Russians got $7.2 million. America got the vast, uncharted wilderness of Alaska. Politicians and the public howled. They called the purchase "Seward's Icebox." The Alaskan Klondike Gold Rush (1897) changed their minds.

Seward was a distinguished secretary of state. He was a skilled diplomat who was able to convince European powers not to support the South during the Civil War. Before becoming a presidential cabinet member, Seward was a two-time governor of New York and a U.S. senator. He was a strong-minded abolitionist.

In 1865, when John Wilkes Booth killed President Lincoln, a fellow assassin attacked William Seward at home. The secretary of state survived and remained in office through President **Andrew Johnson**'s administration.

"Seward's Folly"—Alaska— proved to be one reason William Seward went down in history.

Colonel Robert Shaw insisted his troops receive the same pay as their white peers. This bronze relief of Shaw and the 54th in the Boston Common was dedicated in 1897. Joshua Smith, a fugitive slave who became a Massachusetts state representative, raised the funds for it.

Robert Gould Shaw

Civil War colonel ★ 1837—1863

Robert Gould Shaw came from a wealthy, free-thinking, abolitionist family in Boston, Massachusetts. He distinguished himself in several Civil War battles, including the Battle of Antietam (1862). In 1863, he fought a battle on several fronts. Shaw accepted the command of the 54th Massachusetts, the first Northern regiment of African-American volunteers.

Many people were against arming African Americans and thought they would make poor soldiers. Proving them wrong was one reason Colonel Shaw requested that the 54th join in a planned attack against a Confederate stronghold guarding the harbor entrance to Charleston, South Carolina. The 54th slogged through muddy marshes in a downpour and marched under a searing sun to get to the battle site. They had no rest and little food. Still, on July 18, 1863, the African-American soldiers and their white colonel led the charge on Fort Wagner. They were blasted with bullets and shells as they tried to scale the walls. Nearly half of them died, including Colonel Shaw. The Union lost the terrible, bloody battle—but the 54th was victorious. No one could question the valor of the brave black soldiers in blue.

William Tecumseh Sherman
Union general ★ 1820–1891

The Civil War meant total war to General William Tecumseh Sherman. And that meant soldiers, civilians, cities, farms, food, crops, livestock—*everything*—was under attack.

Sherman was General **Ulysses Grant**'s most trusted officer. He was a veteran of Union victories at Shiloh, Tennessee (1862), Vicksburg, Mississippi (1863), and Chattanooga, Tennessee (1863). In 1864, General Sherman led 100,000 soldiers of the U.S. Army of the West from Tennessee to Georgia. When they reached Atlanta, Georgia, the hub of the Confederate railroads, they destroyed the city. Sherman's victory helped get President **Abraham Lincoln** reelected.

With the ruins of Atlanta smoldering behind him, Sherman pressed forward on his famous "march to the sea" to capture Savannah, a city near the coast. Union soldiers hacked a path 50 miles wide through rural Georgia. They stole what they wanted and burned and slaughtered everything else. They tore up rail lines. The twisted, melted tracks they left behind were called "Sherman's hairpins."

William Tecumseh Sherman was a scruffy general. He wore shoes instead of boots and smoked cigars constantly. His hair and beard were messy, and his eyes were wild.

After capturing Savannah, Sherman directed his army north to join Grant's forces surrounding the Confederate capital, Richmond, Virginia. The Carolinas were crushed by Sherman's modern concept of war: victory through total destruction. His radical, harsh, military actions helped bring about the fall of the Confederacy in 1865.

Christopher Sholes
inventor ★ 1819–1890

Fifty-one people before him had built some sort of "writing machine." So why is Christopher Sholes called the "Father of the Typewriter"? Because his invention not only worked, it could be manufactured.

Sholes, working with various partners, invented several machines, including an automatic number-stamping machine (1866), which was used for printing tickets and coupons. Two years later, he patented his first typewriter. Its frame was made from a kitchen table. Sholes tinkered with his invention until the typewriter became smaller and more efficient. By 1873, he had created the "QWERTY" keyboard. Its nickname came from the order of letters on the top left of the keyboard. Sholes figured out which letters people used most often when typing.

Christopher Sholes coined the word typewriter. By 1874, his invention was being mass-produced by the Remington Company.

Then he spread out these frequently used letters across the keyboard. That way, the key bars wouldn't get stuck even during rapid typing. QWERTY is still used on most keyboards today.

Russell Simmons
hip-hop entrepreneur ★ c. 1957—

Russell Simmons cofounded Def Jam Recordings in 1983 with $5,000.

Not everyone can claim to have built "probably the most powerful cultural influence in America." But not everyone is hip-hop entrepreneur Russell Simmons.

In the late 1970s, rap and hip-hop performances were all live. There were few recordings. Simmons presented rap and hip-hop artists at college parties. In 1983, he and Rick Rubin started Def Jam Recordings. It was the first big successful record label to produce hip-hop and rap music. Def Jam signed artists like L.L. Cool J, Run-DMC, and the Beastie Boys. Their music had a whole new sound that broke down the categories that the record industry had applied to music.

Simmons is one of hip-hop culture's savviest marketers and most successful entrepreneurs. His media empire, Rush Communications, is worth around $200 million. In 1993, he debuted his successful Phat Farm clothing line. Simmons helped organize the first and second hip-hop summits (1996, 2001) to discuss violence, censorship, and public and political response to rap music. In 2001, he produced "Def Jam Poetry," a well-received cable television show.

Frank Sinatra
singer, actor ★ 1915—1998

Frank Sinatra recorded nearly 30 albums. He's most famous for his sophisticated songs about life, love, and loss.

His jazzy songs on *Swing Easy!* (1955), his lovelorn ballads on *Only the Lonely* (1958), and his personal anthems "My Way" (1969) and "New York, New York," (1980) all shaped popular American music.

Born in Hoboken, New Jersey, Frank Sinatra toured with big bands in the 1940s before going solo. The suave crooner recorded several hit songs and starred on the popular radio show "Your Hit Parade." But by 1950, things had turned sour. Sinatra was linked to organized crime. His agent, film studio, and fans abandoned him because of his womanizing. Even his voice gave out because of throat problems.

But "Ole Blue Eyes" came back with an Oscar-winning performance in *From Here to Eternity* (1954). In 1959, he won the first of his seven Grammys for his album *Come Dance with Me* (1959). Sinatra appeared on television and in nightclubs, often with the famous "Rat Pack": Dean Martin, Peter Lawford, Joey Bishop, and Sammy Davis, Jr.

Though his work and personal appeal rose and fell from the 1970s on, to many, Sinatra always remained the symbolic "Chairman of the Board of Show Business."

Sitting Bull
Hunkpapa Lakota Sioux leader ★ 1834—1890

As a child, he moved so deliberately that his fellow Hunkpapa Lakota called him "Slow" (Hunkesi). Then the 14-year-old bravely charged ahead of his war party during an enemy raid. He earned his famous tribal name, Sitting Bull (Tatanka Iyotake).

Sitting Bull was renowned for his spiritual power, his strong leadership, and his stubborn refusal to let the white men drive his people from the Great Plains. Around 1867, he was chosen head chief of the Teton Sioux Nation, which included the Lakota.

After **Red Cloud**'s War, the victorious Lakota signed the Fort Laramie treaty with the United States in 1868. The treaty recognized the Lakota rights to parts of Montana, Wyoming, and South Dakota, including the Black Hills. To the Native Americans, the Black Hills were a revered, sacred place. Whites revered it, too—once they discovered gold there.

The Lakota refused to sell their land. The U.S. government, ignoring their own treaty, declared war and told the tribe to leave the area. Sitting Bull, **Crazy Horse**, and a minority of Lakota refused.

Sitting Bull reached out to the Arapaho and the Cheyenne. He convinced Lakota who had given themselves up to rejoin the struggle. Thousands swelled the ranks at his camp at Rosebud Creek in Montana. Sitting Bull led the warriors in the difficult Sun Dance, a ritual to inspire bravery and courage. During this flesh-piercing ritual, the great chief experienced a vision of soldiers falling from the sky into his camp. Shortly after, Sitting Bull moved his camp to Little Big Horn River with plans to ambush the U.S. army. General **George Custer** and his men rode into Little Big Horn on June 25, 1876. They did not ride out.

After "Custer's Last Stand," the government sent many more troops to hunt down the Lakota. Sitting Bull took his people across the border to Canada in 1877. But their exile couldn't last. The buffalo were dying out, and the tribe was starving. In 1881, Sitting Bull surrendered.

Sitting Bull was jailed for two years as a prisoner of war. Then he joined his tribe, who had been forced onto the Standing Rock reservation in North Dakota. For a while, he traveled as an entertainer with **Buffalo Bill Cody**'s Wild West Show.

Sitting Bull was still considered a very powerful leader, which probably contributed to his death. The Ghost Dance movement was sweeping through the Plains tribes. Ghost Dancers believed their ritual would bring back the nearly extinct buffalo, revive relatives long dead, and make the white people vanish. U.S. officials wanted to make sure that Sitting Bull didn't rise to power in the Ghost Dance movement. They sent 43 Lakota policemen to arrest him on December 15, 1890. Sitting Bull's followers surrounded their chief's cabin. A fight broke out, and shots were fired. A policeman's bullet hit Sitting Bull in the head. The great chief collapsed and died.

Bessie Smith
blues singer ★ 1894–1937

Bessie Smith once faced down the Ku Klux Klan when they showed up at a tent concert in Concord, North Carolina, in 1927. Nobody kept Bessie from singing!

Born in Chattanooga, Tennessee, Smith grew up in extreme poverty. But she had a voice. Smith traveled through the South singing in bars, theaters, and tent shows for several years. In 1923, Smith made her first records, *Down Hearted Blues* and *Gulf Coast Blues*. They were big hits. *Down Hearted Blues* sold two million copies. Smith became one of the highest-paid female entertainers of her time. When she starred in *St. Louis Blues* in 1929, she also became one of the first black people cast in a "talking" movie.

Smith recorded with jazz greats like **Louis Armstrong** and Benny Goodman. Her powerful voice, perfect rhythmic sense, and ability to improvise made her a legend. She was an important influence on other great singers like **Billie Holiday** and Mahalia Jackson.

Bessie Smith, the "Empress of the Blues," made 160 recordings during her 18-year career.

Joseph Smith
religious leader ★ 1805–1844

Joseph Smith is the founder of the Church of Jesus Christ of Latter-Day Saints, also called the Mormons. Smith had several religious visions as a teenager in upstate New York. In one, an angel, Moroni, told him of a hidden gospel written on gold plates. Smith said divine intervention helped him find and translate this text into the *Book of Mormon* (1830). Smith established his church that same year.

Smith was an engaging, spirited leader who attracted many followers. The Mormons were hardworking. They opposed slavery. They lived a community-based lifestyle and prospered. This gave the Mormons economic power and meant they could represent a strong voting bloc. Other Americans feared this. Smith and his followers were persecuted. The Mormons moved through the Midwest. In 1840, Smith founded Nauvoo, Illinois. There were soon 20,000 Mormons in the prosperous Mississippi River town, which had its own university.

In 1844, Smith made two startling announcements. He endorsed polygamy (marrying more than one wife), and he announced his candidacy for president. Anti-Mormon groups were outraged. Smith was arrested after he destroyed a print shop run by Mormons who disagreed with him. He was killed when a mob broke into his cell and shot him.

"I dream for a living."

— STEVEN SPIELBERG

Steven Spielberg
film director, producer ★ 1946—

Steven Spielberg asks questions that are fun *and* scary to think about. What if dinosaurs came back? What if an alien lands in the backyard? What if a big shark wrecks the beach party? In Spielberg's movies, ordinary people end up in extraordinary situations trying to figure out these questions. (The answer usually involves some eye-popping special effects!)

Spielberg came to Hollywood's attention when his short film *Amblin'* got him a contract with Universal-MCA to direct television when he was 20. Spielberg's career went into the fast lane with *Duel* (1971), a suspenseful television drama about a menacing 18-wheel truck. Three years later, he made his film debut with *The Sugarland Express* (1974).

In 1975, Spielberg really made a splash . . . with *Jaws*! Moviegoers flooded theaters to watch the horror flick about a huge, hungry shark. *Jaws* became the first summer blockbuster and the first film to gross more than $100 million in the U.S. It changed the way Hollywood thought about budgets and summer releases.

Steven Spielberg on the set of Jurassic Park.

With his next film, *Close Encounters of the Third Kind* (1977), Spielberg moved into science fiction. He wrote the film's spectacular ending first and worked backward. Spielberg then teamed up with **George Lucas** and made *Raiders of the Lost Ark* (1981) and its two sequels.

E.T., The Extra-Terrestrial (1982) is Spielberg's most famous movie and one of the biggest box-office blowouts of all time. The film's star is a three-foot-tall puppet made of aluminum, fiberglass, and rubber and jammed with circuitry. In a master stroke, Spielberg had some of the movie shot from E.T.'s height, to make audiences see how alien our world looks to an alien. *E.T.* was funny, sentimental, and thoughtful. People loved it! They also loved Spielberg's *Jurassic Park* when the dinosaur thriller thundered into movie houses in 1993. Two sequels followed.

In the decade between aliens and dinosaurs, Spielberg directed his first "serious" film, *The Color Purple* (1986), based on Alice Walker's award-winning book. In the 1990s, the director turned out several other highly acclaimed dramas, including the searing Holocaust drama *Schindler's List* (1993), for which Spielberg was finally given an Academy Award for Best Director; *Amistad* (1997), the historical drama of a slave revolt at sea; and the World War II epic *Saving Private Ryan* (1998), which earned him a second directing Oscar.

In 1994, Spielberg helped form the multimedia giant DreamWorks SKG. Hollywood's first new studio in 75 years, DreamWorks has produced major movie hits like *Shrek* (2001).

Mark Spitz
Olympic swimmer ⋆ 1950—

Mark Spitz made a big splash at the 1972 Olympics in Munich, Germany. He won seven gold medals, each win setting a new world record. This was the first time an athlete had ever won seven medals at one Olympics game.

Spitz's signature stroke, the butterfly, was one of the most difficult. But Spitz was good at it . . . and at the freestyle and at relays. By 1968, he could boast of setting 10 world records and 28 national records. At the 1968 Olympics in Mexico City, he won two gold medals for relay events; a silver medal for the 100-meter butterfly; and a bronze medal for the 100-meter freestyle. In 1969, 1971, and 1972, Spitz was named World Swimmer of the Year.

Spitz's Olympic performance in 1972 was outstanding. He broke records in the 200-meter butterfly (2:00.70), the 200-meter freestyle (1:52.78), and the 100-meter butterfly (54.27). He helped set relay records for the 4x100-meter freestyle; the 4x200-meter freestyle; and the 4x100-meter medley. With nine gold medals to his name, Mark Spitz has won more of these top awards for swimming than any other male Olympian.

Bruce Springsteen
rock 'n' roll artist ⋆ 1949—

In 1974, Bruce Springsteen released *Born to Run*. He was on his way to becoming "The Boss"—and one of the world's most famous musicians.

Born in Freehold, New Jersey, Springsteen's small-town, working-class background inspired many of his songs. Cars, girls, and the Jersey shore also figure into the mix. That's where Springsteen got his start in the early 1970s. His first album was even called *Greetings from Asbury Park, N.J.* (1973), after a New Jersey shore town. Best-selling albums like *Darkness on the Edge of Town* (1978), *Nebraska* (1982), and *Born in the U.S.A.* (1984) feature Springsteen's powerful songs about people struggling with work, poverty, bad luck, dashed hopes, and lost love. But his rousing anthems like "Thunder Road," "Rosalita," and "Born to Run" are rocking tributes to surviving . . . and still daring to dream.

Springsteen has won several Grammys, and an Academy Award for his soundtrack single, "Streets of Philadelphia." In 2002, he released *The Rising*, which featured his legendary E Street Band.

Born in the U.S.A. sold 15 million copies and featured seven top-ten singles.

"Women may be the one group that

Gertrude Stein
author ★ 1874—1946

Gertrude Stein's poems, plays, and fiction generated heated discussions in literary circles. Was her writing daring, or was it dull and unreadable?

Stein was born in Allegheny, Pennsylvania. She studied philosophy and psychology at Harvard Annex (which became Radcliffe College) in Cambridge, Massachusetts. In 1903, Stein moved to Paris, France, with her brother, Leo. In 1909, Stein's companion, Alice B. Toklas, moved in, too.

Stein and Toklas opened their home to writers, artists, and intellectuals. Everyone from Pablo Picasso to **F. Scott Fitzgerald** and **Ernest Hemingway** came to call.

Stein's writing was quite modern. Her work was influenced by new ideas about "stream of consciousness," or how a person experiences the world as a flow of events. Her writing style was noted for its repetition ("Rose is a rose is a rose is a rose"). Stein was a very experimental writer. One of her most famous books is *The Autobiography of Alice B. Toklas* (1933). This book was really written by Stein, but from the point of view of Toklas.

Gertrude Stein (l.) and Alice B. Toklas (r.) arrive in New York City in 1934.

In 1933, Stein's opera, *Four Saints in Three Acts*, with music by Virgil Thomson, was staged in America.

John Steinbeck
author ★ 1902—1968

John Steinbeck sympathized with people who had to work too hard for too little, with people everyone else seemed to forget—or never even notice. He turned the stories of these underdogs into literary classics.

Steinbeck was born and lived in Salinas, California. The cowboys, migrant farmworkers, and fish cannery folk he met there had a big impact on his work. So did the bleak conditions of many of their lives.

Tortilla Flat (1935), Steinbeck's first best-seller, was a humorous book, though. It featured several eccentric but endearing drifters who lived together. His next books focused on labor issues and social problems. Steinbeck's famous novel *Of Mice and Men* (1937) is a moving story about two migrant worker friends, one of whom is simpleminded. His masterpiece, *The Grapes of Wrath* (1939), is the powerful story of the suffering of the Joad family, who are forced off their farmland during the Depression. It won the Pulitzer prize. Steinbeck wrote 12 novels, several short-story collections, a screenplay, and nonfiction books. He was awarded the Nobel Prize for literature in 1962.

Gloria Steinem
women's rights activist ★ 1934—

In the 1960s, Gloria Steinem emerged as a very vocal leader of the women's rights movement. At first, the media focused on her good looks. They loved "glamorous Gloria." Steinem used the spotlight to force people to take her and the feminist movement seriously.

Steinem graduated from Smith College in Northampton, Massachusetts. She moved to New York City in 1960 and became a writer. One of her first magazine articles to get attention was "I Was a Playboy Bunny," published in 1963. Gloria had gotten a job as a "bunny" at the Playboy Club. She wrote an article exposing working conditions at this men's club, where as a waitress she had to work in high heels, wear a skimpy "bunny" outfit, and act sexy. Steinem was outraged by this kind of stereotyping, which regarded women like sex objects.

Steinem continued writing. By 1968, she was a contributing editor at *New York* magazine. That same year, she covered the Democratic and Republican presidential conventions. Through her writing and speaking, Steinem had also become a headliner in the equal rights movement.

In 1970, Steinem, **Betty Friedan**, Bella Abzug, and other women's group leaders organized the Women's Strike for Equality. More than 10,000 people marched in New York City to celebrate the 50th anniversary of women's suffrage and to demand equal rights for women. A year later, Steinem, Friedan, Abzug, and other feminists such as **Fannie Lou Hamer** and **Shirley Chisholm** founded the National Women's Political Caucus. Their goal was to elect more women politicians and get women more political appointments.

Steinem was busy in 1971. She and a group of five other women organized *Ms.*, a magazine devoted to exploring all kinds of women's issues. *Ms.* was launched as a special insert in *New York* magazine. It quickly sold out its 300,000-copy print run. One year later, *Ms.* was published as an independent magazine. Steinem was editor-in-chief. During the late 1980s and 1990s, *Ms.* went through several formats and owners, the last of whom stopped publishing it. In 1998, Steinem and a group of women investors formed Liberty Media for Women and bought back *Ms.*, which is now a bimonthly. On April 28, 1993, Steinem and *Ms.* launched "Take Our Daughters to Work Day," an event that encourages young women to explore different job opportunities. It became an annual national event.

Steinem is founder of Voters for Choice, an advocacy group that supports pro-choice political candidates. She is the author of several books, including a biography of **Marilyn Monroe**. Her autobiographies, *Outrageous Acts and Everyday Rebellions* (1983) and *Revolution from Within* (1992) were best-sellers. Steinem continues her work as an activist and an author.

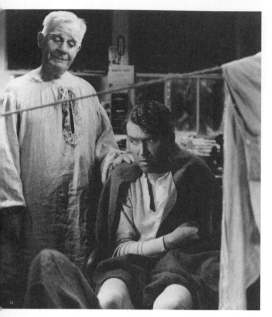

Jimmy Stewart (r.) in It's a Wonderful Life.

James Stewart
actor ★ 1908—1997

Jimmy Stewart was one of Hollywood's top leading men because he was uncommonly good at playing the "common man."

One of Stewart's first big films was **Frank Capra**'s *You Can't Take It With You* (1938). A year later, Stewart played an idealistic senator fighting political corruption in Capra's *Mr. Smith Goes to Washington* (1939). Stewart was nominated for an Academy Award. The following year he won the Academy Award for his role in *The Philadelphia Story* (1940), **Katharine Hepburn** was his costar. Stewart sent his statue home to Pennsylvania for display in the family hardware store.

In 1941, Stewart became a real-life hero. He enlisted in the army during World War II, the first movie star to do so. Stewart flew on 20 bombing missions and became a decorated colonel.

Stewart's first postwar film has proved to be his most lasting legacy. The tall, lanky actor starred in Capra's *It's a Wonderful Life* (1946). Stewart was earnest, funny, frustrated, and sympathetic as George Bailey, an ordinary man who feels he's missed out on life, only to discover how extraordinary his life really is.

Overall, Stewart starred in 80 films, including comedies, westerns, biographies, and four Alfred Hitchcock thrillers. He was awarded a special Academy Award in 1985 for a lifetime of film genius.

Martha Stewart
lifestyles entrepreneur ★ 1941—

Martha Stewart has a degree in architectural history and has worked as a Wall Street stockbroker. In the late 1970s, she opened a catering business. Martha Stewart, Inc., soon became a million-dollar company—and a lifestyles phenomenon.

A series of best-selling books, starting with *Entertaining* (1982), established Martha as the queen of how-to at home. She tapped into a huge audience, ready and eager for her step-by-step instructions to a more elegant life at an affordable price. By 1991, she was running Martha Stewart Living Omnimedia, Inc. She now publishes books and the glossy *Martha Stewart Living* and *Martha Stewart Weddings* magazines. She produces an Emmy Award–winning weekly television show, a daily radio show, and a popular Web site. Her syndicated column, "Ask Martha," appears in newspapers across the country. She also has a very profitable deal with the Kmart store chain, which sells Martha Stewart products for the home. Martha Stewart's empire, once worth an estimated $1.4 billion, was seriously affected when Stewart was investigated in 2002 for her role in the ImClone Systems illegal stock sales scandal.

Lucy Stone
abolitionist, suffragist ★ 1818—1893

When she married, Lucy Stone kept her own name, which was highly unusual at the time.

Even as a bride, Lucy Stone argued for women's rights. At her wedding in 1855, she read a protest against current marriage laws that "refuse to recognize the wife as an independent, rational being."

Independent was the word for Lucy Stone. She worked for nine years to earn the $70 she needed to attend Oberlin College in Ohio. After graduating with honors in 1847, she became a lecturer for the American Anti-Slavery Society. Stone opposed slavery and supported women's rights. Her powerful speech at a Massachusetts convention in 1850 convinced fellow abolitionist **Susan B. Anthony** to join the women's suffrage cause. Stone, Anthony, and **Elizabeth Cady Stanton** worked together for the passage of the 13th Amendment outlawing slavery. But the 15th Amendment drove them apart. All three leaders wanted the 15th amendment, which gave African-American men the vote, to be expanded to include all women. Stone supported the amendment no matter what it finally included. Anthony and Stanton opposed it if it did not give women the vote. Lucy Stone and her supporters founded the American Woman Suffrage Association in 1869 to follow their own political goals. Stone also founded, funded, and edited its weekly newspaper, the *Woman's Journal*. The *Journal* was published for 47 years and was considered "the voice of the woman's movement."

Harriet Beecher Stowe
author ★ 1811—1896

Harriet Stowe's book Uncle Tom's Cabin *sold 3,000 copies the first day it appeared.*

In 1852, Harriet Beecher Stowe fanned the flames of abolition . . . with her pen. Stowe published *Uncle Tom's Cabin*, a story about the injustices of slavery.

Harriet Beecher was born into a prominent Connecticut family of ministers and educators. The Beechers moved to Cincinnati, Ohio, in 1832, where Harriet worked as a teacher. Four years later, she married a professor, Calvin Ellis Stowe. In between doing the household chores and bearing and raising seven children, Harriet Beecher Stowe found time to write sentimental stories and sketches about domestic life. She also read a great deal about slavery. In 1850, the Stowes moved to Brunswick, Maine. A year later, she started the book that would make her famous.

Stowe wrote the last chapter of *Uncle Tom's Cabin* first, and worked backward to the beginning. She said she "worked in a trance," believing she was "the instrument of God." *Uncle Tom's Cabin* was first published in 40 installments in *National Era*, an antislavery newspaper. In 1852, it was printed in book form. More than three million copies were sold before the outbreak of the Civil War in 1861.

Stowe continued writing, producing 11 other novels, biographies, children's stories, and essays.

Barbra Streisand

singer, actress, director, producer ★ 1942—

Barbra Streisand has never let what people think about her looks, her gender, her liberal politics, or her bold ambition stop her. She gets where she wants to go—the top.

Streisand has been a best-selling recording star since releasing *The Barbra Streisand Album* in 1963. As of 2001, she has 44 gold records, 37 Grammy nominations, eight Grammy awards, plus the Grammy Legend (1992) and Grammy Lifetime Achievement (1994) awards. She's also the only woman composer to ever win an Oscar.

On Broadway, Streisand wowed audiences in *I Can Get It for You Wholesale* (1962) and *Funny Girl* (1964). In Hollywood, she won an Oscar for the film *Funny Girl* (1968). She starred in hits like *Hello, Dolly!* (1969) and *The Way We Were* (1973). With *Yentl* (1983), Streisand became the first woman to write, direct, star in, and produce a major motion picture. She also was director-producer-star of *The Prince of Tides* (1991), which was nominated for seven Academy Awards.

With tears and fanfare, Barbra Streisand retired from public singing in September 2000. "We all have to move on in our lives," she said. But that doesn't mean the diva is disappearing. There are new films, records, television shows, and books, as well as other creative projects still to come.

Louis Sullivan

architect ★ 1856—1924

Louis Sullivan was the "Father of Modernism" in architecture. He believed that a building's use should decide its design. He also believed a building could be tall, a "proud and soaring thing." These were bold new ideas in late 19th-century America.

Sullivan, a Bostonian, studied at the Massachusetts Institute of Technology in Cambridge and in Paris, France. He then went to work for Dankmar Adler's architectural firm in Chicago, Illinois. Sullivan and Adler were an impressive team for 14 years. From 1881 to 1895, they produced 120 buildings. Unlike most other people of his era, Sullivan wasn't interested in classical architecture. He designed buildings that would take advantage of new technology like elevators. He thought a building's design should look unified. He wanted the structural lines of a building to show, not be hidden by heavy stonework. He used ornamentation that was both organic and geometric. And he built up. Adler and Sullivan's Wainwright Building (1890–1891) in St. Louis, Missouri, was 137 feet tall, a towering height for its time. This product of Sullivan's genius is often called America's first skyscraper.

"Form follows function." — LOUIS SULLIVAN

Maria Tallchief
ballerina ★ 1925—

Electrifying. Enchanting. Radiant. Those were just some of the adjectives dance critics used to describe Maria Tallchief's performances.

The prima ballerina was born on an Osage reservation in Oklahoma. The family moved to Los Angeles, where Tallchief studied classical piano and then ballet. She began dancing professionally after graduating from high school.

In 1942, Tallchief toured Europe as a soloist for the Ballet Russe de Monte Carlo. While on tour, she met the famous ballet choreographer **George Balanchine**. Tallchief joined Balanchine's company. She also married him. Tallchief was Balanchine's great inspiration. He created or arranged starring roles for her in *The Firebird, Symphonie Concertante, Swan Lake, Allegro Brillante*, and *The Nutcracker*. Tallchief's dancing in these ballets was widely praised. She danced with Balanchine's New York City Ballet as well as other companies for the next 18 years. In 1965, Tallchief retired. She served as artistic director of the Chicago Lyric Opera Ballet and in 1981 founded the Chicago City Ballet company.

Maria Tallchief, shone here in Swan Lake, *won the 1996 Kennedy Center Honor.*

Amy Tan
author ★ 1952—

Amy Tan, the daughter of Chinese immigrants, was born in Oakland, California, but also grew up in Switzerland. She'd studied linguistics (the study of human language), worked with disabled children, and freelanced as a business writer. She also wrote short stories.

In 1985, Tan tried her hand at writing fiction. In a series of short stories, she explored the complexity of being female and Asian-American. Tan's work was published in 1989 as *The Joy Luck Club*. It became a best-seller, was nominated for the National Book Award, and was later made into a movie. In her second best-selling work, *The Kitchen God's Wife* (1991), Tan explored some of the painful mysteries of life in China for women like her mother. In *The Bonesetter's Daughter* (2001), she continued to examine relationships between American daughters and their Chinese mothers. Tan writes about the psychological ghosts that haunted her mother and grandmother because of their experiences as young women in China. This helps her free herself from her own feelings of depression.

In addition to her famous novels, Tan writes stories, essays, and children's books. She's also written about her feelings about being labeled a multicultural author, which she thinks is a burden on a writer.

Elizabeth Taylor

actress ★ 1932—

Elizabeth Taylor has been called the "most beautiful woman in the world."

Born in London to American parents, Elizabeth Taylor moved to Los Angeles when she was a girl. Her British accent and striking violet eyes helped her get a small role in the 1943 film *Lassie Come Home.* She then signed a contract with the MGM studio. Box-office hits like *National Velvet, Jane Eyre,* and *Little Women* followed. By the 1950s, Taylor was a major Hollywood star. Ever since then, the press and the public haven't been able to get enough of her.

In 1961, Taylor won her first Academy Award for *Butterfield 8.* Six years later, she took home another Oscar for *Who's Afraid of Virginia Woolf?* Her costar was Richard Burton, with whom she'd made the epic film *Cleopatra* (1963). Burton and Taylor made 10 films together, were married and divorced twice, and had one of Hollywood's stormier relationships.

Liz Taylor has starred in more than 50 films. She cofounded and helps fund a major AIDS research foundation. In 1993, Taylor received a Lifetime Achievement Award from the American Film Institute. In 2000, she was made Dame Commander of the Most Excellent Order of the British Empire. And she still has star power: In 2001, Taylor appeared in the television movie *These Old Broads.*

Tecumseh

Shawnee leader ★ c.1768—1813

After the American Revolution, white pioneers rapidly began chopping, plowing, and farming their way through tribal lands between the Ohio and Mississippi rivers. Tecumseh knew only one thing could possibly stop them—unity among the tribes.

The respected Shawnee leader traveled from the Great Lakes to Florida, urging Native Americans to unite and form their own great nation to keep the United States from spreading farther west. Tecumseh and his brother, a famous religious visionary known as "The Prophet," founded Prophetstown, near Tippecanoe Creek in Indiana.

Tecumseh was a brilliant commander responsible for several key victories in the War of 1812 between the British and the Americans.

Tecumseh negotiated with U.S. Army General William Harrison to regain tribal lands. The negotiations failed. In 1811, Harrison and the U.S. Army responded and destroyed Prophetstown.

During the War of 1812, Tecumseh sided with the British and brought 700 Shawnee, Sioux, Fox, Winnebago, and other warriors with him. Tecumseh thought a British victory would ensure a good land treaty for the Native Americans. The British forces were eventually overcome. Tecumseh died in the Battle of the Thames River in 1813. His great plan died with him.

"Sell the land? Why not sell the air, the

Shirley Temple
actress ★ 1928—

Shirley Temple once shot at **Eleanor Roosevelt** with a slingshot at a barbecue. She might have been one of the highest-paid Hollywood stars of the 1930s, but she was still a kid!

Temple was curly haired and cute, and had a million-dollar dimpled smile. She sang, danced, and melted hearts. That's what made her Hollywood's biggest box-office draw between 1935 and 1938. At six years old, Temple was earning $2,500 a week starring in films such as *Little Miss Marker* (1934), *The Littlest Rebel* (1935), and *Heidi* (1937). She received a special Academy Award for being "the outstanding personality of 1934."

Temple retired from movies when she was 22 and married Charles Black. Shirley Temple Black became involved with Republican politics in the 1960s and served under four presidents. **Richard Nixon** appointed her delegate to the United Nations General Assembly in 1969. Black served as U.S. ambassador to

Shirley Temple sometimes danced with Bill "Bojangles" Robinson in her movies. Robinson was one of the world's best tap dancers.

Ghana from 1974 until 1976, when President Gerald Ford named her chief of protocol in the State Department. Black served as foreign affairs officer under **Ronald Reagan**; **George Bush** appointed her ambassador to Czechoslovakia. In 1988, Black won the Gandhi Memorial International Foundation Award. In 1998, she was awarded a Kennedy Center Honor.

Sydney, Australia, 2000. Jenny Thompson, second from the left, and her fellow relay swimmers show off their Olympic gold medals for the 800-meter freestyle relay.

Jenny Thompson
Olympian ★ 1973—

With 10 medals (eight gold, one silver, and one bronze), Jenny Thompson is the most decorated female swimmer in the Olympics. In fact, she has more gold medals than *any* other Olympian.

Enrolled in Stanford University, Thompson raced into a record-breaking 19 National College Athletic Association swimming titles. She then power-stroked her way to 23 national titles and was named U.S. Swimmer of the Year in 1993. That same year, Thompson swept the Pan-Pacific Championships, earning six gold medals. At the 1999 Pan-Pacific Championships, Thompson flew through the water in 57.88 seconds to break the world's record for the 100-meter butterfly.

Thompson's Olympic career spanned the 1992, 1996, and 2000 Games. She won three gold medals in the 400-meter freestyle swimming relay (1992, 1996, 2000); three in the 400-meter medley relay (1992, 1996, 2000); and two golds in the 800-meter freestyle swimming relay (1996, 2000). Thompson also medalled in the individual 100-meter freestyle race, taking home a silver in 1992 and a bronze in 2000.

clouds, and the great sea as well?" —TECUMSEH

Henry David Thoreau
philosopher ★ 1817–1862

Thoreau's Civil Disobedience *inspired many abolitionists of his time, as well as modern civil rights leaders from Mahatma Gandhi to* **Martin Luther King, Jr**.

Henry David Thoreau *lived* **Ralph Waldo Emerson**'s ideas about closely observing nature—on Emerson's own land.

Thoreau attended Harvard University in Cambridge, Massachusetts, from 1833 to 1837. There, he was exposed to Emerson's transcendental philosophy, which dealt with nature, individual responsibility, and the personal search for truth. Thoreau embraced Emerson's ideas.

Thoreau was also a bit lost. His beloved brother, with whom he had run a school, had died in 1842. Thoreau then worked as a tutor in New York and at the family's pencil factory in Concord, Massachusetts. Neither job was satisfying. So Thoreau spent $28.12 building a small, rough cabin near a pond on Emerson's property. He moved in on July 4, 1845. Thoreau brought his writing tools to the tiny cabin—and produced two classics of American literature: *Civil Disobedience* (published in an 1849 essay collection) and *Walden, Or Life in the Woods* (1854).

In *Civil Disobedience*, Thoreau argues that people should peacefully resist unjust laws. In *Walden*, Thoreau talks about the simplicity of his life in the cabin and the beauty of nature. It sold only 200 copies when it was published but is now Thoreau's most famous work.

Jim Thorpe
Olympian ★ 1888–1953

When the King of Sweden presented Jim Thorpe with two Olympic medals, he called the Native American the "greatest athlete in the world." Many sportswriters and fans still do.

Thorpe excelled in 10 different sports at the Carlisle Indian School in Carlisle, Pennsylvania. And once the legendary coach Pop Warner got hold of him, he became a football sensation, too. He scored 25 touchdowns and 198 points in one year!

No one else has ever done what Thorpe did at the 1912 Olympics: win the pentathlon *and* the grueling decathlon. But a year after his triumphant ticker-tape parade, Thorpe was stripped of his gold medals. During a break from attending the Carlisle Indian School, Thorpe had once played semipro baseball for $15 a week. He said he did it for the love of the game. A sports union said the money meant he wasn't an amateur.

Thorpe was bitter, but ever the athlete. He played with several major league baseball teams and spearheaded the movement to make football a professional game. He also helped organize what became the National Football League (NFL) and served as its first president. Jim Thorpe's Olympic gold medals were finally restored—30 years after his death.

Jim Thorpe was inducted into five sports halls of fame.

Harry S Truman
33rd president ★ 1884–1972

Polls and the press predicted that President Truman couldn't be elected on his own merit in the 1948 presidential race. They were famously wrong.

Harry S Truman's Democratic presidency (1945–1953) was defined by World War II and postwar problems.

He became president on April 12, 1945, when **Franklin Roosevelt** died. The war in Europe ended shortly after, but the battle still raged in the Pacific. On August 6 and 9, President Truman ordered atomic bombs dropped on Hiroshima and Nagasaki, which killed several hundred thousand people. On August 10, the Japanese requested peace. World War II was over.

In his second term, President Truman raised the minimum wage and provided money for desperately needed housing. He also desegregated the armed forces. Truman recognized that the United States could not remain isolated in the postwar, atomic world. He supported the creation of the United Nations (UN) in 1945–1946. The president issued the Truman Doctrine (1947), arguing that the U.S. had to "contain" the spread of communism. Truman also agreed to form a North Atlantic Treaty Organization (NATO) with European nations as protection against Soviet hostility.

But containment didn't always work. In 1949, Communists took over China. In 1950, the Korean War broke out when North Korean Communists invaded South Korea. President Truman sent in General **Douglas MacArthur**, but was unwilling to expand the conflict to war against China.

Sojourner Truth
abolitionist ★ c.1797–1883

Like many slaves, Sojourner Truth couldn't read or write. She dictated her autobiography, Narrative of Sojourner Truth *(1850).*

Her deep powerful voice rang out: "I could work as much and eat as much as a man—when I could get it—and bear the lash as well. An a'n't I a woman?" The audience at the Ohio Women's Rights Convention (1851) was stunned. They had never heard anyone like Sojourner Truth.

She was born a slave, named Isabella Baumfree, in upstate New York. When slavery was banned there in 1827, she moved to New York City. Baumfree took her new name, Soujourner Truth, following a divine vision. She then spent her life traveling through New York, New England, and parts of the Midwest in the 1840s and 1850s.

Audiences at churches, camp meetings, even street corners heard the tall, gaunt woman's powerful speeches. Truth spoke of divine love and of the need to abolish slavery. Her preaching drew many new people to the abolitionist movement. In 1850, Truth took up the women's rights cause and was equally eloquent and persuasive.

"I can't die but once." — HARRIET TUBMAN

Harriet Tubman
abolitionist ★ 1820—1913

The most famous conductor on the Underground Railroad never lost a passenger. In 19 trips to the South, she brought nearly 300 people out of slavery and delivered them into freedom.

Harriet Tubman was born a slave on a Maryland plantation. Like many slaves, she was overworked, whipped, and abused. She also suffered from blackouts because a white overseer had hit her in the head with a two-pound weight. What she didn't suffer from was a lack of courage.

In 1849, Tubman was afraid she was going to be sold farther down south, where conditions were worse for slaves. She escaped by traveling on the Underground Railroad and staying in secret hiding places or "stations," run by antislavery sympathizers. She then worked for two years in a Philadelphia hotel and earned enough money to return to the South and rescue her family. That was just the beginning. The woman many would soon call "Moses" intended to free as many slaves as she possibly could.

For 10 years, Tubman traveled in and out of slave states, sometimes in disguise, always with her long rifle. She led men, women, and children on the long journey north. They traveled only at night and spent their days hiding in swamps, forests, and abolitionists' "safe" houses. A deeply religious woman, Tubman believed she was guided and protected by God.

Tubman was a master at organizing. She figured out travel routes, forged papers, and found ways to keep a baby quiet during an escape. Because she'd never been taught to read or write, Harriet relied on memory and observation to help her in her work. Slaveholders offered a $40,000 reward for her capture.

During the Civil War, Tubman went to Florida and the Carolinas. She worked as a nurse and a cook, tending to newly freed slaves. The Union army recruited her as a spy and scout. She infiltrated Confederate lines with the same cool resourcefulness with which she'd crossed state lines so many times. Tubman even led Union raids on plantations, one of which freed nearly 800 slaves in 1863.

After the war, Tubman moved to a small farm she owned in Auburn, New York. She had no income, so friends petitioned Congress for a pension in recognition of her war work. She eventually got $20 a month.

Harriet Tubman continued to work tirelessly for improved conditions for African Americans and for women's rights. Her home eventually became the "Harriet Tubman Home for Indigent Aged Negroes," where poor African Americans could find shelter. Tubman died there at age 93. The words on her gravestone read, "Servant of God, Well Done."

Nat Turner
abolitionist * 1800—1831

In 1831, there was an eclipse of the sun and dark sunspots. Nat Turner read these as signs. Now was the time for his planned uprising.

Turner grew up a slave in Southhampton County, Virginia, attended church, and learned to read and write. As a teenager, he began to have strong, terrifying visions. Turner believed that God had chosen him to lead his fellow slaves out of captivity. On August 22, 1831, he and four other slaves killed Turner's owner and his family and rallied other slaves to their cause. They then headed to nearby plantations to do the same. Sixty white people were killed.

On October 30, 1831, Nat Turner was captured at gunpoint by a farmer named Benjamin Phipps.

Turner's destination was Jerusalem, Virginia, where he could seize an arsenal of weapons. Warned by an escaping slave, white owners defended themselves and called in the militia. Fear of slave rebellions quickly spread panic across the South. Reprisals were swift and severe: At least 120 African Americans were killed and the activities of slaves were more restricted than ever.

Despite a $500 reward on his head, Turner hid out for nearly six weeks in a nearby swamp before he was caught, tried, and hanged.

Ted Turner
media owner * 1938—

Ted Turner changed the way the world sees itself. The media empire he built broadcasts television from everywhere to almost everywhere.

In 1970, when cable was a young industry, Turner bought an Atlanta, Georgia, television station. Within five years, he turned it into TBS (Turner Broadcasting System), the first television "superstation." TBS broadcast cable television via satellite. Millions of customers tuned in, and millions of dollars rolled in. Turner used these profits to buy the Atlanta Braves baseball team (1976) and basketball's Atlanta Hawks (1977).

People thought Turner was crazy when he launched a 24-hour cable news network in 1980. But CNN was on the

Ted Turner is a brilliant pioneer, but his outspokenness has earned him the nickname "The Mouth from the South."

spot at history-making events like the explosion of the space shuttle *Challenger* (1986), the Persian Gulf War (1991), and the war on terrorism in Afghanistan (2001–2002). Today CNN is the most widely syndicated television news service.

Turner's multimedia company merged with Time Warner in 1996.

In 1997, Turner pledged $1 billion to the United Nations—and then scolded other rich people to "loosen up their wads." He supports environmental causes through the Turner Foundation. And in 2000, Turner created the Nuclear Threat Initiative, which aims to stop the buildup of nuclear and biological weaponry.

Mark Twain
author ★ 1835–1910

"Mark Twain" is a riverboat term. It means the water is 2 fathoms (12 feet) deep, safe for navigation.

A short story, "The Celebrated Jumping Frog of Calaveras County" (1865), made Samuel Langhorne Clemens a household name. Well, actually it made his pen name, Mark Twain, famous.

Sam Clemens grew up in Hannibal, Missouri, a port on the Mississippi River. All kinds of people lived in Hannibal, including slaves. The shipping trade also brought in an ever-changing, colorful cast of characters. The hustle and bustle of life in a river town, especially the hustles, would have a great influence on Sam's later writing.

As a young man, Clemens worked in print shops throughout the East and Midwest. Occasionally, he wrote newspaper articles. But the mighty Mississippi drew him back. From 1859 to 1861, he worked as a riverboat pilot. "I loved the profession far better than any I have followed since," he declared. When the Civil War halted river traffic, Clemens was adrift.

Clemens ended up in San Francisco, California. He became a newspaperman again, until his jumping frog story made him famous. It was published in newspapers from coast to coast. The author was listed as Mark Twain. Using his new name, Clemens embarked on a new life of literary celebrity.

Twain gave enormously popular lectures. He had a deep understanding of what made Americans so uniquely American and he had a good ear for the way they expressed themselves.

In 1867, he traveled through Europe and the Middle East. Twain wrote ironic, homespun accounts of his trip, which were published as *The Innocents Abroad* (1869). It was a best-seller. Respectably established, Twain married Olivia Langdon, a warm, serious woman. Her wealthy father set them up in a mansion in Buffalo, New York.

Twain was now living an Easterner's high-society life. It was the type of life he himself had made fun of in his book, *The*

> **"The difference between the right word and the almost right word is the difference between lightning and the lightning bug." — MARK TWAIN**

Gilded Age (1873). Over the years, Twain's fortunes rose and fell, often because of poor money management. Through it all he continued to write and lecture.

But Twain, despite his fancy white suits, was still part river rat. In 1876, *The Adventures of Tom Sawyer* was published. Twain had turned memories of his riverbank childhood into what is now a classic American tale. He then finished *Life on the Mississippi* (1883) and two years later came out with his masterpiece, *The Adventures of Huckleberry Finn* (1885, U.S.). In it, Huck Finn, the son of the town drunks, feels suffocated by a local widow's attempt to "sivilize" him. He and a runaway slave, Jim, escape on a raft down the Mississippi. Through Huck and Jim's journey and the friendship that grows out it, Twain comments on the complexity of human behavior.

Rudolph Valentino

actor ★ 1895–1926

Valentino in The Sheik *(1921)*.

Chiseled good looks and smoldering glances made Rudolph Valentino *the* matinee idol of the 1920s.

Valentino was born in Italy. He arrived in New York in 1913, worked as a dancer, and did odd jobs. Four years later, he moved to Hollywood. Three years more and Valentino was the biggest name in movies.

The film that brought him instant stardom was *The Four Horsemen of the Apocalypse* (1921). Set against the backdrop of World War I, Valentino plays a spoiled artist who finds honor through a doomed love affair. That same year, Valentino starred in *The Sheik*. Cast as an Arabian prince, he kidnaps an Englishwoman and takes her to his lavish desert tent. Ultimately, she can't resist his longing gazes and manly embraces. Neither could millions of women moviegoers. They swooned over the passion, the mystery, and the sensuality that Valentino projected onscreen. He was the heartthrob in all his best roles—the sultry Spanish matador of *Blood and Sand* (1922), the dashing Russian Cossack of *The Eagle* (1925), the Arabian heartthrob once again in *The Son of the Sheik* (1926). When Valentino unexpectedly died of an ulcer, there was weeping, wailing, and a near riot at his funeral!

Cornelius Vanderbilt

financier ★ 1794–1877

"Commodore" Cornelius Vanderbilt was the richest man in New York City when he died.

Schooners, steamboats, railroads—Cornelius Vanderbilt kept up with the latest in transportation technology . . . and then bought it.

Vanderbilt borrowed $100 from his mother when he was 16. He started a ferry service between Staten Island and New York. His ferry line prospered by hauling cargo during the War of 1812. "Commodore" Vanderbilt could now afford the biggest schooner sailing the Hudson River. With the arrival of steamboats, he found a way around **Robert Fulton**'s shipping monopoly. Vanderbilt was ruthless when it came to competition. "Beat them, buy them, or ruin them" was his motto.

By the 1840s, Vanderbilt's transportation network included ferries, stagecoaches, and more than 100 steamboats. His boats chugged up and down the Hudson and Delaware Rivers. They docked in Boston, Massachusetts; Providence, Rhode Island; and ports from Connecticut to Cuba. Vanderbilt's boats and coaches brought prospectors to the California gold rush faster and cheaper by going via Nicaragua instead of Panama. Vanderbilt made millions. His competitors often *paid* him to stop running against their routes.

In the late 1850s, Vanderbilt expanded into railroads. In less than 20 years, he controlled several profitable lines.

"I have built my own factory on my own ground."

— MADAME C. J. WALKER

Madame C. J. Walker
cosmetics entrepreneur ★ 1867–1919

For 18 years, Sarah Breedlove, a widow and mother, worked as a laundress in St. Louis, Missouri. Then in 1905, she had a dream. It gave her the idea for a special formula for grooming African-American women's hair. She followed her dream and became one of the nation's first black millionaires.

Breedlove married newspaperman Charles Walker and started calling herself Madame C. J. Walker. She created what came to be called the Walker System. It included a shampoo, her grooming formula, brushes, and hot-iron combs. Madame Walker hired and trained a staff of agents called "beauty culturists" to sell her products. In 1910, she opened a manufacturing company in Indianapolis, Indiana. With 3,000 to 5,000 female employees, it was the country's largest African-American owned business. Many of the hygiene, or cleanliness, rules that Madame Walker insisted her employees follow later became part of laws governing the cosmetology industry.

George Wallace
governor ★ 1919–1998

In his 1963 inauguration speech, Governor George Wallace of Alabama vowed "segregation forever." He personally blocked the doors of the state university to keep out black students. He refused to provide police protection for participants in the Selma to Montgomery civil rights march. He also refused to meet with **Martin Luther King, Jr.**, when the marchers reached the state capital.

Wallace jumped into national politics in 1964 and ran for president as a Democrat. He supported states' rights and opposed the civil rights bill. Wallace was appealing to racists, but he also attracted a whole new body of conservatives. He helped set the stage for conservatives to become a more powerful political force in the South.

In 1968, Wallace ran for president again, this time as a third-party candidate. He got 13% of the votes, carried five states, and nearly deadlocked the race. Four years later, his politics flip-flopped. To keep up with the times—and gather the black votes he needed for another presidential bid—Governor Wallace now said he disagreed with segregation. In the 1972 Democratic primaries, he got more votes than any other candidate. Wallace's national campaign was cut short when a gunman shot and paralyzed him. A four-time governor of Alabama, Wallace served his last year in that office in 1986.

Barbara Walters

television journalist ★ 1931—

The "Today Girl" on NBC's *Today Show* was supposed to be a pretty, perky sidekick with not much airtime. Barbara Walters took over the job in 1964. Things changed. Walters was an experienced, hardworking journalist whose personable interviewing style became popular with audiences. By 1974, she was cohosting the *Today Show*.

In 1976, she was lured to ABC by a $1 million salary, the highest ever paid to a journalist at the time. Walters became the first woman to coanchor an evening news program. But the *ABC Evening News* didn't get the viewer ratings the network wanted. Walters was reassigned and started producing her own television specials. She conducted intimate, emotional interviews with world leaders like Fidel Castro; presidents **Richard Nixon**, **Jimmy Carter**, and **Ronald Reagan**; business figures like **Bill Gates**; and movie stars like **Katharine Hepburn** and **Christopher Reeve**. Walters won two Emmy Awards and later a Peabody Award. Her critics say she's turned television journalism into television gossip. But Walters is one of the most recognizable media figures in the world. She's hosted ABC's *20/20* news program since 1979 and is coproducer and occasional host on *The View*, a news and current events show hosted by women.

Sam Walton

retail entrepreneur ★ 1918—1992

Sam Walton had a clear business philosophy: "There is only one boss: the customer." It worked for him. Walton built a small store in Arkansas into America's biggest retail chain, Wal-Mart.

In the 1940s and 1950s, Walton managed a retail franchise. He expanded operations and eventually ran 15 profitable stores in Arkansas, Missouri, and Oklahoma.

At that time, discount stores were just popping up. Many retailers opposed the idea because they thought they would

lose money. Walton saw discounting as the wave of the future. He opened his first Wal-Mart in Rogers, Arkansas, in 1962. Walton was a savvy manager. He found ways to cut costs so that Wal-Mart stores supported his company motto, "We sell for less, always." He was among the first to computerize store data, which made keeping track of Wal-Mart's products and distributing them cheaper. He scouted key locations for new stores and opened Wal-Marts as fast as possible (a move often criticized by local merchants and townspeople). Then he went to Wal-Mart openings himself to motivate workers and mingle with customers. People responded to Walton's friendly, folksy ways. And they shopped! By 2001, there were 3,054 Wal-Mart stores around the world, selling $104 billion worth of goods . . . at a discount, of course!

"In the future, every person will be

Andy Warhol
Pop artist ★ c.1928–1987

Pop Art was brilliant and insightful. Pop art was boring and silly. In the 1960s, artists, critics, and art audiences were all arguing about this new art phenomenon. Andy Warhol, the world's most famous Pop artist, just coolly watched—and worked.

Warhol was fascinated by the objects and symbols in the world all around him. He created art that made people stop and really *look* at these images. In the 1960s, he painted *32 Soup Cans* (1961–1962). The title said it all. So did the one for his silk screen, *80 Two-Dollar Bills* (1962). Warhol's works were direct and impersonal. They made the familiar seem obsessive. When they were exhibited in a one-man show at the Stable Gallery in New York City in 1962, they made Warhol famous.

Andrew Warhola got a degree in art from the Carnegie Institute of Technology in Pittsburgh,

Self-Portrait *(1986) captures Warhol's famous look: the cool stare, the slightly parted lips, and the wild, platinum white wig.*

Pennsylvania. He moved to New York in 1949 and worked as a commercial artist. He quickly distinguished himself with his ad illustrations, particularly for shoes. Supposedly, the credit line on his first printed drawing dropped the final *a* from his name. Andy liked the idea.

He also liked the anything-goes atmosphere of New York City in the 1960s and 1970s. Warhol was everywhere: at art galleries, underground rock jams, and all-hours nightclubs. He opened up a studio space nicknamed the "Factory" in 1963. Artists, actors, writers, rock stars, and wannabes hung out there. Warhol kept working. He and his assistants mass-produced art, just like industry mass-produced the consumer objects Warhol often pictured in his work. His subjects included Brillo boxes, cereal boxes, and giant, silk-screened flowers. His signature style became the repeated image, often a photograph, silk-screened in vivid or unusual colors. Warhol used this format for his Death and Disaster series (1962–1964), based on lurid news photos. It also worked for his 1964 series on recently widowed **Jackie Kennedy** and in his Cow Wallpaper (1965-1966).

From 1963 to 1974, Warhol shot more than 60 films. Like Warhol's art, a few of the early experimental films, like *Sleep*; *Kiss*; and *Eat* (all 1963), aimed to make people more aware of the ordinary. Warhol also made a few feature-length films and commercial movies, like the 3–D *Andy Warhol's Frankenstein* (1973).

In 1968, Valerie Solanas, a disgruntled artist, walked into the Factory. She shot and nearly killed Warhol. After the artist recovered, he moved into his Post-Pop period. In the 1970s, he produced portraits of famous people. He silk-screened bold photos of well-known figures, from the Rolling Stones' Mick Jagger to **Muhammad Ali** to China's chairman, Mao Tse-tung. He accented face and body parts with jarring color blocks, jumpy outlines, and frenetic paint strokes. In the 1980s, he produced a series of American "myth" paintings about icons like Mickey Mouse and Superman and another series on endangered animals. Warhol's life and work was cut short when he died after surgery in 1987. But his legacy is long-lasting.

world-famous for 15 minutes." — ANDY WARHOL

Mercy Otis Warren
philosopher, writer ★ 1728–1814

When the nation's first woman historian set to writing her three-volume *A History of the Rise, Progress, and Termination of the American Revolution* (1805), she knew many of her book's characters very well. They had often argued their revolutionary politics at Warren's own home.

Mercy Otis grew up in a prominent Massachusetts family and married a patriot. She counted **Abigail** and **John Adams**, **John Hancock**, and **Thomas Jefferson** among her acquaintances.

Warren took part in the American Revolution armed with pen and paper. She wrote poetry and political pamphlets championing independence. She published several popular, satirical plays with patriotic messages. One of Warren's plays, *The Motley Assemblage* (1779), was the first play written in America to have all American characters.

After the war, Warren kept her quill pen sharpened. She didn't support the proposed Constitution and said so in her essay, *Observations on the New Constitution* (1788). Warren's essay helped convince the Constitution's supporters to add what would become the Bill of Rights.

Booker T. Washington
educator ★ c.1856–1915

Booker T. Washington was the most prominent African American of his time. His autobiography, *Up from Slavery* (1901), was a best-seller.

Born into slavery in Virginia, Washington worked hard to get an education after the Civil War. In 1881, he became head of the Tuskegee Institute in Alabama. At Tuskegee, African-American students learned vocational skills like carpentry, bricklaying, printing, and mechanics. Some also trained as teachers. All Tuskegee students learned to dress, speak, and behave in a way that would make them "acceptable" to white society. Under Washington, Tuskegee thrived. By the time he died, the college had 200 faculty members (including **George Washington Carver**) teaching 40 trades in 100 buildings.

Washington was a tireless fund-raiser and a skilled public speaker. He advised presidents, politicians, and business leaders about racial issues. He stressed that education and economic freedom, rather than politics, would improve the status of African Americans. He believed in compromise, and focused on trade education rather than on academics. Other African-American leaders, like **W. E. B. Du Bois**, criticized Washington because he didn't demand equal rights. Secretly though, Washington funded efforts to overturn segregation laws, protect voting rights, and get African Americans on juries.

"Liberty, when it begins to take root

George Washington
first president ★ 1732–1799

". . . first in war, first in peace, and first in the hearts of his countrymen," said General Henry Lee at George Washington's funeral. Washington himself would probably have been happy with just the second "first." Given a choice, the "Father of Our Country" preferred the quiet, peaceful life of a Virginia gentleman farmer. But he was drawn into the service of his country again and again.

This famous painting of George Washington was saved from fire by **Dolley Madison** during the War of 1812. The portrait was painted by Gilbert Stuart (1755–1828).

Colonel Washington and his Virginia militia fought well in the French and Indian Wars (1754–1763). When the Continental Congress declared independence from British rule, they appointed Washington head of the new Continental army in 1775.

General Washington was an imposing: 6 feet 2 inches tall, nearly 200 pounds strong. His ability to inspire loyalty in his soldiers kept the ragtag Continental army together. Washington and his ill-equipped, ill-clothed, underpaid men were eventually victorious. In 1781, the British finally surrendered at Yorktown, Virginia.

Six years later, Washington presided over the Constitutional Convention in Philadelphia in 1787. He and the other delegates created the three-branch system of government described in the U.S. Constitution. Washington was unanimously chosen president by the state electors.

On April 30, 1789, George Washington powdered his hair, donned a brown suit and dress sword, and headed to the country's first inauguration. He was sworn in as president at Federal Hall in New York City. Washington refused the $25,000 salary that came with the job.

Politically, President Washington favored a strong federal government. He didn't believe in separate political parties, but he did think he should appoint the best advisors for the country. So his cabinet included **Alexander Hamilton** and **Thomas Jefferson**.

President Washington served two terms (1789–1797). During that time, he and the new nation had to deal with questions of federal versus state authority. The president also had to deal with international issues. Washington knew the country was in no military position to become involved in wars with other nations. There was enough trouble at home between Native Americans and the white settlers who were displacing them. Washington also helped pick the site for the nation's new capital. This new federal city in the District of Columbia was named in his honor.

On September 17, 1796, President Washington's Farewell Address was printed in a Philadelphia, Pennsylvania, newspaper. The popular president had refused to run for a third term. He returned to Mount Vernon, his home in Virginia, where he stayed informed about politics. He also enjoyed daily horseback rides around his farm. On December 12, 1799, he took his last ride. Caught in a snowstorm, Washington took ill and died two days later.

is a plant of rapid growth." — GEORGE WASHINGTON

Martha Washington was the first woman portrayed on U.S. paper currency (1886) and on a postage stamp (1902).

Martha Washington
first lady ★ 1731—1802

"Steady as a clock, busy as a bee, and cheerful as a cricket"—that's how Martha Washington described herself when she was where she most wanted to be: at home.

The country's first first lady grew up in Virginia plantation society. Her first husband's death in 1757 left Martha a wealthy widow with two young children. After a brief courtship, she married **George Washington** in 1759. The family moved to Washington's Mount Vernon home. There, Martha oversaw the household, the servants, the dairy, the smokehouse, and the plantation's several small businesses.

Throughout the American Revolution, Martha shared winter army quarters with her husband. Her calm, steady, cheerful spirit was a comfort to the soldiers. So were the knitted socks and shirts she sewed for them. In 1789, George Washington was elected president. "Lady Washington," as Martha was often called, helped her husband create a dignified, elegant atmosphere around the first presidency.

James Watson
zoologist ★ 1928—

Deoxyribonucleic acid (DNA) is the basic molecule that makes the chromosomes found in all cells. It is often called the "code of life" because it passes along hereditary information from generation to generation. In 1953, James Watson and British scientist Francis Crick cracked that code while working at Cambridge University in England. They discovered that DNA is a double helix, a sort of twisted, 3-D spiral staircase. Understanding DNA has opened up new fields of study, including genetic engineering. Watson, Crick, and Maurice Wilkins (a scientist from another lab working on DNA) were awarded the 1962 Nobel Prize for medicine because of their groundbreaking work.

Watson returned home to the United States, where he worked at the California Institute of Technology and later Harvard University. He also published *The Double Helix* (1968), a frank account of the fierce competition that was part of the DNA race.

*To beat **Linus Pauling**, who also was in the DNA race, James Watson (l.) and Francis Crick (r.) adapted Pauling's model-building technique. They built a model of DNA using custom-made metal parts.*

In 1968, Watson was appointed director of Cold Spring Harbor Laboratory, a prestigious biological research center in New York. In 1989, he became director of the Human Genome Project, a monumental, international scientific effort to map all three billion human genes.

John Wayne

actor ★ 1907–1979

John Wayne in Rio Bravo (1959).

Everybody recognizes John Wayne. He's the strong, silent type, the all-American hero of westerns and war films, the superpatriot. But in the 1930s, "The Duke" was just another B-movie star.

Between 1928 and 1938, Marion "Duke" Morrison was the low-paid star of some 80 low-budget films. Along the way, director John Ford got him a break. In 1930, Duke Morrison made it into a big-budget film, billed as John Wayne. Unfortunately, that film, *The Big Trail*, bombed at the box office. Wayne didn't give up and Ford didn't forget him. He cast the tall young actor as the gunfighter Ringo Kid in his now classic film, *Stagecoach* (1939). Ford's movie made a star out of Wayne. He rode tall in the saddle in westerns like *Red River* (1948) and *She Wore a Yellow Ribbon* (1949). He fought the good fight in *Sands of Iwo Jima* (1950) and *Flying Leathernecks* (1951). In 1969, Wayne gave an Oscar-winning performance as Rooster Cogburn, the hard-living, one-eyed marshal of *True Grit*. In 1976, he made his last movie, *The Shootist*, before succumbing to cancer.

Daniel Webster

senator, secretary of state ★ 1782–1852

Daniel Webster was one of the greatest of all American orators. In many of his speeches, he defended the U.S. Constitution and the need for a strong federal government with strong, powerfully worded arguments.

Webster, a lawyer, represented Massachusetts in the U.S. Senate from 1827 to 1841. In 1830, Webster brilliantly argued against **John C. Calhoun** and others who said states could nullify, or ignore, federal laws if they felt it necessary. Webster also thought the federal government should play a role in the economic development of the country. Webster, along with **Henry Clay**, favored protective tariffs, or taxes. He wanted federal funding for new transportation systems and a national bank.

As secretary of state, Webster ironed out a treaty that prevented war with Great Britain. It also defined the coast-to-coast border between the U.S. and Canada.

Daniel Webster, **John C. Calhoun**, and **Henry Clay** were the giants of the U.S. Congress in their time. They all wanted to be president, too, although none of them were ever elected.

Webster supported the Compromise of 1850, which admitted California to the Union as a free state. His fellow New Englanders were outraged by the Fugitive Slave Act included in the compromise. It meant slaves who had escaped to the North could be captured and sent back to their owners. Webster included the act in his compromise because he felt the South had to be satisfied. He wanted to make sure the U.S. government didn't fall in the bitter struggle over slavery.

"Liberty and Union, now and forever,

Noah Webster

lexicographer ★ 1758–1843

Noah Webster believed American language was an important part of American culture. He also fought for copyright laws to protect writers from unauthorized (therefore unpaid) use of their work.

Noah Webster was a Yale graduate who had fought in the American Revolution. He published his spelling book, *A Grammatical Institute of the English Language,* in 1783. It became known as the Blue-Backed Speller because of the color of its cover. Webster, a lexicographer, or dictionary writer, wanted to replace British words and spellings with American ones. The book sold more than 60 million copies in 50 years.

In 1806, Webster published *A Compendious Dictionary of the English Language*, the first American dictionary. In it, the lexicographer simplified many British spellings and added uniquely American words like *skunk*. Over the next 20 years, the great lexicographer learned 26 languages, including Sanskrit. He wanted to thoroughly research the origins of American English. In 1828, he presented his work: the 70,000-word *American Dictionary of the English Language.*

Orson Welles

actor, director ★ 1915–1985

Genius/box-office poison. Creative/chaotic. Praised/panned. Orson Welles—all of the above.

Welles cofounded the Mercury Theatre and its radio show in New York City in the 1930s. His 1938 Mercury broadcast of H. G. Wells's book *The War of the Worlds* was so realistic that people panicked, thinking Martians had landed! The headlines helped Welles land a movie contract.

The youthful director-writer-actor took Hollywood by storm. He was given free creative control on a movie project and an unheard-of 25% of the film's gross earnings. Welles produced *Citizen Kane* (1941), arguably the most influential movie ever made. He was 25.

Citizen Kane is a dazzling masterpiece. It uses extraordinary camera shots and innovative sound and lighting. The story unfolds through flashbacks, different voices, different viewpoints, and even a movie within the movie.

A famous low-angle shot of Orson Welles in Citizen Kane.

Welles was brilliant in the lead role of a ruthless newspaper tycoon. (**William Randolph Hearst**, the model for this character, didn't think so. He used his newspapers to try to destroy the film.)

Orson Welles later had an erratic career. He appeared in nearly 70 films. Classic Welles movies include *The Magnificent Ambersons* (1942), *The Lady from Shanghai* (1948), *The Third Man* (1949), and *A Touch of Evil* (1958).

one and inseparable." —DANIEL WEBSTER

Ida B. Wells
activist journalist ★ 1862–1931

In the 30 years after the Civil War, thousands of African Americans were lynched. These hanging murders did not go unreported. Ida B. Wells made sure of that.

Wells, the Mississippi-born daughter of slaves, led the great anti-lynching crusades of the late 19th and early 20th centuries. In 1895, she published *A Red Record*, the most thorough document on lynchings available at the time. As co-owner of the Memphis, Tennessee, *Free Speech* newspaper, Wells wrote about the rising violence against African-American men and women. Her exhaustive research showed white men were lynching people either because African-American businesses were cutting into their profits or because they feared African Americans would take their jobs. When three of Wells's friends were lynched outside of Memphis in 1892, the journalist stepped up her campaign. An angry mob ransacked her newspaper office and then hoped to lynch her. Wells escaped to New York City. There, she continued her crusade, writing articles for the *New York Age* and speaking all across the country.

In 1895, Wells married and moved to Chicago, Illinois. She worked with **Jane Addams**, continued her fight for the rights of African Americans, and worked for women's suffrage.

Mae West
actress ★ 1892–1980

She sashayed around in silk gowns, feathers, and furs, dripping with diamonds. She had a bold eye and a sultry voice. She was America's most scandalous star—Mae West.

Brooklyn-born Mae West started singing and dancing on New York City stages when she was seven. She was a vaudeville star by the time she was a teenager. West wrote and produced her own plays. Many of them were big hits—before the cops rushed in. Her bawdy stage shows like *Sex* (1926) and *The Pleasure Man* (1928) were too much for censorship groups. The plays were closed, and once West was even jailed. In 1932, she moved to Hollywood, looking for artistic freedom.

West became one of Hollywood's most popular and highly paid stars. Audiences flocked to see West swivel her hips, roll her eyes, and toss out one-liners in movies like *Night After Night* (1932), *She Done Him Wrong*, and *I'm No Angel* (both 1933). West was a great comic star, too, as she proved in *My Little Chickadee* (1940), in which famed comedian W. C. Fields was her costar. And she was a savvy businessperson. In 1935, Mae West made more than $450,000 a year for her tough, sexy roles. She also invested in Hollywood real estate, which made her a very wealthy woman.

George Westinghouse
inventor ★ 1846—1914

He was a brilliant inventor and a smart entrepreneur. That's why George Westinghouse was a leader of the industrial age in the early 20th century.

Westinghouse foresaw that railroads would be essential to America's growth. But the train system wasn't all that safe. In 1869, Westinghouse made it safer. He invented the compressed-air brake, which allowed the engineer to safely stop all train cars at once. He also formed a company to manufacture his air brakes. By 1882, Westinghouse had started another of the 60 companies he would eventually found. This one produced his signal-and-switch system, which also improved train travel.

George Westinghouse held more than 360 patents. His company was also the first to harness the hydro-electric power of Niagara Falls.

Westinghouse moved to Pittsburgh, Pennsylvania. It was a very profitable move because he discovered natural gas in his backyard. The inventor went to work and developed a new system to safely and quickly deliver natural gas, via pipe, from well to customers.

In 1885, he bought patent rights to an electrical transformer. It transmitted electricity using alternating currents (AC). Westinghouse thought this was the cheapest, most efficient way to wire America. **Thomas Edison** did not agree. One of the most famous technological feuds of its time began. In the end, Westinghouse's idea prevailed. AC is still the U.S. electrical standard.

Edith Wharton
author ★ 1862—1937

Edith Wharton, one of America's great novelists, was the first woman to win the Pulitzer prize for fiction. She won it for *The Age of Innocence* (1921), a novel that criticized the upper-class world Wharton came from.

Wharton was born into a wealthy, high-society family in New York City. She married into a similar Bostonian family. Her first successful book was about redecorating her Newport, Rhode Island, mansion.

When she was 40, Wharton turned to serious fiction writing. Her first novel, *The House of Mirth*, was published in 1905. It told the story of a young woman whose life is destroyed by cruel social customs. Critics and readers recognized Wharton as a powerful new literary voice.

Edith Wharton was friends with another important American writer of the time, Henry James (1843–1916).

Many of Wharton's books deal with sharp observations of her own social world. Her novels explore how society can crush an individual. She wrote about a basic conflict she often felt herself: what a person *should* do versus what a person *wants* to do. One of the greatest of her books on this theme is the now classic tragedy, *Ethan Frome* (1911).

Phillis Wheatley
poet ★ c.1753—1784

This picture of Phillis Wheatley is the work of an African-American engraver, Scipio Moorhead, who made it for Wheatley's book, Poems (1773).

America's first African-American poet lived most of her life in slavery.

Phillis Wheatley was named by John Wheatley, the Boston merchant who bought the young African girl in 1761. It is not known where she came from.

Phillis was educated along with the Wheatley children. She could read the Bible and literature by the time she was 12. By 13, she was writing poetry.

During the 1760s and 1770s, Wheatley's fame as a poet grew. Many people upheld her as an example of why African Americans should not be enslaved and that they were not intellectually inferior.

The Wheatleys freed Phillis when she was in her 20s. Her book *Poems on Various Subjects, Religious and Moral* was published in 1773. *Poems* had a forward signed by 18 prominent men, including **John Hancock**. It confirmed that Wheatley was the book's author, in case anyone doubted the talents of a former slave. During the American Revolution, she wrote a poem dedicated to General **George Washington**. Washington himself invited Wheatley to meet with him.

James McNeill Whistler
painter ★ 1834—1903

James McNeill Whistler, an American painter who lived in Paris, France, and London, England, believed in "art for art's sake." He thought paintings should be appreciated for their beauty, not for their moral lessons.

Whistler was interested in the harmony of form, pattern, and color. He was also influenced by Japanese art. Some of Whistler's most famous paintings include *Symphony in White No. 1, The White Girl* (1862), in which he used primarily white tones. In the 1870s, he painted a series of dreamy, atmospheric paintings of the Thames River in London, like *Nocturne in Blue and Gold: Old Battersea Bridge* (1872–1875). In *Nocturne in Black and Gold: The*

James McNeill Whistler's most familiar painting, Arrangement of Gray and Black, No. 1: Portrait of the Painter's Mother (1872), is commonly called Whistler's Mother.

Falling Rocket (1875), his work became even more abstract. Whistler used musical terms in naming some of his paintings because he believed his art created a mood, just like music did.

Whistler's works were rejected at first by art academies, galleries, and customers. Once, he lavishly repainted the leather-bound walls of a dining room while the homeowners were away. That disputed work, *The Peacock Room*, is now at the Freer Gallery of Art in Washington, D.C.

carols I hear . . ." — WALT WHITMAN

Walt Whitman
poet ★ 1819—1892

When **Ralph Waldo Emerson** read Walt Whitman's first book of poems, he was thrilled. *Leaves of Grass* was real "American" poetry.

Whitman's work didn't rhyme, it rollicked. It wasn't sentimental, it soared. He didn't use fancy language. The self-proclaimed "poet of the people" used the voice *of* the people, in all its slangy, twangy glory.

Whitman grew up in New York. He worked there for several years as a printer and a newspaper editor. He lost more than one job for his outspoken abolitionist views. In 1848, he was offered a job in New Orleans, Louisiana. Whitman rode the rails, boarded stagecoaches, and floated down the Mississippi River on a paddleboat steamer. He was inspired by the brawny energy and hurly-burly of American life. "The United States themselves are essentially the greatest poem," he declared. In *Leaves of Grass*, he captured that poem. For the rest of his life, Whitman continued to revise and add new poems to the collection. *Leaves of Grass* went through nine editions (1855–1891).

During the Civil War, Whitman devoted himself to caring for wounded soldiers in Washington, D.C. With his bag of oranges and other treats, he was a much-beloved figure. His wartime experiences influenced his later poems, which dealt more with death and life's sorrows.

Eli Whitney received a patent for his cotton gin in 1794. Southerners declared, "Cotton is king!" By the 1860s, this crop accounted for two-thirds of the national revenue.

Eli Whitney
inventor ★ 1765—1825

Eli Whitney was a mechanical genius.

In 1792, Whitney headed south to become a schoolteacher, but he saw another opportunity. It took a person a full day to pick seeds from *one* pound of short-fiber cotton. Within a year, Whitney had invented his seed-picking cotton gin. His machine did the work of 50 people. The cotton gin changed the economy of the South, but Whitney didn't share in all the profit. He held the patent, but too many people illegally copied and used his invention. Whitney turned to another project, making badly needed muskets.

Eli Whitney was the first to see that creating the right tools would allow production of interchangeable parts. These parts could be assembled, so that goods, like a musket, did not have to be made individually by hand. In 1798, Whitney promised to deliver 10,000 guns to the U.S. government in two years. It actually took him 10 years to create the machinery, build the factory in Connecticut, train the workers, and turn out the muskets—but he revolutionized American business.

"...to remain silent and indifferent

Elie Wiesel
activist, author ★ 1928–

Elie Wiesel survived the horrors of the Nazi concentration camps. The inhumanity of his experience turned him into one of the world's great humanitarians.

Born to a Jewish family in what is now Romania, Wiesel was 15 when he and the people of his village were deported in 1944. Unlike other members of his family, Elie lived to see Allied forces liberate the concentration camps.

After World War II ended, Wiesel went to Paris, France. He worked as a journalist until an influential French writer convinced him to write a memoir. In 1958, Wiesel published his first book,
Night (La Nuit). Wiesel's searing account of "those moments which murdered my God and my soul and turned my dreams to dust" stands as one of the most powerful works of Holocaust literature. *Night* was translated into 30 languages and received universal praise.

Wiesel, who became a U.S. citizen in 1963, is now the author of some 40 books of fiction and nonfiction. He has dedicated his life to honoring the memories of those lost in the Holocaust and to fighting racism and genocide internationally. Wiesel was awarded the Nobel Peace Prize in 1986.

Elie Wiesel (c.) has been on the faculty of Boston University since 1976. He was chairman of the U.S. Holocaust Memorial Council (1980–1986).

Laura Ingalls Wilder was 17 when this photo was taken.

Laura Ingalls Wilder
author ★ 1867–1957

Little House in the Big Woods was an immediate best-seller when it was published in 1932. Its author was 65 years old.

Laura Ingalls Wilder was encouraged by her daughter to write down stories about her pioneer childhood. Wilder had grown up on the frontier in the Midwest and what is now South Dakota. Like many of the families of the time, Laura's built their own houses, dug their own wells, raised and preserved their own food, and made most of their own clothes. They never had enough money. Laura took jobs to help her family get out of debt. She also helped take care of her oldest sister, who was blind. Laura sewed shirts in town, and when she was 16, she became a teacher. She married Almanzo James Wilder in 1885. Eventually, they bought a small farm in Mansfield, Missouri. Laura started writing newspaper columns for the *Missouri Ruralist*.

Wilder drew on her experiences in writing her popular books like *On the Banks of Plum Creek* (1937), *By the Shores of Silver Lake* (1939), *The Long Winter* (1940), and *Little Town on the Prairie* (1941). In the mid-1970s, these books inspired a hit television series, *Little House on the Prairie*.

is the greatest sin of all." — ELIE WIESEL

Emma Willard
educator ★ 1787–1870

In 1819, Emma Willard wrote a *Plan for Improving Female Education*. In it, she argued that women had the right to education, which would "bring its subjects to the perfection of their moral, intellectual, and physical nature." Willard spent a lifetime making this argument.

In 1814, she founded the Middlebury Female Seminary. The schoolhouse was her Vermont home. Willard taught women mathematics, science, history, geography, and other traditionally "male" subjects.

Willard had a hard time getting government funding to expand her school. But the city of Troy, New York, offered her $4,000. In 1821, she started the Troy Female Seminary. Within 10 years, enrollment grew from 90 to 300 young women. Throughout her life, Emma Willard traveled and lectured to encourage politicians to establish state-funded education for girls.

Hank Williams
country western singer ★ 1923–1953

Honky-tonks and heartache. Love and loneliness. The blues. Hank Williams didn't just sing sad songs, he lived them. In his brief life, Williams wrote more than 100 songs, including country classics like "Your Cheatin' Heart," "Cold, Cold Heart," and "I'm So Lonesome I Could Cry." Once in a while, he got happy and put out a finger-snapping song like "Hey, Good Lookin'" or a down-home celebration like "Jambalaya."

Williams grew up poor in Alabama. In 1937, he formed a band, the Drifting Cowboys. Drift they did, from roadhouse to bar. Sometimes they'd get a radio gig. In 1946, Williams wrote songs for Acuff-Rose, a well-known music publisher in Nashville, Tennessee. A record contract with MGM followed and Williams broke onto the charts with "Move It on Over." But his real chart-buster was his yodeling "Lovesick Blues." It hit number one and Hank Williams hit the big time: He was invited to play at Nashville's Grand Ole Opry, *the* showcase for country music. Williams was at his peak, but he drifted too far into alcohol and drugs and died of a heart attack at age 30.

Hank Williams sang with a tear in his twang. He was the first artist elected to the Country Music Hall of Fame (1961).

"Forced worship stinks in God's nostrils." —ROGER WILLIAMS

The Narragansett greet Roger Williams.

Roger Williams
founder of Rhode Island ★ c.1603—1683

Puritan minister Roger Williams was banished from Massachusetts in 1635. To the Puritans, it was bad enough that Williams preached about "soul liberty," as he called freedom of religion. But, even worse, he thought Native Americans should be treated fairly.

Williams and a small band of followers fled Massachusetts in January 1636. The Narragansett tribe helped them through the long, cold New England winter. Williams and the Native Americans had long respected one another, and he spoke their language. The Narragansett gave Williams land. He founded a settlement called Providence.

Williams bought more land from the tribe and what became the colony of Rhode Island grew. Puritans, Quakers, Catholics, Jews, and even atheists were welcomed. So were poor colonists. Roger Williams was elected president of Rhode Island in 1654 and served three terms.

Venus and Serena Williams
tennis players ★ 1980— (Venus); 1981— (Serena)

The Williams sisters burst onto the professional tennis tournament scene in the 1990s. They were a fresh new kind of tennis champ. The young women are African American and from inner-city Los Angeles. Their first coach was their father. The sisters are often doubles partners.

In 1997, Venus became the first unseeded (unranked) player to make the U.S. Open finals. In 1999, Serena defeated Martina Hingis to win the U.S. Open. She was the first African-American woman to win a Grand Slam victory since **Althea Gibson**. It would not be last Grand Slam for the sisters. By the end of 2002, Venus had won four Grand Slam victories (2 Wimbledon; 2 U.S. Open) and Serena had added three more Grand Slam trophies (French Open; Wimbledon; U.S. Open) to her collection.

Venus Williams (r.) defeated her sister Serena (l.) in the 2001 U.S. Open Women's singles.

Venus also won the gold medal for singles at the 2000 Olympics.

The sisters are equally successful when they pair up for doubles matches. They boast an impressive record of 5 Grand Slam doubles titles. They also brought home the Olympic gold medal for doubles in 2000.

Ted Williams

baseball player ★ 1918—2002

The "Splendid Splinter" was the Boston Red Sox's outstanding outfielder and home-run hero for 19 years.

Tall, thin Ted Williams joined the minor leagues in San Diego, California, in 1936. Two years later, the Red Sox bought his contract.

Williams studied the techniques of his batting heroes. He also had extraordinary eyesight. No matter how tricky the throw, Williams was the best at picking out good and bad pitches and batting accordingly. He had a career total of 2,019 walks, a record topped only by **Babe Ruth**. His lifetime batting average was .344. In 1942, Williams scored the Triple Crown, topping the league in batting, home runs, and RBIs (runs batted in). In 1947, he wore that crown again.

Williams kept up his sensational stats, despite two patriotic breaks in his career. From 1942 to 1945, he was a Marine Corps pilot during World War II. Williams was flying instead of batting in 1952 and 1953, during the Korean War, too. He returned to the Red Sox in 1954 and played for six more seasons. Williams last career hit? A home run.

Red Sox fans teased Ted Williams as a rookie. He swore never to tip his hat to them, as is customary after a home run—and he never did.

Woodrow Wilson

28th president ★ 1856—1924

Woodrow Wilson was a man of religious faith, high ideals, and strong principles. He brought all these traits to his job as president of the United States (1913–1921).

In his first term, Wilson worked with Congress to modify high tariffs, or taxes. This introduced a national income tax for the first time. He supported the Federal Reserve Act, which controlled money and credit to help prevent economic crises. He also backed labor reform to improve working conditions.

World events had a major impact on Wilson's second term. The president kept a neutral position when World War I broke out in Europe in 1914. But once Germany threatened U.S. ships and tried to form an enemy alliance, or partnership, with Mexico, there was no other choice: Wilson asked Congress to declare war in 1917.

After the war, Wilson proposed a "League of Nations" to help avoid future world conflicts. He spent six months in Paris, France, negotiating the postwar Treaty of Versailles (1919). He won the 1919 Nobel Peace Prize for his international efforts but was less successful at home. A majority of U.S. senators wanted the U.S. to stay out of foreign affairs. In 1920, they voted down the treaty because of the League of Nations clause. European countries did sign the treaty. But without U.S. backing, the League of Nations never really worked.

"Being able to communicate

Oprah Winfrey
media entrepreneur ★ 1954—

Time called her one of the 100 most influential people of the 20th century. *Newsweek* named her "Woman of the Century." Media maven Oprah Winfrey commands the respect of her peers. She also draws unwavering loyalty from her audiences. Every week, nearly 22 million people in the U.S. tune in to *The Oprah Winfrey Show.* So do viewers in more than 113 other countries.

With her life story, Oprah could be a guest on her own show. She grew up poor, living with her grandmother on a farm in Kosciusko, Mississippi, that didn't even have plumbing. When Oprah went to live with her mother in Milwaukee, Wisconsin, she was sexually abused by male family members and acquaintances. Things improved when she went to live with her father in Nashville, Tennessee. He insisted she get a good education. Winfrey was still a sophomore at Tennessee State University when she became the first African American in Nashville to anchor the local evening news show. She eventually moved to Chicago, where she became host of WLS-TV's *A.M. Chicago* show in 1984. One month later, it was the number one talk show in the area. One year later, it was renamed *The Oprah Winfrey Show.*

Since her show's national debut in 1986, Oprah has continually brought creativity and imagination to its programming. Oprah's shows support her message that "you are responsible for your life." Her style is inspirational and motivational. *The Oprah Winfrey Show* has won 34 Emmy Awards and Oprah was given the National Academy of Television Arts & Sciences' Lifetime Achievement Award in 1998.

"The Queen of Talk" is also the queen of media. Winfrey heads her own company, Harpo Entertainment Group, which produces her talk show. The company has contracts with ABC for television movies and with **Walt Disney** for films. Winfrey was nominated for an Academy Award for her role in the 1985 film version of Alice Walker's *The Color Purple*, directed by **Steven Spielberg**. Winfrey starred in and produced *Beloved*, a 1998 screen adaptation of **Toni Morrison**'s prize-winning book. In April 2000, she launched her smart, glossy, women's magazine, *O*. It sold out almost immediately and was the most successful magazine start-up in publishing history. Oprah is also the cofounder of Oxygen Media, a cable television and online network aimed at women.

Winfrey works well off-screen, too. A generous philanthropist, she has donated millions to educational institutions and created her own Family for Better Lives Foundation.

Oprah at the party celebrating the first issue of her new magazine, O.

with people is power." — OPRAH WINFREY

Sarah Winnemucca
Native American activist ★ c.1844—1891

Sarah Winnemucca, a Paiute, was a skilled interpreter and peacekeeper. Still, she was unable to prevent the U.S. government from taking the Paiute's land.

In 1878, Winnemucca traveled alone for more than 100 miles to rescue her father, a captive of the Bannock tribe. She spied on the enemy tribe and reported important information to the U.S. Army, which was at war with the Bannock. Then the U.S. government went after the Paiute. Winnemucca's tribe was removed from its Nevada land in the dead of winter. They were forced onto a reservation in Washington state.

Winnemucca traveled to Washington, D.C., and protested to President Rutherford B. Hayes and secretary of the interior Carl Schurz in 1880. Schurz promised the Paiute would be given their own land. Corrupt agents from the Bureau of Indian Affairs refused to honor that promise. Sarah Winnemucca went on a lecture tour to publicize the sufferings of her people and fight for policy reform. She wrote an enormously successful book, *Life Among the Paiutes* (1883). She gathered hundreds of signatures on a petition to the government to grant land to the Paiute. Congress passed a bill ordering it done. No one ever executed the order.

Sarah Winnemucca was fluent in three Native American languages as well as English and Spanish. In 1884, she established the first school for Native Americans in Nevada.

Stevie Wonder
singer, songwriter ★ 1950—

Steveland Morris signed with the Motown record label when he was 11. He played the drums, piano, organ, and harmonica. He had an irresistible voice. In less than a year, he had a number-one single and a new name: Little Stevie Wonder.

Wonder is a musical genius who has been blind since birth. Even as a young singer, he brought flair to hits like "For Once in My Life" and "Signed, Sealed, Delivered." He became one of Motown's hottest talents. In the 1970s, he was songwriter, singer, and producer on his own albums like *Music of My Mind* and *Talking Book* (both 1972), *Innervisions* (1973), and *Songs in the Key of Life* (1976). He often played all the albums' instruments, too! Fans and critics are wowed by the lush sounds and complex arrangements Wonder creates. His music is infused with soul ("You Are the Sunshine of My Life"), funk ("Superstition"), pop ("I Just Called to Say I Love You"), and rhythm and blues ("Don't You Worry 'Bout a Thing").

Stevie Wonder has released nearly 40 albums. He's won 17 Grammy Awards, including a Lifetime Achievement Award in 1996. Wonder has written about race, poverty, violence, and inner-city unrest. He's performed at peace concerts and world hunger relief benefits.

Tiger Woods
golfer ★ 1975—

Eldrick "Tiger" Woods started golfing early—so early that he had to climb out of a high chair to pick up his first club.

By the time he was 11 years old, Woods had won 33 junior golf tournaments, every one he had entered. Four years later, Woods became the youngest U.S. Junior Amateur champ. He turned pro in 1986 and went on to 28 wins in Professional Golf Association (PGA) tours. Woods was named PGA Tour Player of the Year in 1997 and again in 1999.

Tiger Woods made golf history on April 8, 2001. By winning the Masters Tournament, he became the only person in the modern pro era to hold titles to the U.S. Open, the British Open, and the PGA Championship all at once! And the 25-year-old golf genius did it with a record 16 shots under par. (Par is the average number of shots it takes to get the ball in the hole.) In 2002, Woods captured his third victory at both the Masters and the U.S. Open. He became the youngest golfer to win eight professional major championships.

Woods is famous for his intense, almost robotic concentration and cool control. He's also got a near-perfect golf swing that can move the club's head at 120 mph His youth, style, and success have made him enormously popular. Woods has also attracted more African Americans to golf.

F. W. Woolworth
retail entrepreneur ★ 1852—1919

Frugal housewives, new immigrants with low-paying jobs, anybody who had a dime but not a dollar to spend, knew where to shop in 1910—at any of F. W. Woolworth's 1,000 stores.

Frank Woolworth, a farm boy from New York, opened his first five-and-dime in Utica, New York, in 1879. His "Great Five Cent Store" lasted two weeks. Woolworth opened another store in Lancaster, Pennsylvania, a month later. A sign in the store window read "Any article in this window 5¢." The Lancaster store took off.

F. W. Woolworth opened his five-and-dime stores across the country. They had bright red-and-gold store signs and colorful display windows filled with low-cost items. Each Woolworth's Five-and-Dime was stocked with candy and other small goods that Woolworth himself sought out and bought in bulk.

Frank W. Woolworth's first successful five-and-dime store was in Lancaster, Pennsylvania.

Incorporated in 1911, Woolworth's was worth $65 million. F. W. Woolworth built the ornate, Gothic-spired Woolworth building in New York City. At 792 feet, it was then the world's tallest building.

 "I would hurl words into darkness

Frank Lloyd Wright
architect ★ 1867—1959

Frank Lloyd Wright (l.) Baroness Hilla Rebay (c.) and Solomon Guggenheim (r.) look at Wright's model for the Guggenheim Museum.

Frank Lloyd Wright dropped out of architecture school in his home state of Wisconsin. He arrived in boomtown Chicago, Illinois, in 1887 with $7.00 in his pocket. Within a few months, he was drafting architectural drawings for **Louis Sullivan**. By 1903, he had his own architectural business.

Wright believed buildings should be functional and inventive in their design and materials, and in how they interacted with their environment. From 1900 to 1910, he built 50 "prairie houses." They had low, sweeping roofs and big, open floor plans. They brought to mind the serenity and space of the rolling Midwest prairies. Robie House (1906) in Chicago is considered his prairie-style masterpiece.

One of Wright's most famous home designs is Fallingwater (1936) in Bear Run, Pennsylvania. This dramatic house is built directly into a cliff. The horizontal concrete-and-glass rooms look like they are suspended over a waterfall and river. Opening a door in the living room floor lets in the river's cool air.

Wright also designed public buildings. The Solomon R. Guggenheim Museum (1943–1959) in New York City is one of the most famous.

Richard Wright
author ★ 1908—1960

He forged a white man's signature to borrow books. African Americans weren't allowed to use the Memphis, Tennessee, libraries.

That was just one form of racism Richard Wright experienced as a young man growing up in the South in the 1920s. He'd seen a family member lynched, or hanged. He'd been denied work opportunities. When he moved to Chicago, Illinois, in 1927, the only job open to him was postal worker.

In Chicago, Wright continued his self-education, and he started writing. In 1938, his short-story collection, *Uncle Tom's Children,* was published. In these realistic stories, the African-American characters are stunted by harsh lives and bitter choices. These themes would be even more powerfully developed in Wright's first novel, *Native Son* (1940).

Native Son is the story of Bigger Thomas, a young African American who accidentally kills a white woman. This plunges him into a downward spiral of fear and violence. It sold 215,000 copies in just three months. Five years later, he brought out an autobiographical novel, *Black Boy*. It firmly established him as a leading voice of the African-American experience.

Richard Wright was frustrated with life in America. He moved to Paris in 1946 and stayed there for the rest of his life.

and wait for an echo." —RICHARD WRIGHT

Wilbur and Orville Wright

inventors ★ 1867–1912 (Wilbur);
1871–1948 (Orville)

Before takeoff, Orville (in the plane) and Wilbur Wright (standing) set up photography equipment to document their historic flight on December 17, 1903. This photograph was later colorized.

The December 6, 1903, edition of *The New York Times* predicted that people wouldn't fly for another 1,000 years. It was off by 999 years, 356 days.

On December 17, 1903, at 10:35 A.M., Wilbur and Orville Wright launched the world's first successful airplane from a beach near Kitty Hawk, North Carolina. Orville was at the controls of *The Flyer*, the Wrights' 600-pound plane with a 40-foot wingspan. He turned on the 12-horsepower engine that the brothers had built themselves. Wilbur steadied the wood-and-cotton wings as the plane ran down its track. Liftoff! *The Flyer* traveled 120 feet in 12 seconds.

The Wright brothers became interested in flying as children. Their father gave them a whirling helicopter toy. The brothers immediately started making copies of it. As the boys grew older, they kept tinkering. In 1889, they opened a printing shop. Three years later, they opened the Wright Cycle Company in Dayton, Ohio, to cater to the new craze for bicycles.

In 1899, aeronautics, the study of flight, was just taking off. The Wright brothers eagerly followed the experiments of several inventors working with gliders. They realized that balance and control posed the most dangerous problems in staying airborne. They also realized that, like the birds they so carefully observed, a craft's wings would have to be able to adjust in flight.

Orville and Wilbur started building gliders in their bike shop. In 1900, they began flying (and crashing) controlled gliders at Kitty Hawk. The Wright brothers continually modified their ideas about controls and movable tail rudders. In 1902, Orville and Wilbur piloted hundreds of smooth glides. They decided to add a motor and propellers. When they did, they made aviation history.

After their amazing flight in *The Flyer*, the Wright brothers devoted themselves to building a stronger, practical airplane that

> "... insects, reptiles, birds and mammals were flying every day at pleasure, it was reasonable to suppose that man might also fly." — ORVILLE WRIGHT

could fly longer. By 1905, they had succeeded. Their *Flyer III* plane stayed in the air 39 minutes and survived multiple landings and takeoffs. The Wrights tried to interest the U.S. Army in their invention. The army didn't respond at first, but the French government did. In 1908 and 1909, Wilbur flew 100 demonstration flights in France. Meanwhile, Orville awed onlookers with test flights in Virginia. (The army had come round and offered a contract.) The two opened the Wright Company in Dayton to manufacture and sell their aircraft. Within a few years, Orville and Wilbur were front-page news. So was the new era they helped launch, the Age of Flight.

Chien-Shiung Wu
physicist ★ 1912–1997

Through her groundbreaking research, Dr. Chien-Shiung Wu updated some long-held physics theories.

Born and raised in China, Dr. Wu earned her Ph.D. in physics from the University of California at Berkeley. She joined the scientific staff of the Division of War Research at Columbia University in New York City in 1940. Dr. Wu was among the scientists who worked on the Manhattan Project, which developed the first atomic bomb.

For more than 30 years, scientists had believed that particles and anti-particles should behave in the same way. In 1956, Dr. Wu worked on a theory proposed by two of her peers. She performed a long, complicated experiment with startling results. Particles and anti-particles *did not* behave identically! Wu's discovery had a profound effect on the field of nuclear energy.

In 1957, Wu became a full professor of physics at Columbia. She was the first woman to win the Comstock Award from the National Academy of Sciences (1964) and the first to win the Research Corporation Award (1958). Dr. Wu was named Woman of the Year by the American Association of University Women in 1962 and elected president of the American Physical Society in 1975. She also won the National Medal of Science that year.

Rosalyn Yalow
physicist ★ 1921–

In 1945, Dr. Rosalyn Yalow became one of the few women to earn a doctorate in physics. She went to work for the Veteran Administration (VA) Hospital in the South Bronx, New York, in 1947.

Dr. Yalow began research into the use of radioactive materials in medicine. She sometimes had to design her own radiation detection instruments. At the VA Hospital, she met Dr. Solomon Berson, and the two worked as a research team for 22 years, until Berson's death in 1972. Their work led to the invention of radioimmunoassay (RAI) in 1959. RAI is a medical tool that uses radioactive particles to help measure blood levels of hormones, enzymes, drugs, and other microscopic substances. RAI technology helps doctors diagnose many different problems, such as diabetes and hepatitis. RAI has earned millions of dollars for corporations but not for the two scientists. They didn't patent their work.

In 1976, Yalow became the first woman to win the prestigious Albert Lasker Medical Research Award. In 1977, she was awarded the Nobel Prize for medicine. Dr. Yalow teaches at Mount Sinai School of Medicine in New York and continues her work at the VA medical center.

Jerry Yang and David Filo
Internet entrepreneurs * 1968—(Yang); 1966—(Filo)

Chief Yahoos Jerry Yang (l.) and David Filo (r.) in 1997.

How many executives have a business title like "Chief Yahoo"? Then again, how many executives became billionaires before 30? Chief Yahoos Jerry Yang and David Filo did.

In 1994, Yang and Filo were working on their Ph.D.s in electrical engineering at Stanford University in California. They did a lot of Internet surfing between studies. The Web at the time was like an uncharted sea. Yang and Filo started creating a navigational system. They categorized and organized their favorite Web sites into "Jerry's Guide to the World Wide Web." Thousands of people started accessing their guide through the Internet. Yang and Filo renamed their guide Yahoo! (Yet Another Hierarchical Officious Oracle), put their Ph.D.s on hold, and went into business.

Yahoo! was incorporated in 1995. It was the first—and is now the largest—online Internet navigational system. Filo directs Yahoo!'s technical operations. Yang oversees Yahoo!'s surfers and other content development. They have rapidly and successfully expanded the Yahoo! business. More than 200 million people around the world use Yahoo! every month.

Chuck Yeager
pilot * 1923—

When pilots in the 1940s got close to Mach 1, the speed of sound, scary things happened. Their controls froze, and their planes shook violently, or worse, exploded. So when decorated World War II pilot Chuck Yeager agreed to test a top secret Army plane, he knew that test flight could be fatal.

On October 14, 1947, a B-29 took off from Edwards Air Force Base in California. The rocket-powered X-1 plane was in its belly. Yeager got into the X-1's cockpit. He had to close one door

Chuck Yeager's X-1 plane, Glennis, is exhibited at the Smithsonian National Air and Space Museum in Washington, D.C. Glennis was Yeager's wife.

with a broom handle. His reach was limited because he'd broken two ribs on October 12. The gutsy pilot kept his injury a secret rather than be grounded. The X-1 was released at 26,000 feet.

At .87 Mach, the X-1 started wildly vibrating. Yeager forced the plane to go even faster until he broke through Mach 1. *Boom!* Observers below heard proof, the sonic boom. Yeager landed safely, after a few celebratory stunt rolls.

Yeager continued as a test pilot and served as a military pilot during the Vietnam War.

"OK, Babe's here! Now who's

In 1903, Cy Young threw the first pitch of the first-ever World Series. His team, the Boston Red Sox, beat the Pittsburgh Pirates and won the series.

Cy Young
baseball player ★ 1867—1955

As a young player, his pitches had such speed and impact that it felt like a cyclone just whirled through the stadium. That's how Denton True Young got his nickname, "Cy."

Cy Young has pitched more innings (7,377) and won (511) and lost (313) more major league games than any other pitcher in baseball history.

A farm boy from Ohio, Young did farm chores to stay fit between seasons playing with the Tri-State League's Canton, Ohio, team and in 1890, with the National League's Cleveland Spiders. The 1890 season was the first of 14 straight seasons in which he won more than 20 games a year.

In 1901, Young signed up with the Boston Puritans (who later became the Red Sox) in the brand-new American League. His winning streak continued. Young led the league in strikeouts, ERA (earned run average), and wins. He continued playing into his mid-40s, pitching shutouts and his third career no-hitter, and thrilling baseball audiences across the country. Today, the best pitcher in the American League and the best in the National League are given the annual Cy Young Award, in honor of this legendary pitcher.

Babe Didrikson Zaharias
athlete ★ 1914—1956

Babe wanted to be the greatest athlete who ever lived. Many people would say she succeeded. ESPN put her at number 10 on their list of Top 100 North American Athletes of the Century. *Sports Illustrated* named her the best female athlete of the 20th century.

Mildred "Babe" Didrikson Zaharias was an outstanding athlete in several sports. After high school, she played semipro basketball and was named All-American three times. Babe won eight out of 10 track-and-field events at the Amateur Athletic Union meet in 1932. That same year, she competed in the summer Olympics. She easily shattered world records in

In the 1932 Olympics, Babe Didrikson threw the javelin a record-breaking 143 feet, 4 inches.

the javelin throw and 80-meter hurdles, winning two gold medals (plus a silver for high jump).

Babe took up golf next and took the 1946 National Women's Amateur title. The next year, she became the first American to win the British Women's Amateur golf title. During her career, Babe won 82 tournaments, including 10 majors. Zaharias helped start the Ladies Professional Golf Association around 1948.

gonna finish second?" — BABE DIDRIKSON ZAHARIAS

GLOSSARY

abolition The 19th-century movement to abolish, or prohibit, slavery.

Allies/Allied forces The group of countries, including the United States, the Soviet Union (Russia), Great Britain, and France, that fought together during World War I (1914–1918) and World War II (1939–1945).

anarchist A person who believes in anarchy, the idea that all forms of government should be abolished.

antitrust Regulation of trusts, which are groups of companies that form to control wages, prices, and competition in an industry.

Black Power An African-American movement that encouraged black pride through establishing black cultural and political institutions. The Black Power movement arose in the 1960s.

boycott To refuse to buy goods or use services as a means of protest.

cabinet The president's advisory group, made up of the heads of various government departments and other advisors.

capitalism An economic system where business is privately owned rather than controlled by the government.

civil rights movement The social and political struggle to ensure that all Americans receive the rights they are entitled to as citizens. The U.S. civil rights movement was sparked by African Americans in the 1960s who staged marches, sit-ins, boycotts, and other forms of peaceful protests.

Cold War The rivalry and competition between Communist countries, like the Soviet Union, and non-Communist countries, like the United States. The Cold War started after World War II. The Soviet Union and its allies promoted the spread of communism; the U.S. and its allies tried to prevent it.

collective bargaining Negotiations between a business or industry and workers who have organized to represent their interests as a group, or union.

color barrier A public, private, legal, or an informal agreement that keeps a person from participating in something because of his or her race.

communism An economic system business is owned and controlled by the government or community. Under communism, the market is regulated and the profits are shared by all members of the society.

Constitutional Convention The 1787 national political meeting where delegates from most of the states met in Philadelphia, Pennsylvania, to create a constitution, a plan to govern the newly formed United States. The U.S. Constitution established the executive, legislative, and judicial branches of the federal government.

Continental Congress The government assembly of colonial America that met in Philadelphia, Pennsylvania, in 1774 to discuss independence from Great Britain and self-governance. The Second Continental Congress met in Philadelphia in 1775 and governed during the American Revolution and the early postwar years until the U.S. Constitution was ratified in 1789.

defect To leave one's country of birth, usually for political reasons.

desegregation The act of getting rid of segregation in public places or institutions.

Dust Bowl Parts of the Midwest that became desert-like in the 1930s because of severe drought, dust storms, and poor land use.

emancipation Freedom from bondage, particularly slavery.

Equal Rights Amendment (ERA) A constitutional amendment, first proposed in 1923, in that guarantees that civil rights are "not denied or abridged . . . on account of sex." The ERA was approved by Congress in 1972, but then had to be ratified by 38 states to become an amendment. It missed ratification by three states.

Federalist A person who believes in a strong central, or federal, government; a member of the Federalist political party of the 1790s.

Great Depression The sharp drop in the U.S. economy that started with the stock market crash in 1929 and caused widespread unemployment, business failures, and poverty during the 1930s.

impeachment The act of charging a political official with misconduct and subject him or her to an appropriate trial.

improvisational Something created on the spot, without prior practice. Improvising is an important element of jazz music.

integration Bringing together people of different races, ethnic origins, gender, etc.

monopoly A group that completely controls a business or industry.

New Deal The programs and plans introduced by President **Franklin Delano Roosevelt** and his administration to help pull the U.S. out of the Great Depression.

pacifist A person who is opposed to war as an answer to settling disputes.

patent A government grant to an inventor that guarantees him or her the exclusive right to manufacture or sell his or her invention.

progressive Supportive of government, social, political, or educational reforms to improve conditions.

Prohibition The period from 1920 to 1933 when the manufacture and sale of alcohol was banned in the U. S. by the 18th amendment.

radical Proposing extreme or violent change, usually in politics or government.

ratification The process of approving, often by voting, and making valid.

recession A slowdown or decline in economic and business activity.

Reconstruction The post–Civil War period from 1865 to 1877 when the U.S. federal government controlled the states that had belonged to the Confederacy.

reforms Improvements, often in politics, labor, education, or the social welfare of a community.

segregation The act of keeping one group of people separate from other groups of people often because of race.

socialism A political and economic belief that factories and other industrial production should be owned by the public or workers.

suffrage The right to vote.

tariff A government tax put on imported or exported goods.

temperance movement The 19th-century drive to ban the sale of liquor because alcoholism was on the rise and women and children had little legal protection from abusive, alcoholic husbands and fathers.

transcendentalism A type of philosophy that says reality can be better understood through meditation and closeness with nature, rather than only through everyday experience.

treason Betrayal of one's country, especially by helping an enemy.

Underground Railroad A secret network of "safe" homes and hideaways through which escaped slaves passed on route to freedom in nonslave states or in Canada.

union A labor group formed by workers in a similar business or industry to help those workers negotiate wages and working conditions with their employers.

United Nations An organization created after World War II to help settle international conflicts and help promote human rights and economic development worldwide.

SELECTED BIBLIOGRAPHY

This selected bibliography lists some general works that are particularly good for children and young adults.

Book Series

Biography Today. Omnigraphics, Detroit, Michigan.

Giants of . . . Blackbirch Press.

Great Lives. Atheneum Books for Young Readers. Simon & Schuster.

In Their Own Words. Scholastic Inc.

Lives of the . . . by Kathleen Krull. Harcourt Brace & Company.

Scholastic Encyclopedia of. . . Scholastic Inc.

Individual Titles

Bolden, Tonya. *Strong Men Keep Coming: The Book of African American Men.* John Wiley & Sons, Inc., 1999.

Bredeson, Carmen. *American Writers of the 20th Century.* Enslow Publishers, Inc., 1996

Carlin, Richard. *Rock and Roll: 1955–1970.* Facts on File, 1998.

Carroll, Andrew. *Letters of a Nation: A Collection of Extraordinary American Letters.* Kodansha America, Inc., 1997.

Glenn, Patricia Brown. *America's Favorite Architects.* John Wiley & Sons, Inc., 1996.

Greenberg, Jan and Jordan, Sandra. *The American Eye: Eleven Artists of the Twentieth Century.* Delacorte Press, 1995.

Hansen, Joyce. *Women of Hope: African Americans Who Made a Difference.* Scholastic Inc., 1998.

Knapp, Ron. *American Generals of World War II.* Enslow Publishers, Inc., 1998.

Littlefield, Bill. *Champions: Stories of Ten Remarkable Athletes.* Little, Brown and Company, 1993.

Macy, Sue and Gottesman, Jane. *Play Like a Girl: A Celebration of Women in Sports.* Henry Holt & Co., 1999.

Mayo, Edith P. *The Smithsonian Book of the First Ladies.* Henry Holt & Co., 1996.

McKissack, Patricia and Frederick. *Black Diamond: The Story of the Negro Baseball Leagues.* Scholastic Inc., 1994.

———— *Rebels Against Slavery: American Slave Revolts.* Scholastic Inc., 1996.

Monceaux, Morgan. *Jazz, My Music, My People.* Borzoi Books/Alfred A. Knopf, Inc., 1994.

Morey, Janet and Dunn, Wendy. *Famous Asian Americans.* Cobblehill Books/Dutton, 1992.

———— *Famous Hispanic Americans.* Dutton, 1996.

Mour, Stanley. *American Jazz Musicians.* Enslow Publishers, Inc., 1998.

Rennert, Richard, ed. *Pioneers of Discovery.* Chelsea House Publishers, 1994.

Robertson, James I. Jr., *Civil War!* Alfred A. Knopf, 1992.

Sherrow, Victoria. *Great Scientists.* Facts on File, Inc., 1992.

Sugar, Bert Randolph. *The 100 Greatest Athletes of All Time.* Citadel Press/Carol Publishing Group, 1995.

Web sites

A&E's Biography: http://www.biography.com

History Channel: http://www.historychannel.com

Library of Congress, American Memory
   http://memory.loc.gov/ammem

National Women's Hall of Fame
   http://www.greatwomen.org

PHOTO CREDITS

t = top b = bottom

© Bettmann/CORBIS: 4t, 5b, 7t, 7b, 9b, 13, 19t, 39b, 47t, 65t, 68, 78t, 98t, 137b, 138t, 141t, 150b, 151t, 175b, 177b, 178t, 180b, 181t, 192t, 212t, 224, 235b, 244b, 245b, 248b, 249b; © Photofest, NY: 4b, 60b, 130b, 217t, 225t; © AP/Wide World Photos: 5t, 6t, 8b, 9t, 10, 12b, 14t, 15b, 16t, 18b, 22b, 24b, 27t, 31b, 32t, 35t, 35b, 40t, 40b, 43b, 45t, 45b, 47b, 54t, 55t, 58b, 64, 66t, 69t, 69b, 71b, 84t, 84b, 85t, 86t, 93t, 93b, 94b, 96t, 97b, 102t, 104t, 104b, 107b, 110t, 112, 117t, 118, 122b, 123t, 123b, 124, 125t, 126t, 127b, 129t, 134, 139t, 141b, 142b, 143b, 144t, 147b, 148t, 148b, 150t, 152b, 153t, 157, 159t, 160t, 160b, 161t, 161b, 163, 166t, 168t, 170t, 172b, 173t, 183t, 184b, 185t, 186t, 187t, 188t, 188b, 190b, 191, 192b, 195, 197b, 198, 199t, 200t, 200b, 201b, 203t, 207t, 211b, 213, 214b, 216t, 217b, 219b, 226b, 227t, 238t, 240b, 241t, 242, 243b, 244t, 248t; © North Wind Picture Archives, Alfred, ME: 6b, 8t, 11t, 20b, 28b, 29b, 34b, 43t, 46t, 52t, 54t, 63t, 76, 77t, 80b, 95t, 99t, 111b, 131t, 133, 145t, 149t, 158t, 176b, 178t, 183b, 187b, 189t, 203b, 204t, 205t, 208, 209b, 215b, 222, 223t, 229t, 233t, 237b, 240t, 241b; © Library Company of Philadelphia, PA: 11b; © NYPL/Schomburg: 12t, 56b, 73t, 128b, 197t, 226t; © The Frank Driggs Collection, Brooklyn, NY: 14b, 23t, 44b, 58t, 102b, 171b, 209t, 239b; © NASA: 15t, 113t, 165, 190t;

© Kobal Collection/RKO: 16b, 214t, 233b; © National Portrait Gallery, Smithsonian Institution/Art Resource, NY: 17t, 37t, 41, 62, 108t, 220b; © The Granger Collection, NY: 17b, 20t, 27b, 74t, 75t, 78b, 108b, 111t, 114t, 117t, 120b, 135, 144b, 151t, 159b, 164b, 172t, 180t, 216t, 221b, 229b, 238b, 245t, 246; © New York Historical Society: 18t; © Kobal Collection/CBS-TV: 19b; © Library of Congress: LC-USZ62-108565 21t, LC-99-Z2-28608-B 21b, LC-USZ62-122966 22t, LC-USW3-014843-C 23b, 30t, LC-USZ62-106337 33b; LC-USZ62-95040 36b, LC-USZ62-114627 38b, LC-USZ62-42538 42b, LC-USZ62-28947 49t, 61t; LC-USZ62-110141 61b, 65b, 79b, LC-USZ62-122091 83b, LC-USZ62-130656 85b, LC-H822-T-1822 87b, 91t, LC-USZ62-93807 97t, LC-USZC4-7503 100t, LC-USZ62-112435 106t, LC-USZ62-110029 106b, LC-USZ62-53343 109t, LC-USZC4-2389 116t, LC-USZ62-95653 128t, LC-USZ62-93443 136t, 143, LC-USZ62-111236 145b, LC-USZC4-4597 146b, LC-USZ62-16956 154t, LC-USZ62-8571 156b, LC-

USZ62-42559 158b, LC-USZ62-123323 167b, LC-USZ62-46915 170b, LC-USZ62-20176 174t, LC-USZ62-26653 177t, 186t, LC-USZ62-24168 215t, LC-USZ62-35413 231t, LC-USZ62-110179 232b, LC-USZ62-093492 235t, LC-USC4-5316 236t; © Brown Brothers, Sterling, PA: 24t, 44t, 49b, 50t, 71t, 72b, 82t, 92b, 103t, 132b, 149b, 169t,182b, 193b, 207b, 218b, 220t, 239t; © Agrilink Foods, Inc., Madison, WI: 25t; © New York Academy of Medicine, NY, NY: 25b; © Simon Bruty/Allsport: 26t; © Seneca Falls Historic Society, Seneca Falls, NY: 26b; © Kobal Collection/Warner Brothers: 28t;

© The Estate of Margaret Bourke-White: 29t; © Kobal Collection/Paramount: 30b, 146t; © Canada Post Corp., 1986, Reproduced with permission: 31t; © Globe Photos, NY: 32b, 184t; © The Cleveland Indians: 33t; © United States Senate Historical Office: 34t; © American Museum of Natural History, NY, NY: Neg #296833 36t; © Maryland State Archives, Annapolis, MD: 37b; © The Senate Office of Ben Nighthorse Campbell: 38t; © Kobal Collection: 39t, 87t, 147t, 155t, 218t, 219t, 232t, 234b; © Bridgeman Art Library, NY: 42t; © National Baseball Hall of Fame Library, Cooperstown, NY: 46b, 60t, 249t; © The White House: 48; © Union Pacific Railroad Museum, Omaha, NE: 50b; © Smithsonian Institution: Neg #80-12873 51t;

© Connecticut Historical Society, Hartford, CT: 51b; © Nell Dillon-Ermers, Photographer, NY, NY: 52b; © The Everett Collection: 53t, 91b; © Superstock Images, Jacksonville, FL: 53b, 73b; © Merce Cunningham Dance Foundation, NY: 55b; © National Archives: NWDNS-ANSCO-CA-10 56t, NWDNS-111-B-5140 57b, NWDNS-111-SC-83726 83t, NWDNS-111-B-36 89b, NWDNS-306-55M-4D 185b, 206; © Kobal Collection/20th Century Fox: 57t; © Chicago Eagle Lithographing Co./CORBIS: 59t; © Robert Frost Library-Amherst College, Amherst, MA: 59b; © Timepix, NY, NY: 63b, 75b, 82b, 88b, 89t, 96b, 99t, 105b, 107t, 113b, 125b, 126b, 127t, 129t, 139b, 171t, 182t, 193t, 202t, 202b, 212b, 223b, 225b, 247b; © Longyear Museum and Historical Society, Boston, MA: 66b; © Edison National Historic Site, West Orange, NJ: 67; © Corbis: 70, 72t, 152t, 173b; © Dian Fossey Gorilla Fund Int., Atlanta, GA: 74b; © Schlesinger Library-Radcliffe Institution, Harvard University, Cambridge, MA: 77b; © Kobal Collec-

tion/Selznick/MGM Collection: 79t; © Kobal Collection/MGM: 80t; © AFP/CORBIS: 81; © Chicago Historical Society: #DN-3882 86b; © London Features: 88t, 98b, 110b, 116b, 196b; © Kobal Collection/Wark Producing Company: 90t; © Tony Duffy/Allsport: 90b, 119b, 132t; © Scholastic Photo Archives: 92t, 109b, 194; © Independence National Historical Park, Philadelphia, PA: 94t; © Getty Images: 95b; © Underwood & Underwood/CORBIS: 100b; © Hershey Community Archives, Hershey, PA: 101t; © Intel Corp.: 101b; © Francis G. Mayer/CORBIS: 103b, 105t, 140b; © The Lyndon B. Johnson Presidential Library, Austin, TX: 114b; © Allsport USA: 115t, 137t; © David Leah/Allsport: 115b, © Denver Public Library: 119t; © Kobal Collection/United Artists: 120t; © John F. Kennedy Library, Boston, MA: 121, 167t; © Photographer John Cohen, Putnam Valley, NY: 122t; © Retna, NY: 131; © Hanover House Publishing: 136b; © Culver Pictures: 140t; © UPI/CORBIS: 142t, 221t; © Vassar College Library, Poughkeepsie, NY: 153b; © John Storey/Allsport: 155b; © Kobal Collection/Mirisch-7Arts/United Artists: 156t; © The Isamu Noguchi Foundation, Long Island City, NY: 164t;

© Courtesy George Eastman House, The Alfred Stieglitz Collection purchase from Georgia O'Keeffe: 166b; © Newberry Library/Superstock: 168b; © Hulton-Deutsch Collection/CORBIS: 169b; © California Institute of Technology, Pasadena, CA: 174b, 189b; © Jonathan Daniel/Allsport: 175t; © Bill Ross/CORBIS: 176t; © Leonardo de Selva/CORBIS: 179; © National Gallery of Art/Superstock: 181b

© Daniel Nauke: 196t; © Massachusetts Historical Society: 201t; © San Diego Historical Society: 204b; © Lee Snider; lee snider/CORBIS: 205b; © State Historical Society of Wisconsin, Madison, WI: 206b; © Gregory Heisler/CORBIS/Outline: 210

© Hulton Getty/Allsport: 211t; © Wal-Mart Stores, Inc. Bertonville, AR: 227b; © The Andy Warhol Foundation/Art Resource, NY: 228; © New Bedford Public Library/Superstock: 230; © A. Barrington Brown/Science Photo Library, Photo Researchers: 231b; © University of Chicago Library: 234t; © Musee d'Orsay-Paris/Superstock: 236b; © Stock Montage/Superstock: 237t; © Nevada Historical Society: 243t; © AIP Emilio Segrè Visual Archives, College Park, MD: 247t

INDEX

Subject Index